ENGLAND

A GUIDE TO POST-WAR LISTED BUILDINGS

FOREWORD

The quality and diversity of England's historic built heritage is well known and documented. Our cities, towns and villages contain a wonderful collection of buildings dating from every era of the last millennium and beyond, the best of which are given protection by being included in the statutory list of buildings of architectural or historic interest. But we are still building, and it is vitally important that we do not ignore or neglect the best architecture of the twentieth century.

The post-war era was a time of experiment and new directions, and the most exciting architecture of the period reflects this magnificently. Many of the listed buildings contained within these pages illustrate the use of innovative techniques and materials in their construction, and all are significant for their architectural vision and flair. The evidence presented by these buildings demonstrates very clearly that the best of modern architecture ranks with that of the past, and will equally stand the test of time.

ALAN HOWARTH

FOREWORD TO THE SECOND EDITION Much has happened in the two years since my predecessor wrote the foreword for the first edition of this guide. My department has produced 'A Force for our Future', a policy framework for the future of the historic environment, while the newly created Commission for Architecture and the Built Environment has quickly become a respected voice for modern architecture.

This book contains a selection of the very best of post-war architecture. The buildings included have already achieved formal recognition through the statutory listing process. Yet they deserve to be recognised more widely. The value of this publication is as a quick and easy reference that will engage a wider audience and stimulate a greater interest in the modern urban landscape. I hope you enjoy it.

TESSA BLACKSTONE, DEPARTMENT FOR CULTURE, MEDIA AND SPORT

ENGLAND

A GUIDE TO POST-WAR LISTED BUILDINGS / ELAIN HARWOOD

BATSFORD

A CIP RECORD FOR THIS BOOK IS AVAILABLE FROM THE BRITISH LIBRARY

PUBLISHED BY B T BATSFORD   A member of **Chrysalis** Books plc
64 BREWERY ROAD, LONDON N7 9NT
WWW.BATSFORD.COM
DESIGN CLAUDIA SCHENK

FIRST PUBLISHED 2000 BY ELLIPSIS LONDON
REVISED AND EXPANDED EDITION PUBLISHED 2003
COPYRIGHT © 2003 ENGLISH HERITAGE

ISBN 0 7134 8818 2

PRINTING AND BINDING IN ITALY

FOR A COPY OF THE BATSFORD CATALOGUE OR INFORMATION
ON SPECIAL QUANTITY ORDERS OF BATSFORD BOOKS PLEASE
CONTACT US ON 020 7697 3000 OR SALES@CHRYSALISBOOKS.CO.UK

ENGLISH HERITAGE

Elain Harwood 2003

CONTENTS

INTRODUCTION

In 1951 Nikolaus Pevsner, in one of his first architectural guides, called the Hoover Factory 'perhaps the most offensive of the modernistic atrocities' in west London. He refrained from even mentioning the still more art deco Firestone Factory. Yet it was the demolition of Firestone over a bank holiday in 1980, just as it was about to be listed, that brought building preservation to popular attention for the first time. People with little interest in medieval castles and Georgian country houses found they cared passionately for cinemas and lidos, because they were a part of their neighbourhood, their culture. This groundswell of opinion helped to galvanise the government into action. Within six months 150 underground stations, cinemas, factories and other quintessential inter-war buildings had been identified for listing. Today Hoover is listed grade II*, a rare accolade for a building of any period.

But why should listing stop at the 1930s? Architects like Giles Scott, designer of Liverpool Metropolitan Cathedral and the red telephone box – subject of another popular campaign in the 1980s – went on after the Second World War to design Bankside Power Station, now converted to house the modern-art collections of the Tate Gallery. Bankside, long threatened with demolition, remains unlisted. Had it been, more of Scott's subtle massing might have been preserved in Herzog and de Meuron's scheme of reuse. Bankside, the National Union of Miners' building on Euston Road, the Financial Times' offices (Bracken House) opposite St Paul's Cathedral: the post-war buildings threatened with demolition in the mid-1980s were not aggressive, brutal or even made of exposed concrete. It was a revelation to find this coterie of refined, rationalised classical buildings, clad in brick and highly decorative. They remind us that the 1950s were not entirely dominated by modernism, and concentrated research showed that the early post-war years were characterised by a more gentle synthesis of modernism and fine brick building than had hitherto been appreciated. The NUM building, now stripped of its built-in works of art, is a paradigm for the denudation of the British coal industry. But Bracken House, built in 1955–59 to the designs of Sir Albert Richardson and decried by critics since its design was first exhibited, was the first completely post-war building to be listed, in August 1987. Listing saved it from demolition, and instead Michael Hopkins was brought in to remodel it as offices. His new centrepiece shows how a listed building can be treated radically, yet retain its integrity – at Bracken House the old and new gain significantly from their relationship with each other.

An opinion poll in 1996 showed that two-thirds of those canvassed supported the idea of post-war listing. Nevertheless, experience has shown that listing has to be one step ahead of fashion if future Firestone catastrophes are to be avoided. In 1988 Chamberlin, Powell and Bon's curtain-walled seed factory in Witham, Essex, and Ernö Goldfinger's cinema at the Elephant and Castle in London were little lamented when, like Firestone, they were demolished while being considered for listing. That year English Heritage had proposed 70 buildings from the early 1950s for listing, but only 18 were accepted by the government. Out of these failures came a high-profile research programme by building type, supported by leading academics and with exhibitions and booklets on our proposed listings. This work has proselytised both the government and the public, and losses are now less likely: the RC Thanksgiving Shrine of Our Lady of Lourdes by F X Velarde in Blackpool was saved from demolition in 1999 in just 48 hours after a request for listing was made by local residents.

There is now a vogue for the 1960s, and listing has strengthened the popularity of flats in Goldfinger's Trellick Tower and CPB's Golden Lane Estate. Ten years ago Patrick Gwynne's Serpentine Restaurant in Hyde Park was demolished. Now his smaller Dell

Restaurant there is listed, as are most of his surviving houses, and his own house has been acquired by the National Trust.

What makes a building listable? The Secretary of State is required to consider only a building's special architectural or historic interest. A building must be designed with flair, sensitivity and attention to detail; and it must have fulfilled its original brief. Technological innovation, whether in the use of materials or a method of construction, may be a factor, though it must be coupled with design finesse. What matters for any recommendation, whether for a modern or a traditionally styled building, whether it is a church, a school or a factory, is that it demonstrates a clear idea worked all the way through with a consistency of quality down to every detail.

What does listing achieve? It has prevented the probable demolition of Manchester's Oxford Road station, the Wills Factory in Newcastle and Denys Lasdun's Keeling House in Bethnal Green, London. The sale of Keeling House for £1.3 million to a private developer shows the benefit of listing 'buying time' while a new owner or use is found for a building, and how the most controversial public housing can be revitalised. More numerous still are the buildings saved from unsympathetic alteration and partial demolition. Remember the extra storeys that were going to be added to the Smithsons' Economist Building? The external lifts on the side of Centre Point? The demolition of a walkway from the façade of Lasdun's National Theatre? You probably don't, because listing persuaded their owners to think of a more careful solution to their needs.

In the 1980s the idea that the post-war era was about more than welfare-state modernism was a crucial message, and one amply demonstrated by the work of architects such as Donald McMorran and Raymond Erith, as well as by Richardson and Scott. Even more important was the idea that modernism could be good. So much had been forgotten, or ignored by architectural historians of the generations after Pevsner, that English Heritage's research programme was a process of rediscovery starting almost from scratch. We were fortunate in being able first to concentrate on the early 1950s, to look anew at the values and styles personified by the Festival of Britain, with its aspirations in the gentle Scandinavian styles and social democracy of the late 1930s. A similar reappraisal can be seen in the new architecture of the 1990s. The study of the Macmillan years (1957–63), in which England 'never had it so good', was still more important, for never were our towns and cities so radically transformed. Few people realise that more churches were built then than at any time since the 1860s, so overwhelmed were they by the shopping centres, houses, flats and car parks which were also constructed.

Recent media concern has focused on the commercial interests of listing tall office blocks, and on public housing. Research by the Royal Institution of Chartered Surveyors indicated that listing had no adverse impact on the performance of commercial property. Where it *is* having particular value is in the regeneration of urban centres and housing estates, and not only in fashionable central London or emerging Bethnal Green. The listing of Balfron Tower and parts of the Lansbury Estate in the East End, and subsequent local-authority interest in declaring Conservation Areas there, has attracted regeneration grants from an exceptionally wide variety of housing and urban funds. The listing of Park Hill, Sheffield, has so far stabilised a community that had thought its estate might be demolished, and reaffirmed a sense of pride. Public consultations have revealed support for listing among the vocal core of residents at most of the housing schemes which are now protected.

Today the issue is not whether we should list post-war buildings but whether we should be listing more. Three suggestions a week from members of the public are testament to the interest the research programme has generated. Surveys are continuing, with studies of communications, road and airport buildings now with the DCMS. Schools, private homes and the major university expansion programme of the 1960s are now under scrutiny.

STOP PRESS Just listed, on 16 October 2002, was Benjamin Britten's studio at Chapel House, Horham, Suffolk. Here he composed his last works, between 1971 and 1976. Although a simple brick structure erected by local builders, the studio was listed for its historical associations. Chapel House, to which Peter Collymore made additions in 1972, is already listed.

WHAT IS LISTING?

The 1944 and 1947 town and country planning acts required the government to maintain a list of buildings of 'special architectural or historic interest'. Today that power is vested in the Secretary of State for Culture, Media and Sport. English Heritage is the government's architectural advisor and assesses suggestions made by members of the public in addition to conducting its own research. In the past it concentrated on geographical surveys of towns and villages but increasingly it has focused on the types of building under greatest threat, for example textile mills, cinemas and public houses. The post-war programme pioneered this approach back in 1992.

The post-war studies are unique in having the support and expertise of a voluntary steering group of architects, engineers and historians – specialists in the subject – who assess all proposals for listing. Their selection is then debated by English Heritage's Historic Buildings and Areas Advisory Committee, and by commissioners, before final recommendations are made to the DCMS. Since 1994 the public, including owners and occupants, has been invited to comment on post-war listing proposals. This system is neither a poll, nor does it offer a right of veto to owners, for the final decision is that of the Secretary of State.

Although most of the post-war buildings so far listed have been identified as part of a building-type survey, a number have been listed individually, or 'spotlisted' when under threat of alteration or demolition. Anybody can ask for a building to be spotlisted. You should write, enclosing recent photographs, a map and, if appropriate, a contact telephone number for the building to Department for Culture, Media and Sport, Listing Branch, 2–4 Cockspur Street, London SW1Y 5DH. By December 1999 there were 370,000 listings in England, ranging from long terraces of houses to individual tombstones and boundary markers. In all, 551 individual buildings and sculptures from the years since 1940 are listed, including several groups of buildings, notably for education or housing, which form single entries in this guide.

There are three grades of listing. The highest, grade I, is reserved for buildings of international stature and, in all, only 2.5 per cent of buildings are so designated. Those graded II* are defined as 'outstanding' and comprise 5.5 per cent of present listings. Most listed buildings are grade II, for their 'special' interest and national significance.

The date work began on the foundations is that used to determine the age of a building for listing. A building can be listed if it is more than 30 years old and – exceptionally – if it is more than ten years old, provided that it is both under threat and 'outstanding'. Buildings between ten and 30 years old are thus normally only listed if they are of grade II* or grade I importance. This is one reason for the relatively large proportion of highly graded post-war buildings; another is that the buildings meriting high grades tend to be the best known and have already been identified, while grade II buildings are still being discovered.

Listing does not mean that a building has to remain unchanged, but it does require that alterations and additions are thoughtfully designed and not detrimental to its special character. Such work requires listed building consent, from the local planning authority for grade II buildings and from English Heritage for buildings graded II* or I. Five post-war listed buildings have been demolished, one following its near-destruction by fire. Listed buildings may be eligible for relief from VAT for approved works of alteration, and grants may be available for repairs from local authorities, English Heritage, the National Lottery and other sources. Scotland, Wales and Northern Ireland have their own listing systems, with broadly similar criteria for the selection of post-war buildings.

Listing does not require a building to be opened to the public, and the buildings in this guide are strictly private except where access is noted otherwise.

FURTHER READING

The Buildings of England series founded by Sir Nikolaus Pevsner remains an invaluable starting point. It is fascinating to watch Pevsner's own changing appreciation of modern buildings, fulsome in the 1950s, wary of Stirling and brutalism in the 1960s, measured in the 1970s. Recent revisions have brilliantly assimilated his text with new research and reassessments. Robert Elwall's *Building a Better Tomorrow* (Wiley-Academy, 2000) is a well-illustrated introduction.

Large numbers of books were published on the new architecture at the time. Trevor Dannatt's *Modern Architecture in Britain* (Batsford, 1959) and with a distinguished essay by Sir John Summerson, selects the best 1950s buildings, an exercise repeated for the

1960s by Robert Maxwell with *New British Architecture* (Thames and Hudson, 1972). A more international perspective is provided by the special issue of *Zodiac* (no.18, Milan, 1968) devoted to 'English brutalism'. Dannatt was the main editor of the *Architects' Year Books* (Elek Books) which between 1945 and 1968 give an indication of the principal issues and buildings that were preoccupying architects. Ian Nairn's *Modern Buildings in London* (London Transport, 1964) is quirky yet incisive. Studio Vista's City Buildings series is helpful, as is Bruce Allsopp's *Modern Architecture of Northern England* (Oriel, 1969). Best of all these 1960s studies are Nicholas Taylor's *Cambridge New Architecture* (privately published, several editions from 1964 onwards) and Lewiston's and Bellingham's *Coventry New Architecture* (privately published, 1969). On churches Peter Hammond's *Liturgy and Architecture* (Barrie and Rockcliff, 1960) was hugely influential. However, perhaps the most profound scholarship of the period was that of Rayner Banham, of whose works *The New Brutalism* (Architectural Press, 1966), *The Architecture of the Well-Tempered Environment* (Architectural Press, 1969) and *Megastructure* (Thames and Hudson, 1976) are most relevant.

More recent books have concentrated on specific building types, or on individual architects. Andrew Saint's *Towards a Social Architecture* (Yale, 1987) on schools, is an incisive account of the camaraderie and social commitment that stimulated architects and clients in the austere 1940s. Glendinning's and Muthesius' *Tower Block* (Yale, 1994) offers an alternative view of post-war housing, concentrating on the mass of public building rather than the exceptional schemes which have been listed. Andrew Saint's *Park Hill: What Next?* (Architectural Association, 1996) is a critical essay on the most provocative listed housing, and his is the name fronting *London Suburbs* (Merrell Holberton, 1999), which includes a chapter on post-war housing. *Twentieth-Century Architecture*, the journal of the Twentieth-Century Society, has so far looked at post-war industrial buildings, churches, houses, *The Festival of Britain* and *The Sixties*. The Phaidon Press series, *Architecture in Detail*, includes excellent studies on the Royal Festival Hall and Leicester University Engineering Building, both by John McKean, and the former Willis Faber and Dumas Building by Gabriele Bramante.

Books on architects are more numerous and varied. A definitive study is John Allan's *Lubetkin* (RIBA, 1992). Pioneering back in 1983 was James Dunnett's and Gavin Stamp's *Ernö Goldfinger* (Architectural Association), still the best work on this distinctive figure, and the AA also published a retrospective, *Lyons Israel Ellis Gray* (1988). Alan Powers's *In the Line of Development* (RIBA, 1992) is unique in surveying a big 1950s practice, Yorke, Rosenberg and Mardall, and it was followed by our collaboration on *Tayler and Green, Architects* (Prince of Wales Institute of Architecture, 1998). More traditional architects have been well served by their offspring, with Lucy Archer's *Raymond Erith* (Cygnet Press, 1985) and Peter Pace on *The Architecture of George Pace* (Batsford, 1990). Most numerous are books on the Smithsons, including their own *The Shift* (Academy Editions, 1983) and *The Charged Void: Architecture* (Monacelli Press, 2002), and on James Stirling, about whom Mark Girouard's *Big Jim* (Chatto and Windus, 1998) is an entertaining introduction.

Ultimately, however, students of the period have invariably to consult the contemporary magazines, a task made easy by the 'grey books' indexes of the British Architectural Library at the RIBA.

ABBREVIATIONS AND CONVENTIONS USED IN THE TEXT

Housing and schools developed their own jargon during the 1950s, which we have endeavoured to keep to a minimum.

AA Architectural Association

ACP Architects' Co-Partnership

CIAM Congrès Internationaux d'Architecture Moderne

CLASP Consortium of Local Authorities' Special Programme

CPB Chamberlin, Powell & Bon

DETR Department of the Environment, Transport and the Regions

GLC Greater London Council

HKPA Howell, Killick, Partridge and Amis

LB London Borough

LCC London County Council

LMS London, Midland & Scottish Railways

MB Metropolitan Borough

MHLG Ministry of Housing and Local Government

RC Roman Catholic

RDC Rural District Council

RFAC Royal Fine Arts Commission

RIBA Royal Institute of British Architects

SCR Senior Common Room

UGC University Grants Committee

YMCA Young Men's Christian Association

YWCA Young Women's Christian Association

The 1950s and 1960s were a pre-metric age, and imperial measurements have been used where necessary. The names of practices are those in operation when the building began on site, as too are the names of architects who were subsequently knighted or ennobled.

Access to many post-war buildings is extremely difficult. Few churches are open except for services and most schools and – particularly – houses are strictly private.

INTRODUCTION

Listing in England does not carry with it any requirement that a building must be available to the public, unless a grant has been given. Where the words 'Access none' have been used, the building is not visible from the road, and the owners' privacy must be respected.

As a building's age for listing is determined by the date construction started, this, not the design date, has been used throughout.

The name of the nearest station is given where it differs from the name of the town.

ACKNOWLEDGEMENTS

The first edition of this book was the personal suggestion of Alan Howarth, then minister for the arts, and was co-funded by the Department for Culture, Media and Sport and English Heritage.

It fulfilled a long-standing ambition of the Post-War Steering Group, which has been skilfully chaired since its foundation by Bridget Cherry. It is a pleasure to acknowledge her support, and also that of Martin Cherry (no relation), English Heritage's Chief Buildings Historian, both of whom have enriched the text by their comments and corrections. I would like to thank the Steering Group, a loyal body of unpaid experts originally including Ron Brunskill, Catherine Croft, Trevor Dannatt, Alan Powers, Martin Robertson, Andrew Saint, Gavin Stamp, James Sutherland and Geoffrey Wilson, for years of dedication to assessing the significance of many difficult buildings. By 2002 they had been joined by Peter Aldington, John Allan, Peter Beacham, Louise Campbell, Jeremy Gould, Neil Jackson, John Partridge and Pete Smith. The research programme was initiated by Diane Kay whose knowledge and enthusiasm gave the programme its impetus and high standards. It has benefitted from the expertise of many consultants, among them Christopher Dean, Bronwen Edwards, Paul Francis, Roger Harper, Julian Holder, David Lawrence, Suzanne Marston, Mervyn Miller and Bill Smyth. Over all these years Alan Powers, Andrew Saint and Pete Smith have been particularly generous with their time and stimulating in conversation. Nigel Corrie, Alastair Ward and Mike Williams have supplied additional photographs.

Elain Harwood

October 2002

NORTHERN ENGLAND

WYTHENSHAWE BUS GARAGE
MANCHESTER

A new garage for 100 double-decker buses was planned to serve the Wythenshawe Garden Suburb, but on completion it was first commandeered by the Ministry of Aircraft Production for building Lancaster bombers.

It is the second large reinforced-concrete shell roof structure built in England – the first, a hangar at Doncaster Airport, was demolished c. 1990. The equations for shell domes and cylindrical shell roofs were published in England in 1930 and again in 1935, but as the system was both innovatory and German the patentees, Chisarc and Shell D Ltd, found few clients.

Wythenshawe's concrete arches have a span of 165 feet, are 42 feet high and are 42 feet apart. The innovation is that the shell roof between them is just $2^1/_2$ inches thick. It was particularly daring to then pierce such a tensile structure with rooflights. To the rear are washing bays and a taller repair hall, whose roof is formed of seven longitudinal shell cylinders, again with roof lights.

The late 1930s and early 1950s saw the building of many bus garages as tram services were phased out, and shell construction was a cheap way of achieving broad, uninterrupted spans. This was the pioneering example of the means of construction, and the model for the larger shells at Bournemouth and Stockwell (see pages 328 and 674). It is now used for warehousing.

LISTED grade II*, 13 July 2001
ADDRESS Harling Road, Manchester
ENGINEERS H G Cousins with Chisarc and Shell D Ltd
NEAREST STATIONS East Didsbury/Parr's Wood
ACCESS exterior only

Manchester City Architect's Department, under G Noel Hill 1939–42

ADAM RAILWAY VIADUCT
WALLGATE, WIGAN

The Adam Viaduct is the earliest prestressed railway bridge in England - worldwide only examples in Switzerland are certainly earlier. The LMS had opened a pioneering research institution in 1932 at Derby, where it developed the use of precast concrete. Precast units were strong, long-lasting and cheap, and could be installed quickly. But the large depth of the beams required for large spans made the technique of limited use for underbridges and viaducts, where traffic has to pass underneath. Prestressing meant that beams could be more slender. They were used for emergency repairs in the war, but this was their first use in a wholly new structure.

The Adam Viaduct spans a river and bridle path close to the Wigan Pier canal basin, and forms part of an embankment west of the town centre. The new structure replaced a timber bridge. It has four spans, and a deck formed of prestressed I-beams supporting the track. The precast concrete parapet and handrail survive on the eastern elevation. Though not elegant, the massive piers – novel for being of vibrated concrete – have a heavyweight quality faintly reminiscent of John Vanbrugh. High-tensile rods tie the beams so they act together under live loads. Tests made in 1947 showed that the bridge could take a load of $26^1/_4$ tons, 50 per cent more than that for which it was designed.

LISTED grade II, 23 March 2001
NEAREST STATIONS Wigan North Western/Wigan Wallgate
ACCESS any reasonable time

London, Midland and Scottish Railways, W K Wallace, Chief Engineer 1946

W D AND H O WILLS TOBACCO FACTORY
NEWCASTLE UPON TYNE

The Wills Factory's sturdy classicism is reminiscent of American factory design from more than a decade earlier. The image was appropriate for a firm with an American product, which was resisting American competiton while introducing many of its ideas of branding, advertising and egalitarian working conditions.

Cecil Hockin was architect to the Imperial Tobacco Company, of which Wills' formed a part. Imperial had decided to decentralise their manufacture and distribution network before the Second World War, but in the 1940s benefitted from grants encouraging new industry to Tyneside, which explains how they could obtain a rare building licence for so large and impressive a structure. The site is a busy bypass, itself constructed in the 1930s and an appropriate location for streamlined architecture with strong, 'go-faster' horizontals. The centrepiece is of stone, raised half a storey to give a greater monumentality. Here was architecture as corporate advertising, moderne yet dignified, in a perfect location for road and rail communications.

The building was originally much larger, with carefully planned factory ranges at the rear housing the shredding, blending and cigarette-making processes. Listing did not prevent these from being demolished in 1995. A subsequent application to demolish the front office block was challenged, and after years of dereliction and vandalism, it has been successfully converted to flats.

LISTED grade II, 17 November 1986
ADDRESS Coast Road, Newcastle upon Tyne
GETTING THERE train to Howdon or Newcastle Central, then bus; at east edge of city, on A1058
ACCESS exterior only

Cecil Hockin 1946–50

TYNE PEDESTRIAN AND CYCLE TUNNELS
HOWDON AND JARROW

The idea of a road tunnel under the Tyne was approved by Northumberland and Durham County Councils in 1937 and authorised by Act of Parliament in 1946. The road tunnel was not begun until 1961, but in 1947 work started on pedestrian and cycle tunnels to serve the large numbers of men then working in the shipyards on both sides of the river.

Both tunnels are 900 feet long. The pedestrian tunnel is 10 feet 6 inches in diameter, the cycle tunnel 12 feet. At 85 feet the escalators were the longest in Britain and perhaps the world when installed. A speed ray regulator, part of the original equipment, controls their speed, so that they go more slowly when nobody is using them. Lifts and 153 stairs are for emergencies. The modest circular entrance pavilions, of brick and concrete, survive with little alteration to their original internal finishes of tile, aluminium and ivory plastic. The tunnels themselves are lined with cast-iron segments and tiled in sea-green and cream, a pattern interrupted only at mid-point where the boundary between the two counties is marked in black lettering. So much green tiling creates an eerily misty effect, not for the claustrophobic. But the survival of the original machinery and internal finishes make the tunnels a unique experience to explore, and they now form part of a long-distance cycle route.

LISTED grade II, 13 April 2000
LOCATION between Bewicke Street, Howdon, North Tyneside and Tyne Street, Jarrow, South Tyneside
NEAREST METRO STATIONS Howdon/Jarrow
ACCESS open 24 hours

Mott, Hay and Anderson 1947–51

39–73 (ODD) GRAHAM PARK ROAD
GOSFORTH, NEWCASTLE UPON TYNE

In 1948 Gosforth Urban District Council voted to build flats 'of a superior type... for better-class people' on a small bomb site near its southern boundary. Its model was the middle-class flats built in the 1930s in London's outer suburbs. Wyld prepared his designs the following year.

The 18 flats have a strong Festival of Britain quality, with circular windows and tiled dados to the staircases, projecting canopies and balconies. At one end is a shelter for prams. Inside the flats have glazed screens between the living and dining areas, with a hatch to the kitchen, and many retain their original fitted cupboards. Wide skirting boards were designed for ease of cleaning. Letter boxes and rubbish chutes were carefully built in. The flats had garages from the first, and their high standard of finish testifies to the care with which this scheme was designed for its target market.

The concept of building council flats to be let at commercial rents was popular in the immediate post-war years, but relatively few were built. This example survives unusually completely, and the conscious emulation of southern England is itself rare. Though such flats proved popular in cities, in the new towns planners found that most people wanted houses and only in the 1960s were more flats built, to bring a population to the town centres.

NORTHERN ENGLAND

LISTED grade II, 11 July 2001
NEAREST METRO South Gosforth
ACCESS exterior only

Clifford Wyld, Gosforth Borough Architect 1951–52

THE SHIPPON
SOUTHPORT

Although he was unable to begin work on Meols Hall until 1960, Roger Hesketh discovered in 1952 that he could obtain a building licence for agricultural buildings. The result was a cow house – traditionally termed a shippon – for his herd of prize Jerseys.

Hesketh's understanding of classical proportion and detailing, subsequently displayed at Meols Hall, is already evident in this extraordinary design. It is a remarkable design for its date: at once austere yet supremely inventive. Hesketh produced a symmetrical Palladian composition, with a two-storey centrepiece flanked by cow byres and low-end pavilions under hipped roofs. The gaunt central block is reminiscent of Raymond Erith, but in a grittier northern vein made more convincing by the reuse of old bricks and stonework.

LISTED grade II, 15 July 1998
ADDRESS Meols Hall, Botanic Road, Churchtown, Southport
NEAREST STATION Meols Cop
ACCESS none

Roger Fleetwood Hesketh 1952

LOVELL TELESCOPE
MACCLESFIELD

Radio astronomy, pioneered in the 1930s, evolved in Britain out of radar. In 1945 Bernard Lovell installed a radar transmitter at Manchester University's botanical station, Jodrell Bank, and proved that meteors were part of the solar system.

Lovell then constructed a huge paraboloidal reflector on the ground. Its success in detecting radio waves from the Andromeda galaxy prompted him to propose a giant telescope that could be pointed to any part of the sky. Charles Husband designed a 76-metre dish that could be tilted from supports on either side, and moved on a circular track. As construction commenced discoveries elsewhere demanded a more precisely finished bowl so as to detect wavelengths of a few centimetres. A solid steel dish was produced from 7100 welded panels, 2.1-mm thick.

The telescope achieved immediate fame when in 1957 it tracked the first satellite, Sputnik I. Though used for tracking space probes, astronomical study – particularly of pulsars – remains its principal function. In 1970–71 two circular wheel girders were placed under the bowl as additional supports. It is now the third largest fully steerable radio telescope in the world, after those at Effelsberg, Germany, and Green Bank, West Virginia. It can also be linked to seven other dishes across England.

LISTED grade I, 13 June 1988

ADDRESS Nuffield Radio Astronomy Laboratories, Jodrell Bank, near Macclesfield, Cheshire

NEAREST STATION Goostrey

ACCESS visitor centre open daily; call 01477 571339 for information

NORTHERN ENGLAND

Bernard Lovell, astronomer; Charles Husband, engineer 1952–57

FARNLEY HEY
HUDDERSFIELD

Farnley Hey is Britain's best-known example of the American 'contemporary' style, mixing traditional rough-stone walls and floors with vast picture windows, and natural wood with fashionable modern materials such as Formica and opaque glass. It is the principal English work by Peter Womersley, a Newark-born architect who later settled in Scotland, and was designed for his brother. Remarkably, most of Womersley's original fixtures and internal finishes survive.

The expansive windows, together with the terraces and porches that colonise the hillside, suggest that the house is larger than it is: the planning and degrees of enclosure account for the house's spaciousness. Apart from a small landing between bedroom and bathroom, there is virtually no circulation space; the staircase with its Formica panel is as much a piece of furniture as a link between levels. The double-height living room, daringly cantilevered mezzanine gallery and 'zoned' bedroom and bathroom wing are an early demonstration of the exciting possibilities of free planning. Fittings include original silk lampshades and special hi-fi units.

In style Farnley Hey suggests the influence of Le Corbusier's Pavilion Suisse, and of Frank Lloyd Wright's free planning and use of materials, brought to a dramatic site in the Pennines. It also typifies the best of the 1950s in its lightness, sense of the picturesque and optimistic stance.

NORTHERN ENGLAND

LISTED grade II, 15 July 1998
ADDRESS Farnley Tyas, near Huddersfield, West Yorkshire
NEAREST STATION Honley
ACCESS none

Peter Womersley 1953–54, extended 1956

HEATON PARK PUMPING STATION
SALFORD

An Act to bring water to Manchester from the Lake District was secured in 1919, and a dam to form the Haweswater Reservoir was completed in 1934. It was only in 1947–55 that an aqueduct and pipeline were built to bring the water to the city, a distance of 82 miles and costing £14 million. The building of the aqueduct is recorded in panels along the walls of the little pumping station, designed by Alan Atkinson, head of Manchester City Engineer's Department, and opened in June 1955 at the end of the pipeline at Heaton Park Reservoir. Appropriately, the building was constructed of Yorkshire sandstone and Westmorland greenstone.

Most evocative of all is the mural carved along its main wall. Mitzi Cunliffe, a prolific designer of architectural sculpture, depicts the bringing of water from Haweswater to Manchester with a curious flat relief designed to be seen from below. The inclusion of contemporary figures commemorates those who constructed the aqueduct as well as the route from the Lake District.

The interior of the pumping station is completely preserved. It is lined in beige and green marble, and features a relief diagram in sycamore wood tracing the route of the pipe. It is extraordinary to find so much artwork on a humble industrial building, especially one in an unfrequented suburban location. It serves as a tribute to the preoccupation with public art of the early 1950s.

LISTED grade II, 15 April 1998
ADDRESS Heywood Road, Prestwich, Salford
NEAREST STATION Besses-o'-th'-Barn
ACCESS exterior only

Manchester City Engineer's Department 1954–55

RC THANKSGIVING SHRINE OF OUR LADY OF LOURDES
BLACKPOOL

The Shrine of Our Lady of Lourdes, patron saint of the diocese of Lancaster, was conceived by Bishop Thomas Flynn as a thanksgiving for the diocese's relatively unscathed survival through the Second World War. Every parish in the diocese subscribed to its cost of £50,000 – considerably more than most parish churches at the time. Blackpool was chosen for its central position and convenience for visitors, and a local builder, William Eaves, donated the site.

Velarde's work was described as 'original', but with 'its roots in the Ancient Romanesque Architecture'. This undervalues its diminutive jewel-like quality that transcends conventional church formulae. The exterior is dominated by a central carved relief and figurative corner pinnacles, all the work of local sculptor David John. The exceptional integration of art and architecture is continued in the sumptuous interior, which has gilded mosaic columns and a painted ceiling. The Romanesque style and use of gilded decoration is reminiscent of Velarde's contemporary church at St Theresa, Up Holland (see page 40).

Spotlisting – in just two days – pre-empted the shrine's demolition by the Diocese, who had already stripped the interior of its pews and movable fittings. The building has now been given to the Historic Chapels Trust.

LISTED grade II*, 30 June 1999
ADDRESS Whinney Heys Road, Blackpool
GETTING THERE train to Blackpool North; off B5266 on east of town
ACCESS exterior only at time of writing

Francis Xavier Velarde 1955–57

RC ST THERESA OF THE CHILD JESUS
UP HOLLAND

Francis Xavier Velarde was an influential architect in the 1930s, but his later churches were not published and have remained little known. Most architects whose work spanned the Second World War were compromised by the smaller budgets available in the 1950s into building more modest works. Not Velarde. His later work has a strength lacking in his earlier churches, achieved using traditional materials expressively, and by adopting the Romanesque style. His windows are deliberately small and round-arched to heighten the sense of massiveness. Velarde had a Spanish father and closely studied that country's early churches, and it is this influence which came increasingly to the fore.

St Theresa's has a remarkable quantity of external carving, with reliefs, a pietà and a line of angels topping the buttresses. This sculpture is by Herbert Tyson Smith, who worked on many of Velarde's churches. The composition is offset by a campanile, whose round-arched openings are a Velarde characteristic.

However, it is the interior which is most impressive, for its exceptional sense of darkness and richness, and for its use of gilding and touches of brilliant colour. The long low hall is reminiscent of the earliest Christian churches. This is achieved by the massive construction and small windows, and by an aisle of round, gilded columns. Their blue capitals complement the painted ceiling and altar fittings.

LISTED grade II, 9 December 1999
ADDRESS Up Holland, Lancashire
GETTING THERE train to Orrell or Up Holland; just off A577 to north of town, towards Roby Mill
ACCESS open regularly; call 01695 622516 for more information

Francis Xavier Velarde 1955–57

FORMER SUGAR SILO
LIVERPOOL

The storage of granular substances such as grain poses particular problems due to their fluidity. In the USA around 1900 reinforced concrete was found to have the necessary strength for silos, and the skylines of Minneapolis and Buffalo were transformed by the giant bins later celebrated by Erich Mendelsohn and Rayner Banham.

In Britain only a few silos have been built. At Billingham, Imperial Chemicals built a series of silos to store fertilisers in the 1920s using a parabolic arched construction inspired by Eugene Freyssinet's hangars at Orly, and which conformed to the natural shape of a mound of phosphate or grain. The same principle was adopted in Liverpool by David Bailey, of Tate and Lyle Engineer's Department, for a tunnel silo to store sugar.

At 161-metres long and 26.5-metres high this is the largest parabolic silo in England. It is constructed in twelve ribbed sections, each with an expansion joint. The interior is smooth. Raw sugar was loaded via a system of conveyor belts from the dockside, and reclaimed by gravity through a band of hoppers set down the centre of the floor into another conveyor below. Although the parabolic arches were not innovatory the silo's prestressed floor was an advance over the Billingham models, and its very size and shape is impressive. Today it is used to store grain.

NORTHERN ENGLAND

LISTED grade II*, 23 September 1992
ADDRESS 173 Regent Road, Liverpool
NEAREST STATION Sandhills
ACCESS exterior only

Tate and Lyle Engineer's Department 1955–57

UNIVERSITY LIBRARY AND ARTS TOWER
SHEFFIELD

Sheffield University was unique in the post-war years in holding a public competition for its new buildings, in 1953. This is now remembered for the unplaced schemes by the Smithsons and by James Stirling which signalled the emergence of a new British architecture. The winners were more inspired by the American office architecture of Mies van der Rohe and Gordon Bunshaft, and no other British firm achieved the simplicity of American curtain walling with such confidence. With the loss of GMW's most important London buildings, the Sheffield buildings have added significance.

The buildings were completely redesigned after the competition, as was the overall plan. The library was built first, of Portland stone and tinted glass, and the outstanding interiors have an opulence rare in university buildings. They comprise a progression of spaces, increasing in size and dramatic effect until they reach a climax on arriving in the main reading room, overlooking Weston Park. Light-weight mezzanines have been successfully incorporated to provide extra study space.

The library's low bulk acts as a foil to the 19-storey Arts Tower. Although the debt to Bunshaft's Lever House and Union Carbide buildings followed a later revision, a tower featured in GMW's first proposals. There are lecture theatres in the basement, with tutorial rooms in the tower. The complex dramatically fulfills the university's original aim of creating a prominent landmark.

NORTHERN ENGLAND

LISTED grade II*, 30 March 1993
ADDRESS Western Bank, Sheffield
GETTING THERE train to Sheffield, then tram to University
ACCESS exterior only

Gollins Melvin Ward and Partners 1956–59, 1961–65

RUNCORN-WIDNES BRIDGE
RUNCORN GAP

This bridge replaced the transporter bridge of 1901 that linked Runcorn and Widnes across the Mersey. When built it was the largest steel arch in Europe and the third largest in the world, with a main span of 330 metres. The side spans are of 76 metres, and with end cantilevers the total length of the bridge is 496 metres. The final cost was £2.467 million.

The bridge is designed as a two-pinned arch, the side spans being continuous with it. To meet the movements that arise in large-span bridges, a joint was designed consisting of a series of steel plates laid on edge across the carriageway, inlaid with rubber cushions. Forty-two of these units were laid together and prestressed.

The bow-arch bridge shares the powerful aesthetic found in inter-war bridges, such as the same firm's Sunderland Bridge of 1929, and Sydney Harbour Bridge of 1929–32. Here, however, there are no stone terminal towers, so that the engineering stands for itself, elegant and expressive of the new England encapsulated in the road's very name of Queensway. It remains the principal road link between Liverpool and the south.

LISTED grade II, 29 March 1988
ADDRESS Queensway, A533 at Runcorn Gap
NEAREST STATION Runcorn
ACCESS any reasonable time

Mott, Hay and Anderson, engineers 1956–61

CIVIC CENTRE
NEWCASTLE UPON TYNE

A new city hall was first proposed in 1939, and plans were prepared in 1950. The building was consequently considered old-fashioned when it was completed and was little published, but it is now appreciated as an exceptional civic ensemble of art and architecture.

The Civic Centre is part office building, part function suite. First came the Rates Hall range at the rear, with murals by Victor Pasmore, then teaching at the university. Next followed the 12-storey central office range and finally the council chamber and public halls (1965–69), where the sculptural enrichment is particularly lavish. The centre is best approached via the Ceremonial Way, with nine symbolic flambeaux by Charles Sansbury, who also designed metal screens to the internal courtyard and the lift doors. The entrance is dominated by the *River God Tyne* by David Wynne, and opens on to the council chamber on one side. The banqueting hall on the other side features a John Piper tapestry.

Dominating the entrance is a carillon tower, culminating in a series of copper fins sporting seahorses and crowns from the city's coat of arms. These exemplify the overall Scandinavian tone of the building, which uses Norwegian stone, and which is reminiscent of Oslo City Hall (1940). Appropriately, King Olav V of Norway performed the opening ceremony.

NORTHERN ENGLAND

LISTED grade II*, 16 November 1995
ADDRESS Barras Bridge, Newcastle upon Tyne
ACCESS call 0191 232 8520 for guided tours

George W Kenyon, city architect 1956–69

RHODESWAY SCHOOL
BRADFORD

Rhodesway is an unusually serious piece of architecture for a school. This is especially apparent in its use of materials, where a heavily polluted atmosphere prompted the choice of black-painted steel, tiles and grey engineering bricks. These are combined well with natural stone. The boiler-house chimney, in grey brick, acts as a counterpoise to the long main range and the abutting teaching wing to its left.

The planning is compact. A square central block houses the assembly hall and gymnasium, which is separated by a landscaped courtyard from the administrative offices and sixth-form rooms. Classrooms are in wings to either side, while workshops have a separate range to the south. Such is the academic success of the school that a series of additions have been made to the side and rear, none of which interfere with the architectural presence of the main range. This is dominated by the school's principal decoration, to the side of the fully-glazed entrance hall: a mural by Joe Mayo in iridescent tiles.

Architecturally, the combination of natural materials with a Miesian aesthetic places Rhodesway midway between Denis Clarke Hall's school at Richmond (1938) and the Smithsons' high school at Hunstanton (see pages 230–232). There is a warmth in the flexibility and informality which many may prefer to Hunstanton's rigorous courtyard box, while the quality of the design gracefully embraces the great range of materials.

NORTHERN ENGLAND

LISTED grade II, 30 March 1993
ADDRESS Oaks Lane, Bradford
GETTING THERE train to Bradford Forster Square or Interchange; to west of city off B6145
ACCESS exterior only

Bradford City Council Architect's Department 1957–59

PARK HILL
SHEFFIELD

No other authority produced a greater range of housing in the post-war years than did Sheffield under Lewis Womersley, city architect from 1953 to 1964. He had few models for comprehensive city redevelopment, save for the Quarry Hill Flats (1935–39, demolished 1978) in the rival city of Leeds. Womersley's enterprise owed much to his rejection of system building in favour of one-off designs for specific sites, as only London and Southampton (in part) were also to do. His reputation attracted the young Jack Lynn and Ivor Smith, who had been designing student projects for 'streets in the sky' – total communities of housing, shops and pubs on several levels. Lynn had also made an unsuccessful entry for the Golden Lane competition (see page 598), where a similar scheme by the Smithsons received considerable attention.

The idea was uniquely suited to the sheer slopes of 'Little Chicago', a notorious slum which had been cleared before the war but not redeveloped. Street decks work at Park Hill as nowhere else because all save the topmost of the three walkways give on to street level at some point. The development ranges from four to 13 storeys with the fall of the land, while maintaining a constant roofline. It has 994 flats, designed on a three-bay, three-storey unit, with an access deck every third floor and comprising a one- and a two-bed flat below the deck level, with a two- and a three-bed maisonette on and above it. There are also four pubs, a shopping parade and a community centre. John Forrester, an abstract artist, advised on the design, though the architects boasted that no complete elevations were ever drawn. The tough concrete frame is infilled with bricks in a progression of colours from dark to light, and each flat has a balcony.

Park Hill's completion attracted widespread publicity, including three BBC documentaries that gloried in the little milk floats which ran along the decks. It signified Sheffield's post-war renewal, along with cleaner air and a new shopping centre. It was

Sheffield City Architects' Department 1957–61

also the first large-scale slum clearance project anywhere, and the first with wide access decks as raised streets where children could play. What is remarkable is not that Park Hill has problems – there have always been too few lifts, the concrete is spalling and the shops are underused – but that it has worked as well as it has.

The listing of Park Hill has attracted more media attention than any other decision, but has been staunchly supported by Sheffield City Council as a key to its regeneration. Proposals for the building's refurbishment are currently being sought. It has proved popular with students of nearby Sheffield Hallam University, and they may be the key to the building's future.

LISTED grade II*, 22 December 1998
ENGINEER Ove Arup and Partners
ADDRESS Park Hill, Sheffield
ACCESS exterior only

Sheffield City Architects' Department 1957–61

ST PAUL
SHEFFIELD

Austere St Paul is the most refined of all Spence's parish churches. All have their genesis in three small churches commissioned for new Coventry suburbs in 1955 by Bishop Gorton, using War Damages Commission compensation for a single bombed church. Spence and Gorton were developing ideas for a fully glazed west end at Coventry Cathedral, which would allow people to see in and out, and Spence had experimented with the idea in little churches for the Coventry suburbs. Glazed ends were subsequently made fashionable by the Sirens' Otaniemi chapel of 1957, which overlooks virgin Finnish woodland.

St Paul is glazed at both ends, though the western window is bisected by the gallery carrying the choir and organ. The slightly undulating walls are of brick, while the segmental barrel roof is criss-crossed with diagonal steel bracing from which simple bulbs are strung. The roof appears to float on glass, so transparent and minimal is the design. The fittings are by Spence, who personally gave the altar ornaments of hammered iron. Outside, the church's presence is denoted by an open bell tower, linked by a covered way. The church is remarkably little altered.

This is an architectural lemon sorbet, the perfect place for tranquil contemplation. The real world is oddly visible through the window, but nevertheless set apart.

NORTHERN ENGLAND

LISTED grade II*, 25 September 1998
ADDRESS Wordsworth Avenue, Sheffield
GETTING THERE train to Sheffield, then bus. Wordsworth Avenue runs due north of the A6102, north of the city centre
ACCESS open for services

Basil Spence and Partners 1958–59

ST CATHERINE OF SIENA
SHEFFIELD

This is the second and larger of Spence's two parish churches in Sheffield. It was funded by the War Damages Commission, in compensation for a bombed city-centre church, who insisted on a 'plain church' for 500 worshippers. A folding screen means that the adjoining church hall can be opened into the nave for major festivals and provide the full complement of seating. The unusually rich fittings testify to the church's relatively generous funding.

The sanctuary is carefully staged. Spence's simple architecture achieves its effect through directed clerestory lighting and white plastered walls, the last forming a theatrical cyclorama in the apse behind the liturgical fittings. Altar, pulpit and the fossil limestone font stand in a line, and thus attain equal prominence. The ceiling, running over laminated timber beams, slopes gently upwards to the chancel where a hidden window shines light directly on to the altar.

The 23-metre bell tower is formed of two curves of brickwork, designed as an eye on plan. An incised inscription by the slate-hung entrance is by Ralph Beyer, who was then carving those for Coventry Cathedral. A bronze Crucifixion was later fixed to the tower.

Since the building was listed the porch has been extended, with coffee facilities in their own apse, and the hall has been modified.

NORTHERN ENGLAND

LISTED grade II, 13 June 1997
ENGINEER Ove Arup and Partners
ADDRESS Richmond Road, Sheffield
GETTING THERE Richmond Road runs between the A57 and A616 to the south-east of the city centre
ACCESS open most days for services and events; call 0114 239 9598

Basil Spence and Partners 1958–60

HOLLINGS COLLEGE (THE TOAST-RACK)

MANCHESTER

Hollings College, universally known as The Toast-Rack for the extraordinary shape of its teaching block, was built as Manchester's Domestic and Trades College. It was designed in three parts around courses in catering and fashion design, but is dominated by the six-storey classroom block, whose tapered form was inspired by the need for rooms of different sizes. Its concrete parabolic arched construction is testimony to Leonard Howitt's particular fascination with using concrete technology to create picturesque forms. He was a local lad who worked his way up to become chief architect, and his interest in structure can be seen in public buildings across the city. The result is an early example of the 'pop architecture' of concrete and glass in geometric forms developed in the 1960s in office buildings such as Centre Point, London (see page 546).

The tailoring workshops were placed in a separate steel-framed building at the rear to minimise disturbance from their noisy machinery. The low range in front was built as a circular hall for cat-walk shows with a restaurant wrapped around it – to which the public were invited as guinea pigs for the cookery course. In 1995–96 this hub was raised a storey by Mills, Beaumont, Leacey, Channon to create a library and information technology centre, its neat design an appropriate response to its sensitive location.

LISTED grade II, 24 April 1998
ADDRESS Manchester Metropolitan University, Wilmslow Road, Manchester
GETTING THERE train to Oxford Road, then bus (see page 74)
ACCESS exterior only of interest

NORTHERN ENGLAND

Manchester City Architect's Department 1958–60

UP HOLLAND HIGH SCHOOL
UP HOLLAND

In 1953 Lyons Israel Ellis won a competition for a school in Cornwall, which exploited the local granite aggregates in a tough design of concrete, brick and glass. Under Tom Ellis the firm was among the first consistently to exploit the idiom of exposed concrete frame and brick infill that was a peculiarly British development of Le Corbusier's Maisons Jaoul (1953–55). The evolution of this brutalism is best seen in a series of secondary schools, of which this is one of the most mature.

The site was a tight one, bounded by an earlier school and an infilled quarry. Moreover, the brief imposed a limit of two storeys. Ellis's team produced a system of pale-brick cross walls, spaced 24 foot 6 inches apart, from which the classrooms, science laboratories and handicraft rooms are formed like a series of half-open drawers – some long, some shorter – which give the school its distinctive profile. Three units make up the rear assembly hall. The ends of each unit are fully glazed above thick timber dados. The glazed entrance, reached via steps and ramps set round a mature tree, is a particularly satisfying composition.

Built for 240 pupils, the school now has more than 900. The main building has been extended, but this has been done using the same pale-brick-and-concrete idiom.

LISTED grade II, 30 March 1993
ADDRESS Sandbrook Road, Up Holland, Lancashire
NEAREST STATION Orrell
ACCESS exterior only

Lyons Israel Ellis 1958–60

SCARGILL CHAPEL
NORTH YORKSHIRE

Scargill House was bought by a group of Anglicans from Manchester as a holiday home and conference centre. Pace was already acquainted with its beautiful setting, and conceived a chapel that would 'appear to grow out of the dale'. The brief was for a building easy enough for the founding enthusiasts to construct it themselves, though it was eventually entrusted to a local builder for lack of time.

The chapel is built of local limestone, in keeping with the dry-stone walls of the surrounding hillsides. Its simplicity has great power, especially in the relationship between the square hall and its curved entrance passage and staircase, and its sweeping roof of cedar shingles. The interior is equally austere, and the feeling for the local vernacular tradition is continued by the use of timber crucks to support the roof. The church was an early demonstration of the liturgical movement, with the altar set forward of the long side wall. Lessons are read and sermons preached from the same position, for there is no lectern or pulpit.

The unusual brief gave Pace freedom to explore new ideas, and it marked a turning point in his career. Here he developed the personal language of rough stonework, unadorned timber stanchions and liturgical planning that made his subsequent churches like St Mark, Chadderton (see page 90), so extraordinary.

NORTHERN ENGLAND

LISTED grade II*, 25 September 1998
ADDRESS near Kettlewell, North Yorkshire
GETTING THERE train to Settle; off B6180 south-east of Kettlewell
ACCESS open daily, services on Sunday afternoons; call 01756 760 234 for details

George Gaze Pace 1958–61

ST MARK
SHEFFIELD

W H Crossland's large church of 1868–71 was bombed in 1940, leaving only its tower, which has long been listed. However the rebuilding has produced one of Pace's most impressive parish churches, a rare opportunity to build on a large urban scale.

In 1949 Pace was appointed surveyor to the diocese of Sheffield, and while his schemes to extend the cathedral were frustrated, he secured a handful of commissions for new or replacement churches in the area. His first design for St Mark was made as early as 1950–51. It was followed by a more experimental scheme of cantilevered concrete construction, and it was a reduced version of this that was finally built.

The exterior is faced in local stone, and has the characteristic thick, rectangular piercings for windows that are the most typical arts-and-crafts features of his work. The plan is a very irregular hexagon, made broad to accommodate a large choir to the side of the sanctuary. The interior is unexpectedly modern, impressive in its scale and lack of clutter, a vast white interior suffused with light. It is a synthesis of expressionist concrete trusses and limed oak furniture. All the furniture was designed by Pace himself. The interior is dominated by the organ case, and concentrated blocks of colour by means of east and west windows by Harry Stammers and John Piper.

NORTHERN ENGLAND

LISTED grade II, 9 December 1999

ADDRESS Broomfield Road, Broomhill, Sheffield

GETTING THERE train to Sheffield, then tram to University. The church is just south of the A57

ACCESS open daily until 17.00; call 0114 267 0362 for further information

George Gaze Pace 1958–63

ROSEHILL THEATRE
WHITEHAVEN

Sir Nicholas 'Miki' Sekers was a Hungarian émigré who opened silk mills near Whitehaven in 1937. He also had a passion for the arts, which led him to found the Friends of Glyndebourne, and he supplied silk to the designer Oliver Messel. When Sekers decided to build a 'Glyndebourne of the North' Messel was the natural choice. Rosehill is his only building in Britain, though he later worked extensively in Barbados and Mustique.

The auditorium is a nineteenth-century barn, which was extended with a stage and large foyer. It was intended to incorporate parts of a local music hall, the Royal Standard, then being demolished. But when part of the barn collapsed on the salvaged timber only some painted panels survived, and the final building is more completely Messel's. The most dramatic feature is the classical portico that forms the proscenium arch. This and Messel's lighting sconces display the deliberately two-dimensional, fey classicism that informed his celebrated stage and cinema design from the 1930s onwards. The walls are lined in silk.

Sekers attracted a galaxy of stars to Rosehill. The opening concert on 3 September 1959 featured the Mozart Players and Dame Peggy Ashcroft, and impressive concert seasons continued into the 1970s, supplemented with the professional and amateur theatrical productions that continue today.

NORTHERN ENGLAND

LISTED grade II, 12 June 1998
ADDRESS Moresby, near Whitehaven, Cumbria
ACCESS regular performances, by appointment
on 01946 694039

Oliver Messel with Gavin Paterson and Son 1959

1 PARK LANE
SHEFFIELD

The designer David Mellor was raised in Sheffield, and returned to work and teach there after studying at the Royal College of Art. Guest was working for Gollins Melvin Ward on Sheffield's College of Technology and University (see page 44).

The workshop and studio originally occupied two-thirds of the house. Mellor was then a bachelor and the kitchen was set into a corner of the lounge, divided by a wardrobe that incorporated a pull-out bed. Bedrooms were added after he married. But the combination of living and working functions set in one simple brick and timber rectangle has proved surprisingly flexible. The store and photographic studio have become utility rooms, and the drawing office is now the kitchen.

The workshop is set down five steps on the sloping site, and as a constant roofline is maintained extra height is achieved. The brick crosswalls are painted rather than plastered, the ceilings are of cedar, while full-height teak doors and glass screens make the entrance hall – originally the receptionist's office – most impressive.

Between 1960 and 1972 Mellor produced all his designs here, and made all his limited editions and prototype works. The house has the same clarity as Mellor's tableware or, as *House and Garden* said, 'how pleasant for one's house to be a complete reflection of one's practical work and philosophy of design.'

NORTHERN ENGLAND

LISTED grade II, 20 December 2000
NEAREST STATION Sheffield
ACCESS none

Patric Guest 1959–60

ENTWOOD
BIRKENHEAD

Entwood is one of the least known and most remarkable private houses of the late 1950s. Dewi Prys Thomas was one of a distinctive group of architects working in the north-west who experimented with unorthodox plans and novel roof structures, and this is the first house of its kind to be listed.

The house is formed from a group of linked pavilions on a pin-wheel plan, with quarter-pyramid roofs. The entrance is in an angle between the house and garage, suggesting a continuous turning motion which gives the house an interesting shape from every angle. The white-painted Tyrolean rendered brick walls also suggest vernacular influences, which made Thomas's work stand out from his contemporaries.

Dewi Prys Thomas was a lecturer at Liverpool School of Architecture, and was noted as a charismatic and inspirational teacher.

NORTHERN ENGLAND

LISTED grade II, 15 July 1998
ADDRESS Westwood Road, Birkenhead, Wirral
NEAREST STATION Upton
ACCESS none

Dewi Prys Thomas 1959

OXFORD ROAD STATION
MANCHESTER

The creation of British Railways in 1948 had little impact on the architects' departments of its four constituent companies, who continued to design independently. Leslie Martin had established the London, Midland and Scottish Railways as the 'cradle of prefabrication' with three stations in 1945, and when in 1957 electrification of the lines between Manchester, Liverpool and London began, his successors adopted a light-weight steel system for the smaller stations north of Crewe.

Manchester Oxford Road was the only large station rebuilt by prefabricated methods, chosen because a light structure was dictated by the weakness of the viaduct on which the station sits. Max Clendinning of British Railways Midland Region turned to the Timber Development Association, who in 1956 had appointed the engineer Hugh Tottenham to research timber-shell roofs. Oxford Road is Tottenham's finest achievement, a laminated timber structure of three conoid shells, ranging between 13 and 29 metres in span, supported on a cruck-like frame. Similar crucks support the curved canopies over the platforms. Timber is also used for the shop fronts, café and bench seating – giving the station its remarkable cohesion and a sense of warmth that belies its exposed site.

Timber-shell roofs were a peculiarly English achievement, popular for school halls but never developed so dramatically elsewhere as here at Oxford Road. Clendinning went on to a successful career in furniture design. Listing has prompted careful restoration of the station.

LISTED grade II, 24 November 1995
ADDRESS Oxford Road, Manchester
ACCESS any reasonable time

British Railways London Midland Region 1959–60

NORTHERN ENGLAND

CO-OPERATIVE INSURANCE SOCIETY/NEW CENTURY HOUSE
MANCHESTER

This group of smart office buildings still stands out with streamlined elegance on the Manchester skyline. It consists of a 25-storey office tower for the CIS, together with a 14-storey building for the Co-Operative Wholesale Society over a large conference hall for shareholders' meetings.

Sir John Burnet, Tait and Partners were chosen after a careful study of comparable buildings in London and North America. The brief was for modern offices for 2500 staff, to be made as open-plan as possible and with furnishings by the Design Research Unit. The intention was clearly to create a prestigious headquarters for the north that was comparable with anything in London. In this the CIS succeeded admirably. The massing, materials and detailing are disciplined to the highest standards, with Italian mosaic and glass curtain walling selected as the cladding materials, with aluminium mullions to withstand the grimy air for which Manchester was then still notorious.

By virtue of its prominent site and projecting lift tower the taller block rears over its not inconsiderable neighbour. It also has the larger and more transparent entrance hall, which still features a mural by William Mitchell of patinated bronze fibreglass that extends its full width. The more subdued conference hall is a darker mass alongside, and has decorative panels by Stephen Sykes.

LISTED grade II, 24 November 1995
ADDRESS Miller and Dantzic Streets, Manchester
ACCESS exteriors only

Sir John Burnet, Tait and Partners with George S Hay 1959–62

THE SOLAR CAMPUS
WALLASEY

This school is one of the earliest, largest and most successful passive solar-energy buildings in the world.

It was designed as a boys' school, but merged with the adjoining girls' school before it opened. There are two ranges, cranked slightly apart and facing south-south-east and south-south-west. Both have a double-glazed solar wall, which together is 70 metres long and rises some 12 metres. This has two skins of glass, about 610 millimetres apart, the inner one translucent and with some reversible aluminium panels which are painted black on one side to absorb heat in winter. A window in each room can be opened for ventilation. Additional heat was provided by the electric lighting and the students' body heat, and the roofs were insulated with 127-millimetre foamed polystyrene. Radiators incorporated at the behest of the Ministry of Education were seldom used.

The massively built walls give the school its distinctive appearance. The technical specification was kept out of the architectural press; when Morgan died suddenly in 1964, he was applying for patents and the mathematics behind the design were never revealed. In the 1970s a monitoring programme by Liverpool University showed that the massive construction ensured equable temperatures, although ventilation was limited.

In 1994 the school was closed by Wirral Metropolitan Borough Council, but has subsequently reopened privately.

LISTED grade II, 22 January 1996
ADDRESS Leasowe Road, Wallasey, Wirral (see Entwood, page 72)
GETTING THERE train to Wallasey Village
ACCESS exterior only

Emslie A Morgan 1960–61

MEOLS HALL
SOUTHPORT

For its mix of old and new, Meols Hall has been acclaimed as one of the most convincing country houses created since the Second World War. Though it has been in the Hesketh family since the Middle Ages, it largely served as a second home or agent's house until in 1938 it was inherited by Roger Fleetwood Hesketh, who had studied architecture but never practised. The next year he inherited the family portrait collection, but had nowhere to hang it. The war, rationing and a political career delayed his remodelling of Meols Hall for another 20 years.

Hesketh believed that the only appropriate style was Palladio's, as adapted to the English country house in the eighteenth century. He was fortunate to rescue the stonework and a doorcase from a demolished wing at Lathom, near Ormskirk, by the first English translator of Palladio's *Il Quattro Libri dell' Architettura*, Giacomo Leoni, and contemporary bricks from Tulketh Hall, Preston. The staircase balustrade came from nearby Harrock Hall, and other details copy Alberti or local eighteenth-century motifs. It is this mixture of textbook Renaissance models and Lancastrian variations that gives Meols the illusion of organic growth that makes it so convincing.

In the grounds Hesketh erected two brick gazebos modelled on an eighteenth-century original at the family's former home at nearby Rossall, and a Shippon which is separately listed (see page 30).

(see page 30)

LISTED grade II*, 15 November 1972
ADDRESS Botanic Road, Churchtown, Southport
NEAREST STATION Meols Cop
ACCESS open daily mid-August to mid-September; groups at other times by appointment on 01794 228326

Roger Fleetwood Hesketh 1960–64

PILKINGTON BROTHERS' HEAD OFFICES
ST HELENS

Pilkingtons dominate St Helens, with glass works and offices across the town. This was still more true in the early 1950s, until the company concentrated six offices into a single prestigious headquarters. An open valley outside the town was selected in 1953 and Maxwell Fry was appointed, perhaps through the auspices of Liverpool University. He immediately proposed a lake. His curtain-wall office tower and canteen are integrated within a refined landscape of water and greenery that gives the buildings added stature. The 48-metre office tower is a scintillating advertisement for Pilkingtons' products. Its aluminium glazing system was specially devised for its elegant profile and simple fixing, while the glass panels are an opaque blue at subtle variance with green slate cladding. A white vitrolite canteen block closes the northern end of the lake, where the first-floor restaurants enjoyed spectacular views.

The quality of the environment is matched by the art within it. The original canteen retains two abstract reliefs in wood – one painted, the other not – by Victor Pasmore. Both buildings feature glass panels, some back lit, by Charles de Vic Carey, Don Foster, Barbara Jones and, in the main entrance hall, Avinash Chandra.

Pilkingtons is one of the best and earliest examples of a headquarters building on a green-field site, and is Fry's principal post-war work in England.

LISTED grade II, 24 November 1995
ADDRESS Borough Road, St Helens, Merseyside
GETTING THERE train to St Helens Central; off A58 south-west of town
ACCESS exterior and museum

Fry, Drew and Partners 1960–64

WENTBRIDGE VIADUCT
WAKEFIELD

This prestressed-concrete viaduct carries the A1 over the beautiful gorge of the River Went. The span of the viaduct is 94 metres between supports and 143 metres between the centres of its outside bearings. The deck is divided by sharply inclined supports into two side spans of 43 metres and a centre span of 58 metres. The deck is of concrete cellular construction, with cantilevered footpaths on both sides, and is fixed at the south abutment while left free at the north abutment. Considerable horizontal thrust can be caused at the fixed end by unsymmetrical loading of the bridge, which is combatted by 14 hemispherical bearings. It is claimed to be the first use in England of precast concrete hinges, and of prestressing cables placed outside the concrete within the hollow deck.

This was the largest structure of its kind in Europe when built, and in 1964 it was recognised by the Museum of Modern Art in New York as a structure of significance in twentieth-century engineering: 'At last Britain has a bridge to show which by virtue of its sheer size, its taut, paired-down elegance, its dramatic impact, can hold its own with any of the great bridges of the continent – a bridge of Maillart-like excitement, which even the Autostrada del Sole cannot better.'

NORTHERN ENGLAND

LISTED grade II, 29 May 1998
ENGINEERS F A Sims with Maynard Lovell
ADDRESS A1 near Darrington, Wakefield, West Yorkshire
NEAREST STATION Pontefract; on A1 east of Darrington

West Riding County Council Bridges Department 1961

UNIVERSITY SPORTS PAVILION
LIVERPOOL

This is an elegant little bar and café set on two levels with views of the surrounding rugby and football pitches. It is linked to changing rooms and stores on one side, and to concrete terracing on the other which serves as a grandstand.

The site of Wyncote House was given to Liverpool University as a sports ground in 1922, but was developed with new pitches and a running track only in 1957. Gerald Beech was a lecturer at the School of Architecture, and his work is noted for its thoughtfulness and imagination. The buildings are set beside a pond and trees, which mask the greater bulk of the changing rooms. A bridge at first-floor level leads from this unremarkable range to the bar and café, set one above the other and which dominate their surroundings despite their tiny scale. They are striking for their sleek, continuous glazing, extending round the corners and set within delicate steel supports. *The Architects' Journal* questioned 'whether the best place to hold a post-rugger bottle party is a glass box', but the building has survived unaltered and is much appreciated.

LISTED grade II, 2 December 1997

ADDRESS Geoffrey Hughes Athletics Ground, Wyncote, Allerton, Liverpool

NEAREST STATION Mossley Hill

ACCESS by appointment with the university on 0151 7244948

Gerald Beech 1961–63

SUNDERLANDWICK HALL

GREAT DRIFFIELD

Sunderlandwick Hall was Johnson's own favourite commission. His beautifully executed design replaced a heavily altered eighteenth-century mansion which had burned down during VJ Day celebrations in 1945.

Johnson was commissioned by his cousin, and her husband Sir Thomas Ferens. They asked for a house which would hold its own against the 1840s stable block when seen from across the park. Johnson produced an 'L'-shaped plan, with the drawing room, dining room and study facing the park. This main front has an elliptical bow in the centre flanked by tripartite windows under blind arches, one of his favourite motifs. It has an air of comfortable largesse under its hipped roof: there are no unnecessary gimmicks or details, and neither is there the pinched quality found in many post-war ventures into classicism. This confidence is continued inside, and the fireplaces, pedimented doorcases and curved staircase strengthen the semblance of a c. 1800 villa. On one side is a pedimented garden pavilion; on the other a linked staff house is more clearly in a 1950s idiom.

Francis Johnson lived in Yorkshire virtually all his life. He designed several churches, and extended St Chad's College at Durham University, but his reputation is based on the lovingly restrained alterations and extensions he made to country houses in Yorkshire and Lincolnshire, working closely with skilled local craftsmen.

LISTED grade II, 15 July 1998
ADDRESS near Great Driffield, East Yorkshire
GETTING THERE train to Great Driffield; off A164, to south
ACCESS none

Francis Johnson 1962–63

ST MARK

CHADDERTON

Pace was a prolific and committed designer of churches and church fittings, mainly in the north of England and in Wales. His work is imbued with his simple faith, which gave him the confidence to be increasingly radical in his design. It is also indebted to the arts and crafts tradition, developed with a long-standing team of Yorkshire craftsmen. There is a strong northern sensibility, reminiscent of Charles Rennie Macintosh or of E S Prior's St Andrew, Roker (1905–07).

Pace's earliest designs are simple rendered halls for a congregation and sanctuary set in a single rectangular space. This changed in the late 1950s. As more non-orthogonal plans from mainland Europe became known, so his spaces became more organic. He expressed his materials – whether rough stone, concrete or brick – with increasing force and honesty. His penchant for punching small rectangular openings through these walls evolved from a Romanesque symmetry to a loose patterning reminiscent of Le Corbusier's Notre Dame du Haut, Ronchamp.

This process reaches its maturity at St Mark, which apes the local industrial aesthetic in its glossy, unadorned engineering brick. Only the saddleback tower is reminiscent of Pace's earlier work. A lattice pattern of windows dominates the interior, whose barn-like quality is enforced with giant forked posts of laminated timber. The church is entirely traditional in spirit – yet Nikolaus Pevsner could rightly term it 'raw and wild' for its very simplicity.

LISTED grade II, 25 September 1998
ADDRESS Milne Street, Chadderton, Oldham
NEAREST STATION Oldham Werneth
ACCESS regular services or by appointment on 0161 624 2005

George Gaze Pace 1962–63

JESMOND BRANCH LIBRARY
NEWCASTLE UPON TYNE

This tiny library is a quiet gem in a buzzing Victorian shopping street. Its round plan was a response to a tight corner site, and the council's requirement that the building line be set back. It also symbolises the panopticon supervision of the librarian from a central desk, which is also circular. The saw-tooth arrangement of the perimeter glazing enables direct daylight to fall along the spines of the books set in the radially placed shelves. This exemplifies the way that every element was carefully considered by the job architect Harry Faulkner Brown.

So neat a concept is only of merit when matched by elegant execution, as here. The steel frame is delicate and sharp, and contrasted with granite aggregate panels and thin glazing bars. The surrounding paving, with granite setts, and the small tree set at the corner of the site, all testify to Faulkner Brown's close attention to detail. A taller rear block houses a study room, book stack and offices.

Jesmond is the best of a group of modern libraries in Newcastle. Williamson, Faulkner Brown and Partners went on to specialise in designing large university libraries.

NORTHERN ENGLAND

LISTED grade II, 24 April 1998
ADDRESS St George's Terrace, Newcastle upon Tyne
NEAREST STATION West Jesmond (Metro)
ACCESS open daily except Sundays

Williamson, Faulkner Brown and Partners 1962–63

KINGSGATE FOOTBRIDGE
DURHAM

Kingsgate Bridge was commissioned by the University of Durham to link the historic city peninsula to new departments across the River Wear. It is an exceptional response to an outstanding setting, spanning the steep gorge below the cathedral, and is remarkable, too, for the eccentricity of its construction.

The bridge was conceived as a thin band stretched taut above the gorge on a pair of slender 'V'-tapered stilts. Each half of the main span was built at right angles to its final position, one on each bank. The two arms were then turned and fixed with neat bronze locks, seen half-way along the balustrade and which serve as expansion joints. For Arup they symbolised the bond between the city and its university. It is the sophistication with which every detail has been handled that makes this such a delightful toy, down to the pink Shap granite aggregate and the chamfered top to the parapet that together make the bridge a pleasure to touch. It forms a symbiotic group with the Architects' Co-Partnership's solid, stepped Dunelm House alongside, complementing each other to the enhancement of both.

Sir Ove Arup himself had a great input into the design of the bridge. It remained a personal favourite from his huge body of work, and his ashes were scattered from here after his death in 1988.

NORTHERN ENGLAND

LISTED grade I, 29 May 1998
ADDRESS New Elvet, Durham
ACCESS any reasonable time

Ove Arup and Partners 1962–63

RC ST MARY
LEYLAND

Leyland became a new town only in 1968, when council offices were grouped to the south of the church to form a civic centre. In 1959 it was a rapidly growing truck-building town, and a new church for over 1200 worshippers was a potent symbol of the optimism of the Catholic church in the early 1960s.

Father Edmund FitzSimons was inspired by progressive Swiss and French churches to conceive a round church centred on the altar. That the building has a continental flavour is due also to the involvement of Polish architects and artists. It is a dramatic space: a drum with a zigzag concrete roof and a central corona, supported on 'V'-shaped columns. A low ambulatory runs all round, and there is a long, narrow weekday chapel of the Blessed Sacrament opposite the entrance and baptistry.

The decoration is of remarkable quality. Most is figurative, yet modern: bronze Stations of the Cross by Arthur Dooley sitting between the spurs of the columns, a tapestry of the Trinity by Jerzy Faczynski, a hanging cross by Adam Kossowski and fine inscriptions by George Thomas. The most dramatic work is abstract, however: 36 panels of *dalle de verre* glass around the ambulatory, based by Patrick Reyntiens on the Creation. Reyntiens was inspired by Fernand Léger's church glass at Audincourt, France, but St Mary's is the more powerful integration of art and architecture.

LISTED grade II, 25 September 1998

ENGINEER Taylor, Whalley and Spyra

ADDRESS Broadfield Drive, Leyland, Lancashire

GETTING THERE 20-minute walk from Leyland station, near civic centre

ACCESS open most days; call 01772 421183 for information

Jerzy Faczynski of Weightman and Bullen 1962–64

HOLY REDEEMER
ACOMB

Many cities with a surfeit of old churches have demolished selectively to endow new suburban parishes, but the procedure has become increasingly controversial. One of the last to go was St Mary Bishophill Senior, York, in 1959, where Pace prepared 22 schemes to incorporate elements into his new church at Acomb.

Holy Redeemer is unmistakably Pace's, but has an unusual richness of texture and decoration that is nevertheless homogeneous. The south entrance front tells the story. There are characteristic oblong windows and a saddleback tower, but also two lancets and a small, round, arched doorway of c.1200 in a wall built largely of medieval masonry. In the porch is another late-twelfth-century doorway. Enter, and you are in a wide nave with two narrow aisles, the left with an arcade of white brick piers and concrete beams, the other with an arcade of round piers from c.1200. The west window is Victorian. The altar end has an iron cross and, set in the middle, a carved Saxon stone. Another decorated Saxon stone is built into the pulpit.

The church demonstrates Pace's commitment to liturgical reform. Its grouping together of altar, font, pulpit and lectern shows, he said, that 'the ministry of the word and the sacraments are of equal importance'.

LISTED grade II, 25 September 1998
ADDRESS Boroughbridge Road, Acomb, York
GETTING THERE train to York; off B1224
ACCESS regular services

George Gaze Pace 1962–65

METROPOLITAN CATHEDRAL OF CHRIST THE KING
LIVERPOOL

The English city with the largest Roman Catholic population was the last to gain a cathedral. An ambitious design was commissioned from Sir Edwin Lutyens in 1930, but by 1940 only the crypt was completed. Adrian Gilbert Scott simplified the concept, but in 1959 it was abandoned and a competition was held for an alternative. Archbishop Heenan requested that the congregation be set close to the celebrant of the mass, one of the first espousals of the Liturgical Movement in the Roman Catholic church in England.

Gibberd's design was the winner out of 289 entries, the assessors concluding that it 'powerfully expresses the kingship of Christ, because the whole building is conceived as a crown'. Gibberd put a flat roof over Lutyens' crypt to make a space for outdoor services, and designed a new church with an underground car park on land to the south. An axis through the principal entrance, denoted by a free-standing belfry resembling that by Marcel Breuer at St John, Collegeville, Minnesota (1956–60), and the large Blessed Sacrament chapel, was intended to link the two spaces. Otherwise Gibberd's church is 16-sided, with a perfectly central altar under a glazed corona. While most cathedrals reveal themselves slowly as you explore them, entering Liverpool is to be struck by a single, arresting image of the cathedral as a vast auditorium, extending from a central altar bathed in coloured light. While a central altar subsequently proved inconvenient for those standing behind the celebrant, the simplicity of the concept remains overwhelming.

John Piper and Patrick Reyntiens designed the glass, which is 25-millimetres thick and set in concrete panels; Gibberd had admired their work at Coventry. Elisabeth Frink designed the altar cross, R Y Goodden the candlesticks and the marble floor is by David Atkins. The stone belfry and bronze outer doors feature relief panels by William Mitchell, and the Chapel of the Blessed Sacrament has a mural by Ceri Richards which forms a triptych with glass by Reyntiens. Their gentler hues contrast with the vivid blues and reds of

Frederick Gibberd 1962–67

METROPOLITAN CATHEDRAL OF CHRIST THE KING

the main scheme. The Lady chapel has traditionally set glass by Margaret Trahearne, and a Madonna and Child by Robert Brumby. Many of these artists had worked at Coventry, yet in this very different context their work is sublimated to an overall effect.

The structure of 16 concrete buttresses tied by ring beams was innovative, and water ingress has proved problematic. Listing has enabled the cathedral to be grant-aided, and for a study to be made of the impervious mosaic cladding behind which water lodges.

LISTED grade II*, 7 February 1994
ADDRESS Mount Pleasant, Liverpool
ACCESS open daily

Frederick Gibberd 1962–67

THE LAWNS
HULL

In Scotland post-war architecture is dominated by the outstanding practice of Gillespie, Kidd and Coia, under Isi Metzstein and Andy McMillan, who specialised in Roman Catholic churches and educational buildings. This group of university halls of residence was their first work south of the border. Financial cut-backs ensured that only half the scheme was built, and an intended lake aborted, while the adjoining social centre was also pared down. Instead the six linked halls enjoy an open parkland setting whose maturity has made it feel complete.

Each hall is cleverly planned: a self-contained quadrangle of three-storey student bed-sitters, with a lower range behind housing the warden and tutorial staff. The medium is brick, with staggered cross walls forming a series of parallelograms defining groups of five single study bedrooms and two double rooms per floor, each of which share a kitchen and 'parlour'. Each room has its own balcony, concealed from its neighbour by the stepped plan, and white French windows contrast with the brickwork. The balconies suggest a generosity that belies the controlling UGC cost limits. There is care and method here, more akin to the work of Hull University's master planner, Sir Leslie Martin, than to the fireworks of Metzstein and McMillan's tortuous church constructions.

NORTHERN ENGLAND

LISTED grade II*, 30 March 1993
ADDRESS Northgate, Cottingham, Hull
NEAREST STATION Cottingham; to north of B1233
ACCESS by application to the Lawns Centre on 01482 847900

Gillespie, Kidd and Coia 1963–67

FORMER CHAPEL AT HOPWOOD HALL COLLEGE

MIDDLETON

Gibberd worked out many of his ideas for the centralised Liverpool Metropolitan Cathedral (see pages 100–102), then under construction, at a small chapel for the De La Salle College at Hopwood Hall, near Middleton. The small scale of the octagonal chapel meant that Gibberd could place the altar under its funnel-like corona, and still arrange the seating in a fan formation. Three of the eight sides are given over to subsidiary spaces, including the organ and a small weekday chapel, so no member of the congregation was seated behind the celebrant. The chapel is now deconsecrated and used as a hall for examinations and induction classes, but the altar, organ and weekday spaces have not been removed.

The structure is a simple one, comprising a reinforced concrete frame with concrete block infill. The copper roof and central glazed corona, filled with simple rectangles of red, yellow and green hues designed by David Atkins, give colour and interest to the building. Though a small building, this conical tower means that it makes a dramatic impact in the semi-open countryside and can be seen from a considerable distance.

NORTHERN ENGLAND

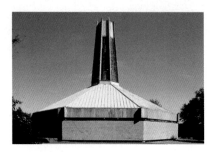

LISTED grade II, 22 January 1996
ADDRESS Rochdale Road, Middleton, Rochdale
NEAREST STATION Castleton
ACCESS by appointment on 0800 834 297

Frederick Gibberd, in association with Reynolds and Scott 1964–65

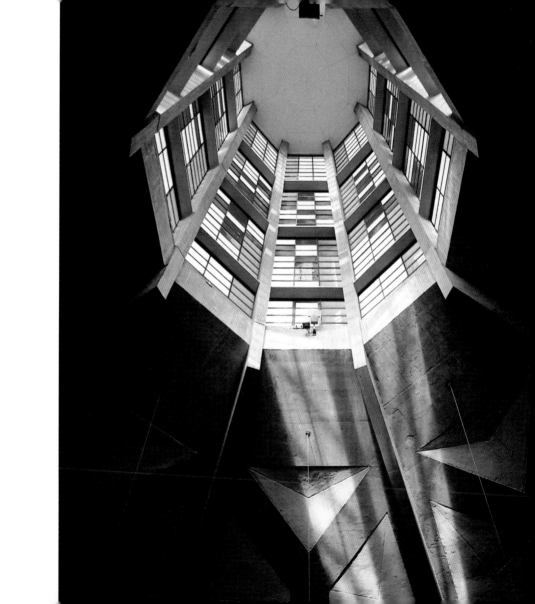

ST PETER
SHEFFIELD

Greenhill is a twentieth-century hilltop suburb overlooking Sheffield, and St Peter's pyramidal spire of 28 metres is a prominent landmark. Although the site was acquired in 1930, the church was planned only in 1963, when Father Andrews asked the local architects to seat 450 people 'as near the sanctuary as possible'. The delay thus enabled St Peter's to become one of the first Anglican churches to be built in accordance with progressive liturgical thinking on church planning.

The building comprises a series of segments which together form a staggered circle, with a raised sanctuary at its centre under the spire. The largest projection houses the weekday chapel, which has a whole wall of abstract stained glass. By placing the vestry and service rooms behind the altar the architects avoided seating the choir or worshippers behind the celebrant, so that it has a greater affinity with Gibberd's Hopwood Hall than with his Liverpool Metropolitan Cathedral (see pages 100–102). The rich collection of fittings fulfills the early-1960s aesthetic of clean simple lines and solid craftsmanship and materials, while the steel cross suspended over the altar is a fitting tribute to Sheffield's principal industry. A new church hall was added in 1995 following the segmental plan and in a similar style; it has not disturbed the impressive interior, in which the top-lit altar dominates every view.

LISTED grade II, 18 February 1999
ADDRESS Reney Avenue, Greenhill, Sheffield
GETTING THERE train to Sheffield, then bus; on south-west of city close to A61
ACCESS regular services or by appointment on 0114 237 2311

Oxley and Bussey 1964–65

WILLIAM TEMPLE MEMORIAL CHURCH

WYTHENSHAWE, MANCHESTER

This is the most challenging and dynamic of Pace's interiors. These qualities are not immediately evident externally, for like all his best churches of the 1960s it resembles a broad low barn, here with high dormers and only a stubby tower derived from Le Corbusier's La Tourette (1957-60). Here, too, are Pace's usual oblong slit windows and sense of introspection.

The difference is Pace's use of steel inside. The rolled joists and posts give the nearly square interior both an industrial aesthetic and a feeling of flexibility within carefully defined areas. The large railed sanctuary, with a curved clerical bench behind, is set diagonally, with salvaged Victorian pews set in two blocks to either side. An enclosed chapel with the choir in front occupies the other corner. In the middle the font is wrapped in another steel framework, which also supports the roof. Every formal element of worship – sanctuary, baptistry, weekday chapel – thus has its own separately defined structure within the single space. It is this sequence of industrial sculptures which is so disarming, in what has been described as 'a workshop for worship'.

LISTED grade II, 25 September 1998
ADDRESS Simonsway, Wythenshawe, Manchester
NEAREST STATION Heald Green
ACCESS regular services or by appointment on 0161 437 3194

George Gaze Pace 1964–65

CUMMINS ENGINE FACTORY
DARLINGTON

The American Cummins Engine Company and its independent associate Chrysler Cummins were attracted to Darlington by a Government Industrial Development Programme. They built separate factories, each with offices and boiler houses, on adjoining sites. Chrysler Cummins (by James Cubitt and Partners, 1963–64) is a good British design of the period, but is totally upstaged by its American-designed neighbour.

The Cummins Engine Factory was the first work by Roche and Dinkeloo, former associates of the late Eero Saarinen. They continued Saarinen's experiments with neoprene gaskets – a means of fixing glazing derived from the car industry – and Cummins is the world's first building to use this system for internal partitions as well as externally. The result is an exceptional totality of design, in which there is no outward differentiation between the offices and the factory floor.

The delicate glazing pattern is contrasted with a truly heavyweight Saarinen material for the welded frame: CorTen steel. CorTen is rich in manganese and vanadium, and oxidises within three years to a tactile rust-brown finish that is maintenance-free. The long, low building, sitting behind a reflective pool in a parkland setting, is a composition of exceptional elegance.

Cummins is the most outstanding post-war factory in England, and among the first in a series that demonstrated the United States' greater sophistication in designing for large corporations.

LISTED grade II*, 23 September 1992
ADDRESS Yarm Road, Darlington
ACCESS exterior only

Kevin Roche and John Dinkeloo 1964–66

BRITISH GAS RESEARCH ENGINEERING STATION
KILLINGWORTH

In 1963 Ryder and Yates had built offices for Northern Gas in Killingworth. They were therefore on hand when each region was invited to submit proposals for the industry's national research station. The discovery of North Sea gas in October 1965 meant that the laboratories and workshops had to be designed with maximum flexibility, as nobody could predict their requirements. They are housed in a steel-framed shell at the rear, for which Ryder and Yates developed a system of demountable partitions and services which they later marketed commercially.

It is the frontage range of offices, set over a car park, which is most remarkable. Yates's admiration for Le Corbusier here came to the fore. The low, cool building appears to float behind landscaped mounds, which are sliced vertically to reveal the car park. Entry is over a drawbridge, and through a square arch, whose acute taper contrasts with the six rooftop funnels which mask the services.

Ryder and Yates, who had worked with Berthold Lubetkin at Peterlee, understood the artistic nature of 1930s modernism as well as its solid, clear proportions, and integrated this sensibility with a belief in the integration of architecture, servicing and engineering that made them one of Britain's first multi-disciplinary practices. Listed when empty and under threat, the building is now the local council's offices.

LISTED grade II*, 27 January 1997
ADDRESS Station Road, Killingworth, North Tyneside
NEAREST STATION Longbenton; off A1056, close to A189
ACCESS exterior only

Ryder and Yates 1966–67

NORTHERN ENGLAND

LIVERPOOL PLAYHOUSE THEATRE ADDITIONS

LIVERPOOL

The Liverpool Playhouse opened in 1911 as one of England's first repertory theatres. It occupied a building remodelled by Sir Charles Reilly and Stanley Adshead from the 1865 Star Music Hall. By the 1960s its minimal foyer and backstage facilities were proving debilitating, and the redevelopment of the adjoining city markets enabled land to be secured for an extension.

A large workshop was built behind the stage, together with five storeys of dressing room and wardrobe space. In front of these workaday areas, a complex of foyers, bars and a restaurant were cantilevered over Williamson Square in two dramatic circular structures which are almost wholly glazed. They are reached via a circular staircase from the entrance and box office tucked underneath.

Though small, the foyers and bars are a fascinating sequence of spaces because of their changing levels and cross vistas between the two circles. The use of glass means that the extension looks exciting without compromising Reilly and Adshead's stuccoed block, and sparkles enticingly when lit up at night. The precise finishes are typical of the work of this elegant but little-known firm of local architects.

Since the building was listed the workshops have been redeveloped as retail spaces, to fund the regeneration of the theatre while disturbing the circular foyers and bars as little as possible.

LISTED grade II*, 14 March 1975 (theatre); 26 March 1999 (extension)
ADDRESS Williamson Square, Liverpool
ACCESS awaiting reopening

Hall, O'Donahue and Wilson 1966–68

PALL MALL COURT
MANCHESTER

Pall Mall Court was commissioned as a prestige headquarters building for the London Assurance Group, for whom Harry Teggin had designed offices in Sloane Streeet (Seker's, see page 644). London Assurance was taken over by the Sun Alliance Group as work began, and the building has always been occupied by a variety of tenants.

In shape the building is an inverted Z, with a five-storey range to King Street sheltering a twelve-storey block and a public piazza to the rear. Teggin says he wanted the building 'to have the impact of a jet stone' by the use of bronze glass, sharp angles and opaque facets in the soot-blackened Manchester atmosphere. The cleaning of the surrounding buildings has tempered its effect; instead it attests to the sumptuousness and mystery that a black building can bring to the streetscape. It has always been admired for its exemplary detailing, achieved by using only the best foremen to lay the dark bricks on the elevations towards the piazza. Brick, too, are the planters in this new public open space.

Teggin went on to design just one further office block in this shiny black and bronze idiom, for Portsmouth City Council. Pall Mall Court was listed, but the adjoining National Westminster Bank by Casson and Conder (1966–69), with which it formed a group, was gutted before it could be considered.

NORTHERN ENGLAND

LISTED grade II, 4 December 2000
LOCATION 55 King Street, Manchester
NEAREST STATIONS Manchester Piccadilly/Deansgate/Manchester Victoria
ACCESS exterior only

Brett and Pollen, Partner in Charge, Harry Teggin 1966–68

THEATRE ROYAL ADDITIONS
YORK

The first theatre here opened in 1744, and the basement incorporates the undercroft from a twelfth-century hospital. The present theatre largely dates from 1879–80, its baronial Gothic exterior more typical of a chapel than a theatre. There was little foyer or workshop space, no common entrance and tiny bars. On the side was a hut for storing scenery, and a garden. The Director, Donald Bodley, realised that part of the garden had to be built on. He came to London to seek advice, and lunched at Gwynne's Serpentine Restaurant in Hyde Park. Immediately Bodley determined that Gwynne should be his architect.

Gwynne says that he was inspired by umbrellas to create the mushroom columns at the Serpentine, which are repeated here as linked hexagons. Two double-height ones, unglazed, advertise the building to the street. Seven more, in two tiers, are set behind black-framed glazing that rises sheer to the roof. Spherical rooflights ensure that people can see inside during the day; at night the building shines, invitingly, like a lantern.

Best of all is the sweeping staircase, cantilevered from a single freestanding post. No calculations could determine if this would work; the engineer Sefton Jenkins made informed guesses – and it worked.

The foyers are a sparkling addition to historic York, and among Gwynne's most accessible buildings. The Serpentine Restaurant was demolished in 1990–91.

LISTED grade II*, 14 March 1954 (medieval remains); 24 June 1983 (theatre); 14 March 1997 (additions)
LOCATION St Leonard's Place, York
ENGINEER R A Sefton Jenkins
ACCESS open Monday to Saturday, 10.00–19.00; 10.00–17.00 when there is a show. Call 01904 632 596 for details

Patrick Gwynne 1967

THE MIDLANDS

394–427 WAKE GREEN ROAD
BIRMINGHAM

There is more public interest in prefabs than any other post-war building type, but so far only this group in Birmingham are listed. They are among the increasingly rare survivors of 156,623 bungalows erected in 1945–48 as part of the Temporary Housing Programme promised by Winston Churchill in March 1944 – a response to an acute housing shortage only acerbated by the war.

The 'temporary prefab' was built to a standard size and a two-bedroom plan determined by the Ministry of Works, who exhibited prototypes at the Tate Gallery in 1944 and 1945. Production versions were erected across Britain, often on sites prepared by prisoners of war. Left-over Anderson shelters were often erected as garden sheds, as here.

Eleven types were manufactured in all, the most numerous being made of scrap aluminium from damaged aircraft. No original detached versions are known to survive in England. All save an American timber model – long gone – had built-in kitchens and bathrooms designed by the Ministry and considered luxurious at the time.

The Phoenix was one of the rarest and least publicised types, but its solid covering of asbestos cement sheeting has made it among the most durable. It was intended to last 15 years, but examples are still popular with residents for their careful planning and large gardens.

LISTED grade II, 15 July 1998
NEAREST STATION Hall Green; off B4146 south of city centre
ACCESS exteriors only

Phoenix (manufacturer unknown) 1945

CLIPSTONE COLLIERY HEADSTOCKS

Clipstone Colliery was opened in 1922. After the Second World War the depth of the mine was increased, and the traditional headstocks for winding access cages up and down the mineshaft were replaced with a set of 'Koepe' winders.

The Koepe winding system, invented by Frederick Koepe in Westphalia in 1877, is powered by an electric motor that can be installed either on the ground or in an upper winding chamber and connected directly to the drive wheel. All earlier winding mechanisms had required heavy engines on the ground, but Koepe's system made this no longer necessary. It introduced a single continuous winding rope which required less power, for the two cages could then counterbalance each other, allowing the falling cage to do much of the work in pulling the rising cage. Less power for braking was also required. The system was first introduced unsuccessfully at Bestwood Colliery in 1883, but became established in the deep pits of the north-east in the 1920s.

Today the Koepe headstocks at Clipstone are the oldest to survive. They are also visually impressive: two giant steel towers each supporting two wheels, one above the other, stand sentinel either side of a central brick powerhouse and operating room.

This local landmark was listed when it was threatened with demolition; its future is uncertain.

THE MIDLANDS

LISTED grade II, 19 April 2000
ADDRESS Mansfield Road, Clipstone, Nottinghamshire
NEAREST STATION Mansfield Woodhouse
ACCESS exterior only

Bolsover Colliery Company 1950–51

LIMBRICK WOOD SCHOOL
COVENTRY

Stirrat Johnson-Marshall left Hertfordshire in 1948 to found a Development Group at the Ministry of Education dedicated to studying new constructional methods. Though preoccupied with secondary schools, he was drawn to the Bristol Aeroplane Company's prototype school at Lockleaze, Bristol, developed from prefabricated aluminium panels and trusses when peace threatened the aircraft industry. Johnson-Marshall thought the system had possibilities, though it still featured ribbons of classrooms set off long corridors.

Donald Gibson, chief architect at Coventry, had been Johnson-Marshall's boss at the Isle of Ely in the 1930s, and offered a site in the new suburb of Tile Hill. As at Cheshunt (see page 212), the infant's department was built first, but here the junior school was entirely separate. Both elements set pairs of classrooms, with cloakrooms, around a central assembly hall, which was cheaper and more informal than BAC's designs thanks to its three-dimensional grid. The 3-foot 4-inch grid and light aluminium structure, originally brightly coloured, lend some elegance to the humble huddle of pitched roofs.

Limbrick Wood is contemporary with Greenfields School, South Oxhey (see page 228), designed by Hertfordshire to a similar plan. Their simultaneous, independent appearance did much to promote a tighter approach to primary-school planning. The classrooms are still considered large and well planned, particularly for their wet areas for paints and mess.

LISTED grade II, 30 March 1993
ADDRESS Broad Lane, Coventry
NEAREST STATION Tile Hill
ACCESS none

Ministry of Education/Coventry City Architect's Department 1951–52

WOODLANDS SCHOOL
COVENTRY

Woodlands is the largest product of the collaboration between Coventry and the Ministry of Education. Coventry's exceptional post-war prosperity enabled it to spend lavishly on its education programme; however, four old direct-grant schools creamed off the best students, and encouraged it to embark on a pioneering comprehensive system for the rest.

Only a large school could provide a viable sixth form; the Ministry of Education insisted on a ten-form entry. Woodlands was built for 1500 boys. Such a large school could have easily become impersonal, but Coventry devised a novel form of house system, each with its own building so that the boys could first relate to a smaller group. The system remains, with six houses and modified dining arrangements, and the single-storey buildings on the periphery still give it a special character.

Between these blocks are set taller classroom and workshop blocks, with a central hall, library and four gymnasia. The informal planning of separate blocks, with mature planting and 52 acres of playing fields, strengthen the school's character. An open shed intended for learning building trades is a survivor of an Arcon prefabricated steel structure. Otherwise the school is a distinguished refinement of the Hills 3-foot 4-inch system developed at St Crispin's School, Wokingham (see page 372).

LISTED grade II, 30 March 1993
ADDRESS Broad Lane, Coventry
NEAREST STATION Tile Hill
ACCESS none

Ministry of Education/Coventry City Architect's Department 1952–54

ST MICHAEL AND ALL ANGELS
WOLVERHAMPTON

The medieval church of Tettenhall Regis survived the war to be consumed by a fire in 1950 that spared only the fourteenth-century tower and the 1882 south porch.

Bernard Miller, long associated with the Liverpool School of Architecture, built many churches in the 1930s with surprisingly art deco flourishes. Tettenhall is very different. The design is strongly arts-and-crafts inspired, with low broad arcades supported on stylised foliage capitals, and boldly reticulated windows which cast pools of light into the church. The wide nave is spanned by a complex timber roof, which harmonises with Miller's intricate furnishings. His symbol of a bee can be found on one of the painted altar rails. Only the massive font, clad in blue mosaics by G Mayer Marten, hints at Miller's earlier idiosyncracies.

The altar has always been in the crossing of Miller's church. It was originally set against a low wall that divided the main space from the east-end Lady chapel, a device popularised in the 1930s, such as in the work of J Harold Gibbons. The present open-timber screen was installed in 1985. The east window is by G Cooper-Abbs.

St Michael's is an exceptionally lavish church, which in its stylistic homage to E S Prior may be compared with the work of George Pace.

LISTED grade II, 29 July 1950 (for the medieval tower)
ADDRESS Church Road, Tettenhall, Wolverhampton
GETTING THERE off A41 west of town centre
ACCESS Sunday services 8.00, 10.00, 11.30, 18.00; Mondays 9.00; Wednesdays 10.30

Bernard Miller 1952–55

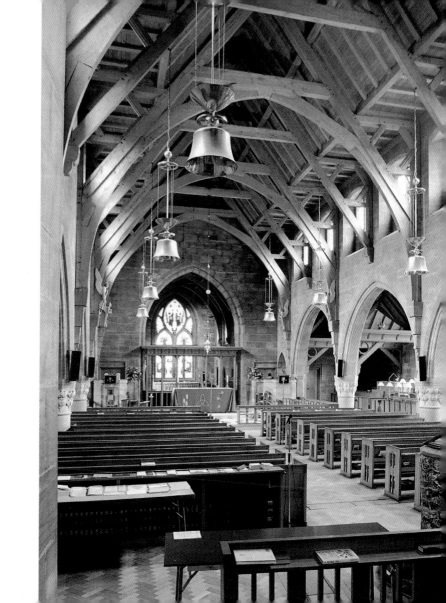

GROSVENOR HOUSE
BIRMINGHAM

This is a rare example of an office building erected before restrictive building licences were revoked in November 1954. It makes the most of its small corner site by means of a wavy, nautical motif reminiscent of the Festival of Britain, with jaunty projecting sills, cornices and balconies. These form an unusually cohesive ripple of contrasting planes, that culminate in a distinctive prow to the corner with New Street. Most prominent of all is an oversailing glass cornice that projects over its uppermost storey. The composition is greatly indebted to Arne Jacobsen's Bellavista flats at Klampenborg of 1931–34.

Cotton, Ballard and Blow were the architectural practice behind Jack Cotton, the Birmingham-born entrepreneur responsible for much city-centre building there in the 1930s and one of England's leading land speculators in the 1960s. His dealings, first as Central Commercial Properties, then as Ravenseft and finally as City Centre Properties, transformed England with shopping centres and speculative offices.

This is an example of rare wit and integrity in the design of speculative office buildings. Centre Point, London (see page 546), is the only other example to be listed.

LISTED grade II, 18 February 1999
ADDRESS Bennetts Hill, Birmingham
NEAREST STATION Birmingham New Street
ACCESS exteriors only of interest

Cotton, Ballard and Blow 1953–54

22 AVENUE ROAD
LEICESTER

When in 1953 Mr and Mrs Goddard commissioned a new house, building restrictions still in force constrained them to a maximum floor area of 139 square metres. This persuaded them not to waste space on a staircase, and encouraged Fello Atkinson and Brenda Walker to create a free-flowing plan without prescribed circulation areas. The result is one of the first houses in England to be inspired by American open planning. The Goddards now find the compactness ideal for their retirement.

Unlike the contemporary theatricality of Farnley Hey (see page 34), there is a timeless quality to Avenue Road. The pale bricks – striking in red-brick Leicester – the inward-facing L-shaped plan around a patio, the understated elegance, anticipate houses of the 1960s. There is little to see from the road: a door, a neatly-lettered gate and a garage door set into a tight, corner-hugging plot.

Inside all is extraordinarily light, and similarly ahead of its time. The fully-fitted tiny kitchen still has its original cupboards and drawers, the colours of contemporary Fiestaware, with a hatch to the living-dining room. Behind the central fireplace is the master bedroom, and these two rooms have full-height glazing on to the patio. The ceiling-high doors and careful window detailing are reminders that Atkinson was an experienced exhibition designer, and brought the same care for detail to this lovingly wrought house.

LISTED grade II, 15 July 1998
GETTING THERE to south of centre on A6
ACCESS none; barely visible from street

James Cubitt and Partners 1954–55

CHRIST CHURCH
COVENTRY

The exuberance of Christ Church is exceptional for any church, but particularly one with so strong an evangelical tradition. The choice of architect was, however, made by the High Church Bishop Gorton. Christ Church replaced a city-centre church bombed in 1941.

The exterior is a linked composition of church hall, tower, church, vestibule, vicarage and caretaker's house, each separately expressed in different materials: concrete panels and black vitrolite for the hall; timber for the tower belfry and glass for the church. The belfry's chequerboard motif is repeated throughout the interior.

The church has nave and aisles of almost equal width, with only a shallow sanctuary. The plaster vault is decorated with wheels and ribbons representing Coventry industries. Square patterns dominate the side walls and particularly the east end, in timber and purple acoustic tiles edged in gold. Gold, too, are the light fittings, inspired by the hanging birdcage in the Lion and Unicorn Pavilion at the Festival of Britain. The sculpture of Christ the Sower, woodcarving and clock are by John Skelton, the Coventry-born nephew of Eric Gill. The thick stained glass depicting the life of Christ is by Pierre Fourmaintraux.

Christ Church was originally described as 'Pleasure Gardens pastiche', but today it is just this Festival charm and wit which make it so enjoyable.

LISTED grade II, 10 August 1998
ADDRESS Frankpledge Road, Cheylesmore, Coventry
ACCESS Sunday services; call 01203 502770 for more details

Alfred H Gardner 1954–58

OFFICES FOR CARR AND COMPANY
SOLIHULL

This diminutive but distinctive office building was designed as prestige headquarters for a paper manufacturer. It is Goldfinger's first truly mature work. Early designs show him systematically abandoning the brick cladding that still dominates his Regent's Park Road flats, London (see page 522), in favour of an unadorned concrete frame distinguished by a high parapet and contrasting planes of glazing. The result is a shallow brise-soleil that anticipates his more sophisticated office elevations in Albemarle Street, London (see page 600).

The water tanks and lift-motor room are housed in a perfect concrete cube raised high above the roof, intended to allow access beneath to a roof garden. Below, another cube, entirely glazed, forms an entrance hall between pilotis. Goldfinger also designed the forecourt planting, set high within a walled podium and now riotously mature. These volumes contrast with the strict rhythm of the overall 2-foot 9-inch grid of concrete and glass that forms the basis of the building. A more delicate note is provided by the concrete spiral escape stairway on the narrow southern flank. The interior was kept deliberately simple, with demountable partitions for maximum flexibility.

The building survives virtually unaltered, a solitary note of sophistication in an anonymous confusion of suburban housing and more recent industrial units. Its concrete, however, shows signs of spalling – rare in a Goldfinger building.

THE MIDLANDS

LISTED grade II, 24 November 1995
ADDRESS off Cranmore Boulevard, Shirley, Solihull
NEAREST STATION Shirley
ACCESS none

Ernö Goldfinger 1955–56

THE PEDIMENT
AYNHO

In Elizabeth Watt, Raymond Erith found an exceptional client, whose interest in paraphrasing Palladianism on a diminutive 1950s scale matched his own. Her commission was for a small house on a relatively large site, and Erith determined that it needed an architectural presence so as not to appear insignificant. His idea of a square house with a dominating pediment was, however, entirely in the spirit of an architectural folly, with what he called 'the charm that one occasionally sees in eighteenth-century buildings when they are at once very small and very architectural'. The thin cornices give a 1950s baldness to what is otherwise a determined Palladian centrepiece without wings. The large size of the stone blocks with which it is faced endeavoured to provide scale, and the flanking slate-capped walls, compensating for wings, tether it to the ground.

Erith designed the interior with the same microscopic attention to detail that he gave the outside. A neo-Gothic niche in the study contrasts with the heavy Palladian stone fireplace in the drawing room.

The house was followed by a series of garden buildings to Erith's design, and he was still designing for Miss Watt at his death in 1973. He also carried out restoration work at nearby Aynhoe [sic] Park.

THE MIDLANDS

LISTED grade II, 29 March 1988
ADDRESS Aynho, Northamptonshire
NEAREST STATION King's Sutton; on A41 in village centre
ACCESS none

Raymond Erith 1956–57

NEWTON BUILDING
NOTTINGHAM

In 1948 Nottingham University College was split between its Highfields campus, which formed the new university, and its original city-centre site, which was developed as a technical college. Howitt designed for both institutions: the university got a students' union and hall of residence, but the outstanding building was for the technical college. It is one half of a larger scheme proposed in 1952, but the college determined belatedly to retain its original buildings by Lockwood and Mawson (1877) on the northern part of the site.

The Newton Building's tall broad bulk of Portland stone is one of Nottingham's principal landmarks, particularly for the great glazed staircase and lift tower which dominates its wedge-shaped corner site. The tower contains classrooms; to either side low stone walls screen single-storey workshops lit by saw-tooth roofs. The result is an unusual interpretation of the slab-and-podium idiom then just becoming fashionable.

T Cecil Howitt was a prolific Nottingham architect, who built extensively for the city council before setting up in private practice. He designed the prominent City Council House. This is one of his firm's last buildings, a stripped-down and more striking interpretation of his style of the 1930s. Many local authorities built vocational colleges in the 1950s, but Nottingham's is the most architecturally ambitious – a reflection of the city's exceptional financial commitment to higher education.

LISTED grade II*, 24 April 1998
ADDRESS Nottingham Trent University, Burton Street, Nottingham
GETTING THERE on north side of city centre
ACCESS exterior only

T Cecil Howitt and Partners 1956–58

BELGRADE THEATRE
COVENTRY

The Belgrade, by Kenneth King for Coventry City Architects' Department, was the first repertory theatre built after the Second World War, and the first built by a local authority. It was provided with its own workshops and scene-painting facilities, and the Corporation Street elevation included 21 bedsits for resident actors, who were expected to become part of the Coventry community.

The principal elevation faces Belgrade Square, where the glazed double-height foyer is particularly attractive by night. Its pendant lights are by Bernard Shottlander.

Best of all is the auditorium, a single gallery over a shallow pit, with rows of boxes either side reminiscent of those at the Royal Festival Hall. Its memorable panelling, moulded into curves to give the excellent acoustics devised by the Building Research Station, gave the theatre its name. On a visit to Coventry President Tito of Yugoslavia promised a gift of beech wood, but the lengths supplied were too short – instead Belgrade timber can be found in local council housing while the theatre used West African hardwoods. A concrete representation of Belgrade, based on a seventeenth-century print, enlivens the corner of Corporation Street.

The Belgrade has a conventional proscenium stage. Its loge boxes and foyers are more reminiscent of the Royal Festival Hall than of subsequent developments in theatre design, but it has a wealth of 'contemporary' detailing.

THE MIDLANDS

LISTED grade II, 12 June 1998
ADDRESS Belgrade Square, Coventry
ACCESS foyers open Monday to Saturday, auditorium for performances only; call 01203 256431 for information

Coventry City Architect's Department 1956–58

CATHEDRAL CHURCH OF ST MICHAEL
COVENTRY

The medieval church of St Michael, raised to cathedral status in 1918, was ruined in the air raid of 14 November 1940, the fiercest on any city centre in the country. No building competes with Coventry Cathedral as a symbol of post-war revival, not only of Coventry but of Britain, and it made Spence a household name.

An ambitious scheme by Sir Giles Gilbert Scott, incorporating the surviving tower and apse, was abandoned in 1946, and land was acquired to the north. A competition was held in 1950. While there was no restriction as to style or materials, or compulsion to retain the ruins except for the tower and two crypts, the building committee and assessors recognised the public's attachment to them.

Spence's winning design, chosen in August 1951, incorporated the ruins as a forecourt to the new building, which was sited at right-angles and orientated north-south. The new cathedral was designed as a stone-walled structure intended to convey an impression of solidity and permanence – a national monument and a war memorial. When it became clear in 1955 that the cost of the superstructure would exceed the available funds, the design was recast. Spence used concrete for the Chapel of Unity, suggested by the radical Bishop Neville Gorton, and Guild Chapel, and substituted concrete blocks for the cathedral interior. He also redesigned the porch as a massive *porte-cochère* visually linking the old and new buildings, having already determined on a great clear-glazed west window.

Spence commissioned the largest works of art in 1951–53. They included Graham Sutherland's east-end tapestry of Christ in Majesty, John Hutton's etched west window and the ten magnificent nave windows by Laurence Lee, Keith New and Geoffrey Clarke. By commissioning the artworks early, Spence ensured they could not be eliminated as budgets became squeezed, but they inhibited subsequent changes, particularly to the

Sir Basil Spence 1956–62

east end. Further major commissions in 1954–55 included John Piper's baptistry window, Jacob Epstein's sculpture of St Michael quashing the devil, and Ralph Beyer's carved inscriptions for the nave recesses in 1957. Last of all, in 1960, came the altar candleholders from Hans Coper, the high altar cross from Clarke, and the lectern eagle and emblems above the bishop's throne and provost's stall by Elisabeth Frink.

The later commissions show Spence moving towards a greater toughness and austerity in his work, as can be seen in his contemporary secular work such as University of Sussex (see pages 448–450). The cathedral, at first found equally unsatisfactory by modernists and traditionalists alike, is now widely enjoyed as one of the great 1950s repositories of art and culture.

LISTED grade I, 29 March 1988
ADDRESS Priory Street, Coventry
ACCESS open daily; call 01203 227597 for information

Sir Basil Spence 1956–62

INTAKE FARM SCHOOL
MANSFIELD

The price of post-war prosperity in Nottinghamshire's booming coalfields was subsidence. In most pit villages the largest building was the school, and these were fracturing as coal was extracted from beneath them. This problem was inherited by Donald Gibson on his arrival from Coventry in 1955.

Gibson adopted the Hertfordshire model, attracting a loyal team of architects who developed a proprietary system to new ends. Here the Brockhouse cold-rolled frame, used by the Ministry of Education at Belper School, Derbyshire, was adapted with pin joints and rocker bases to ride subsidence. Its nickname, the 'rock and roll system', was a topical one. It was then clad with timber and overlapping tiles. Narrow toplights and high-quality timber finishes give early schools a distinctive architectural fillip.

This little primary school, originally called Bancroft Lane, was the pioneer. With its plan of a linked assembly hall and dining room, from which classrooms are offset in pairs, and a mural by Fred Millett (long overpainted), its membership of the Herts/Ministry of Education tradition is clear.

That the Notts system not only solved the subsidence problem but was so commercially successful that it is still in operation was due to Gibson bringing in other authorities to share the costs of its development and of subsequent building programmes. Hence its name: the Consortium of Local Authorities' Special Programme, or CLASP.

THE MIDLANDS

LISTED grade II, 30 March 1993
ADDRESS Armstrong Road, Mansfield, Nottinghamshire
ACCESS none

Nottinghamshire County Council Architect's Department, Donald Gibson 1957

OLDBURY WELLS SCHOOL
SHROPSHIRE

These two buildings are pivotal to the development of Lyons Israel Ellis as the cutting edge of the New Brutalism during this period. Their mature style evolved in these two buildings, originally built as separate schools for boys and girls on opposite sides of the road, but since 1972 combined as a single comprehensive.

The boys' school, built first, is an urbane, curtain-walled building, strengthened by setting the lines of glazing firmly within an exposed concrete frame, and by a line of rooflights over the main hall (now used for teaching). These are the most characteristic features of LIE's work. The firm extended the school in 1964.

The girls' school is one of the firm's most sophisticated compositions, with a dramatic water tank set high over the set-back entrance. The entrance lobby is itself another cube of concrete, expressed as almost freestanding within the building's dominating frame. Something of the building's overall clarity has been lost by extensions made in 1966, but the forcefulness of this entrance remains.

In the 1950s Lyons Israel Ellis served as a 'finishing school' for ambitious young architects who subsequently went on to prominent careers in their own right. The school was one of the first to adopt the brutalist brick-and-exposed concrete aesthetic and was much imitated.

LISTED grade II, 30 March 1993
ADDRESS Oldbury Park Road, Bridgnorth, Shropshire
ENGINEER Ove Arup and Partners
NEAREST STATION Wolverhampton, or (in summer) Kidderminster, then the Severn Valley Railway to Bridgnorth; off B4364
ACCESS exterior only

Lyons Israel Ellis 1957–58, 1959–60

CRIPPS HALL
NOTTINGHAM

Cripps Hall was the first and most ambitious hall of residence built for men at Nottingham University in the post-war period. Founded as a college in 1875 and given its fine suburban site by Sir Jesse Boot in 1921, Nottingham's university status was long obstructed by an over-paternalistic city council. Once awarded in 1948 it prompted a building boom, but while modernism was early accepted for its science area, halls of residence continued to be built in a late-classical idiom until the 1970s. Donald McMorran (1905–65) was among the most imaginative architects to work in the style, with the confidence to be sparing in his detail and to allow the quality of fine materials and proportions to determine the success of his simple quadrangles.

Here, however, some embellishments were made possible through the generosity of the Cripps family of Northamptonshire – motor-components manufacturers – who were later to richly endow St John's and Queen's Colleges in Cambridge. A clock tower of Soanic understatement denotes the central dining hall and giant Ionic columns with taut volutes frame the entrance. Visiting Cripps Hall as an ignorant teenager, the building impressed by its rare timelessness. It still does nearly 30 years later.

McMorran also designed an extensive series of teaching quadrangles for Nottingham, of which only that for the Institute of Education was built, in 1959–61.

THE MIDLANDS

LISTED grade II, 29 March 1988
ADDRESS Beeston Lane, University of Nottingham
GETTING THERE train to Nottingham; close to A52 on north side of main campus
ACCESS exterior only

McMorran and Whitby 1957–59

COLLEGE HALL
LEICESTER

Leicester was the last pre-war foundation to achieve full university status, in March 1957. A master plan by Leslie Martin was published the same day, which focused on the need for accommodation for women students. Land was provided to the south at Knighton.

This is the first in Martin's series of post-LCC collaborations, in which he sought to establish a 'tradition' of modern architecture by attention to every element in the process of planning and design. Dannatt had collaborated with Martin on the Royal Festival Hall (see pages 668–670) and was emerging as an independent designer of similarly unemotional yet natural-feeling buildings. This was achieved at College Hall on a limited budget.

The design follows principles established by the UGC in 1948, but was the first hall to break away from an institutional neo-Georgian idiom. It was planned for 170 women, centred on a dining hall and a small Senior Common Room, set behind the high table, both with low ceilings of natural timber. As the UGC recommended, there are extensive Junior Common Rooms. The smaller games and meeting rooms are reached via a spiral staircase that is the complex's most sculptural feature, and are cantilevered over the entrance. The strongly expressed supporting beams, together with the exemplary signage around the building, were details refined at Dannatt's subsequent Vaughan College (see page164).

LISTED grade II, 30 March 1993
ADDRESS Knighton Road, Leicester
GETTING THERE between A6 and A50 to south of city centre
ACCESS none

Sir Leslie Martin and Trevor Dannatt 1958–60

LINCOLNSHIRE MOTORS, NOW COUNTY LIBRARY
LINCOLN

The motor car transformed English towns and countryside, our working and living patterns, as nothing else in the post-war period. Yet where is its architecture? The 1950s saw the building of many sleek, Miesian showrooms that proclaimed the luxurious image of the limousine. Few survive. Lincolnshire Motors is special because it is a feat of technical construction that makes changes, here a change of use, seem superficial. The former showroom has a reinforced-concrete hyperbolic paraboloid shell roof, supported on columns to provide a clear unobstructed area. It consists of four units, each 50 feet square and $2^1/_2$ inches thick, with the edges thickened to form the supporting framework. It is now the county library service's bookstore. Sam Scorer was one of the first architects to experiment extensively with hypar roofs, and his St John's, Ermine (see page 186) is a later and larger version. The Hungarian engineer Hajnal Konyi pioneered shell construction in Britain following his arrival here in 1936.

Alongside, the garage offices have been converted into a branch library. Although very different internally, the exterior, with its blue curtain walling, is little altered. The circular corner building was once the manager's office, and now houses the Chief Librarian. Alongside, the forecourt canopy now serves only to shelter a small car park.

THE MIDLANDS

LISTED grade II, 9 August 2000
ADDRESS Lucy Tower Street, Brayford Wharf, Lincoln
ENGINEER Dr K Hajnal Konyi
NEAREST STATION Lincoln Central
ACCESS exterior and library only

Sam Scorer of Denis Clarke Hall, Scorer and Bright 1959

SILHOUETTE CORSET FACTORY
MARKET DRAYTON

In 1957 a visit by Félix Candela revitalised interest in tensile concrete shell roofs for bridging large spans, cheap and capable of architectural drama. The simplest expressive form was the hyperbolic paraboloid – two corners up, two corners down – which enjoyed a fashionable esteem in the late 1950s and early 1960s. Britain was perhaps unique, however, in experimenting with laminated timber 'hypars', thanks to the Timber Development Association and its engineer Hugh Tottenham. His first collaboration with the architect Robert Townsend was a carpet factory at Wilton (1957), long demolished.

The corset manufacturer George Lobbenberg saw in Wilton possibilities for a large, open-plan factory with every service – manufactory, offices and dispatch area – under a single, egalitarian roof. At 30,000 square feet Silhouette was nearly three times larger than Wilton, with four hypars supported on a single central pillar. External concrete buttresses supported any lateral movement, and gave the building its massive architectural form. Movement in the hypar led in 1962 to the roof being renewed by Ove Arup and Partners with tie beams in the manner of Wilton. Nevertheless, the building remained striking and novel, and its open plan led to it being adapted successfully for years as a supermarket.

Listing was achieved the day the building was to be demolished, for which permission was subsequently granted by the DETR.

LISTED grade II, 2 August 2000, demolished 2002
ADDRESS Towers Lawn, Market Drayton, Shropshire
ENGINEER Hugh Tottenham/Timber Development Association (TDA)
NEAREST STATION Crewe or Whitchurch, then bus

Robert Townsend 1959–61

VAUGHAN COLLEGE
LEICESTER

Vaughan College is a mature, more refined working of ideas explored by Dannatt with Leslie Martin in their earlier College Hall (see page 158).

The Reverend Vaughan founded a Working Men's College in 1862, and in 1946 it became the university's Department of Adult Education. However, Vaughan's buildings were cleared for a ring road, and their replacement buildings are set on a three-lane intersection. From the road one looks up to St Nicholas' church, behind a substantial chunk of Roman wall, or down to the excavated site of Leicester's Roman baths. Dannatt's scheme had to incorporate a museum at the lower level devoted to explaining the excavation.

The college itself is set on a terrace, a few steps above road level, cantilevered on double beams over the clear glazed museum and its coffered terrace overlooking the dig. It is at once solid, a deliberately low-key foil to the older structures, and yet creates its own atmosphere. It has a calm sense of rightful purpose, particularly in the simple timber-floored interiors. The main building has a hall, library and a common room overlooking the excavations. Beyond are eight classrooms in a separate wing. Everything is still used as originally intended.

Above all, Dannatt has given a sense of place to a quintessentially twentieth-century collision of the ancient and the banal.

LISTED grade II, 30 March 1993
ADDRESS University of Leicester, St Nicholas Circle, Leicester
ENGINEER Ove Arup and Partners
GETTING THERE off A594 (Vaughan Way)
ACCESS exterior and museum open daily except Christmas Day and Boxing Day; Monday to Saturday, 10.00–16.30; Sunday, 13.30–16.30; call 0116 251 7368 for information

Trevor Dannatt 1960–62

NORTH LINCOLNSHIRE CIVIC CENTRE
SCUNTHORPE

Scunthorpe developed as a steel town in the 1930s, when a town hall was first proposed and Charles B Pearson won a competition for its design. Charles B Pearson and his son Charles E Pearson practised extensively around their native Lancaster, but this is probably their finest building. The complex eventually built was very different from their initial scheme.

The building makes expressive use of the local steel, as panels combined with slate and hardwoods, and contrasted with end walls of brick. The plan is 'L'-shaped, with offices facing the busy main road and the council chamber and committee rooms set behind. The council chamber resembles the 'egg in a box' of the Royal Festival Hall (see pages 668–670) and is clad in Portland stone. Its form is fully visible through a tall open screen of square columns down the side street.

The interior is particularly distinguished, with a double-height entrance hall lined in marble and copper, and the council chamber clad with slatted timber to give excellent acoustics. A Roman mosaic pavement, excavated at Winterton, north of Scunthorpe, has been displayed on an entrance wall. There is an air of jauntiness in the interior's use of contrasting materials, suggesting that these are not intimidating offices but a real hub for this sprawling new town.

LISTED grade II, 24 April 1998

ADDRESS Ashby Road, Scunthorpe

ENGINEERS Ove Arup and Partners/R W Gregory and Partners

GETTING THERE to south of centre off A18

ACCESS exterior only

Charles B Pearson, Son and Partners 1960–62

ENGINEERING BUILDING
LEICESTER UNIVERSITY

This is a post-war British building of international significance. In 1958 John Summerson wrote of a shift away from Scandinavian modernism towards a strongly individualistic style. The Engineering Building is remarkable internationally for its Accrington brick and matching Dutch tiles, with aluminium-framed patent glazing, an update of the industrial aesthetics of England's nineteenth-century cities. Comparisons abound with William Butterfield's All Saints, Margaret Street (1849–59), the beatification of the Industrial Revolution. The Engineering Building is an appropriate celebration of the twin 1950s' religions of education and technology, in an overwhelmingly red-brick city.

It is also a response to an awkward site and specific brief. Leicester is the most physically constrained of the post-war universities, and Stirling and Gowan had to squeeze in workshops for heavy machinery, laboratories, lecture theatres, and a high water tank to create pressure for hydraulic experiments. The workshops, covering two-thirds of the area, had to have north-light glazing, but the plot does not run north–south. So while the building uses its space efficiently, the glazing runs at a diagonal through it. Hence its distinctive lozenge-shaped terminals. Inside, the building glows under this outstanding roof, which is most akin to Gropius's Dessau Labour Exchange. Its impact is greatest in the aerodynamics and electrical laboratories that rise over the service road. The roofing was justified as being low-cost, yet it remains an overwhelmingly architectural piece of design (Gowan's) which was engineered by Frank Newby to achieve greater clarity.

Comparisons can also be made with Frank Lloyd Wright's Johnson Wax complex at Racine, the use of saturated light in the workshops comparable to that in Wright's offices, while there are clear affinities in the banded glazing of their respective towers. Wright's glazing has similarly proved uncleanable and prone to leaks. Here, the glazing to the tower circulation areas has been renewed with a thicker profile, and secondary hardwood

James Stirling and James Gowan 1960–63

windows protect the laboratories stacked over the smaller of the projecting lecture theatres. The tower interiors continue the external aesthetic, except exposed concrete was here permitted along with the simple expanses of red paviours. It is impossible rationally to explain the juxtaposition of the two towers, whose shapely forms are usually credited to Stirling, again with Newby making refinements.

While there remains an ambiguity between who did what, the synthesis created gives the surprisingly skinny building its tautness. Its tricky shapes make it seem larger than it really is. Stirling and Gowan dissolved their partnership soon afterwards and, despite their subsequent individual achievements, for most critics Leicester's Engineering Building remains the sublime monument of the New Brutalism.

LISTED grade II*, 30 March 1993
ADDRESS Leicester University
ENGINEER Frank Newby of Felix Samuely and Partners
ACCESS by appointment on 0116 252 2504, or on application to fifth-floor office

James Stirling and James Gowan 1960–63

THE ROTUNDA
BIRMINGHAM

The Rotunda is the most noted landmark of central Birmingham's wholehearted redevelopment in the 1960s. James Roberts was a local architect who worked extensively for the property company Ravenseft, not only in Birmingham but also, for example, in Croydon and central Liverpool. The Rotunda has none of the expressionist foibles of the better-known work of Richard Seifert and Partners, but is a clean, mosaic-clad design, and it is unique in Britain to find an office building designed in such a simple form as a cylinder set on a podium. It exemplifies the move towards simpler shapes found in art and applied art in the early 1960s, but which is rarely met with in architecture. Its white mosaic expresses its search for a clean, crisp image amidst the vulgarity of so much of Birmingham's 1960s' rebuilding. A much lower tower was first planned in 1960, when the foundations were put in; it took its present form of 24 storeys only as work progressed.

There is one fine interior, a banking hall on the first floor reached by escalators, and which is wrapped around the drum of the tower. The curved wall of the drum is entirely sheathed in an abstract mural of *ciment fondu* by John Poole, a local artist who also worked at Coventry, St Paul's and Brentwood Cathedrals.

THE MIDLANDS

LISTED grade II, 9 August 2000
ADDRESS New Street, Birmingham
NEAREST STATION Birmingham New Street
ACCESS exterior and banking hall only

James A Roberts 1960–65

ASHLEY AND STRATHCONA BUILDINGS
BIRMINGHAM UNIVERSITY

Howell, Killick, Partridge and Amis set up in partnership after coming second in the Churchill College competition of 1959. Birmingham was the first of many university commissions that resulted from this early critical success.

The Faculty of Commerce and Social Science was newly amalgamated from different departments. The tall Ashley Building was therefore devised as a means of bringing the disparate staff together by setting the 69 tutors' rooms around a five-storey atrium, through which coils a circular stair. It is built of the full-height precast panels that HKPA were among the first to use, with distinctive projecting sills designed to throw off rainwater. Strathcona is a long curving tail of concrete blocks housing lecture theatres and seminar rooms.

HKPA's other characteristic feature is their exposed method of construction, reminiscent of an eastern timber shrine but wrought of the finest concrete. This is already evident here. The buildings are unified by their pattern of projecting concrete floor beams, punctuating the façades and resembling a timber-kit construction. Inside, this aesthetic is enhanced by what HKPA termed 'Chinese-style' slatted ceilings and staircase joinery, and by random brick texturings. Their subsequent Oxbridge work refined these ideas, but the Birmingham buildings have an earthy panache, and the atrium remains one of their finest spaces.

THE MIDLANDS

LISTED grade II, 30 March 1993
ADDRESS off Pritchatts Road, Birmingham University
ENGINEER Harris and Sutherland
NEAREST STATION University
ACCESS exteriors only

Howell, Killick, Partridge and Amis 1961–62

COVENTRY STATION
COVENTRY

Coventry was the most successful 'special' station built by the London Midland Region. Paul Taylor, a railway architect, admits that they 'put everything into it, because of the status of the city'. The new station replaced a smaller set of buildings which served only two platforms, which were increased to four.

The entrance is striking for its high, fully glazed concourse, at right angles to both the tracks and the enclosed square in front of it. The quality of the Swedish white-tile and timber finishes can be particularly enjoyed on the staircase to or from the further platforms, and which gives a fine first view of the concourse and the city beyond. The station's particular achievement, however, is its unique and distinguished programme of fascias and back-lit signage, using a modified version of the typeface designed by Jock Kinneir for the motorway system and for which Coventry and Glasgow Queen Street were trial stations.

Coventry's special position as symbol of the brighter post-war England and the business expected from the opening of the new cathedral ensured that its station was generously funded and completed as intended. It has a calm timeless quality, and has stood up well to heavy use.

LISTED grade II, 24 November 1995
ADDRESS Station Square, Coventry
ENGINEER Ove Arup and Partners

British Railways London Midland Region (Derrick Shorter) 1961–62

NOTTINGHAM PLAYHOUSE
NOTTINGHAM

Nottingham Playhouse has all the flexibility and theatrical sophistication lacking at the contemporary Chichester Festival Theatre (see page 454). It is also more intimate, its circular shape and large balcony bringing actors and audience close together. An exciting space in which to see a play, it is the finest work by this specialist theatre architect.

In 1948 a repertory theatre was launched in an old cinema under the dynamic directorship of John Neville, with funding from the nascent Arts Council. A permanent theatre was made possible with compensation for the privatisation of Nottingham's gas compnay, though actors' bedsits similar to those at the Belgrade, Coventry, were removed from Moro's initial design.

Moro had worked on the Royal Festival Hall (see pages 668–670), and Nottingham repeats the idea of a square foyer wrapped around a separately expressed auditorium. Though the individually expressed elements have a simpler geometry than the Festival Hall – an oblong, a cylinder and a square – a flytower, workshops and a large backstage area make this a more complicated building. The ancillary accommodation is tucked neatly at the bottom of the steep site, so that the bulk of the flytower is reduced and the auditorium uses the natural fall of the land.

The round auditorium is the key to the Playhouse's flexibility. It is not a theatre in the round. The stage is conventional, but a large apron can be raised from the orchestra pit and seats rearranged to give a large thrust stage. The blocks which make up this apron can be adjusted to make traps and graves as required. A separate lighting rig is suspended over this apron and forms an important architectural element. Moro was the only architect working in Britain successfully to explore flexible staging methods. Here he was assisted by leading stage designer, Richard Southern, who went on to work at the National Theatre.

The decorative treatment of narrow verticals, used as window openings in the

Peter Moro 1961–63

NOTTINGHAM PLAYHOUSE

façade, reappears throughout the interior as timber slats and lighting troughs. The monochrome palette of black, white and grey was typical not only of Moro's buildings but of his own dress and personal effects. In the double-height foyer the drum of the auditorium is decorated with a large metal mural by Geoffrey Clarke. Projecting from the foyer is a long, low block containing rehearsal rooms and a separate restaurant and bar.

Listing was prompted when damaging proposals were made to remodel the foyer, and a more carefully designed lift for the disabled was subsequently installed.

LISTED grade II*, 14 July 1994

ADDRESS Wellington Circus, Nottingham

ACCESS foyer open Monday to Saturday, daily performances; call 0115 947 4361 for information

Peter Moro 1961–63

RC CHURCH OF THE GOOD SHEPHERD

WOODTHORPE

Gerard Goalen, who had worked for F X Velarde while studying at Liverpool University, designed his first church at the Harlow Development Corporation. Our Lady of Fatima, Harlow (1958–59), was much admired by Father Mooney at Woodthorpe, who wanted a new church for his expanding congregation. Goalen was meanwhile working for Frederick Gibberd, and both had prepared designs for the Liverpool Metropolitan Cathedral competition. Father Mooney's commission enabled Goalen to set up his own practice, and was followed by many more fine Catholic churches.

The church is a foreshortened hexagon in plan, supported on four hexagonal shells like inward-blown umbrellas. The result is a broad worship space, which slopes steeply to the sanctuary. It was one of the very first churches to adopt the preferred liturgical solution of a fan-shaped auditorium in which congregation and celebrant are truly close together. There was insufficient funds for stained glass all round the church, but at its eastern end there are three large windows of dark *dalle de verre* glass by Patrick Reyntiens in rich blues, greens and reds. These are not only of exceptional quality in their own right, but strengthen the numinous, organic experience of the church.

The dark tactile quality of the Good Shepherd may be compared with the brightness of contemporary St John, Ermine.

LISTED grade II*, 25 September 1998
ADDRESS Thackeray's Road, Woodthorpe, Nottinghamshire
GETTING THERE to north of centre, just off A60
ACCESS open most days; call 0115 926 8288 for details of services

Gerard Goalen 1961–63

THE FOLLY
LEOMINSTER

The Folly was built for Mrs M A Willis as a *jeu d'esprit*, but now serves as a dower house to the Gatley Park estate. It is one of Erith's most distinctively quirky compositions, best known from the drawing which he exhibited at the Royal Academy in 1961.

The building stands at the head of a narrow wooded valley, and commands an extensive view. Erith described it as 'sited just above the pass, which it dominates like a fortress'. The proportions of the elevations are developed from the circular plan, and Erith also claimed to have been inspired by the lunar cycle. The plan consists of a series of semi-oval rooms, set one above the other and connected by a spiral stair; on the ground floor are low wings linked by a simple Regency-inspired verandah. Most domed roofs are taller than they are wide, to counter the flattening effect of perspective when viewed from below, but Erith deliberately eschewed this conceit in favour of a perfectly spherical dome with a little viewing platform on top.

In 1969 Erith was invited back to add a long low wing at ground-floor level. This is a timeless neo-vernacular ancillary building that fits naturally into the landscape.

Mrs Willis considers the building to be 'the best thing I have achieved in my life'.

THE MIDLANDS

LISTED grade II, 15 July 1998
ADDRESS Gatley Park, Leinthall Earls, near Leominster, Herefordshire
GETTING THERE to east of A4110
ACCESS none

Raymond Erith 1961–64, 1973–76

ST JOHN
LINCOLN

St John's anonymous exterior resembles a whale, mysteriously beached in a suburban housing estate. Inside is a space of surprising theatricality, where the principles of the Liturgical Movement are brought to life.

The first churches to reject the traditional plan of nave and chancel to bring celebrant and congregation closer together set the altar in the middle, only to find that the incumbent then had his back to some of the congregation. A more complex geometry was required. The hexagonal solution adopted here, with the congregation set on three sides round the sanctuary, was also chosen at the contemporary RC Church of the Good Shepherd, Woodthorpe, Nottinghamshire (see page 182). But here the plan is dwarfed by a hyperbolic paraboloid concrete roof just 76 millimetres thick. The two lower ends reach the ground, where pools catch cascading rainwater. The high prows are lopped off because there was to have been a bell tower – never erected because of lack of money.

Inside, the altar, pulpit and font were made of primitive cast concrete by local sculptor Charles Sansbury. The east window is by Keith New, who had designed some of the nave windows at Coventry Cathedral. This is his first brightly coloured work. At St John's, the combination of technical ingenuity and liturgical planning are entirely homogeneous with each other and with the exceptional fittings.

LISTED grade II*, 19 January 1995
ADDRESS Sudbrooke Drive, Ermine East, Lincoln
GETTING THERE north of city between A15 and A46
ACCESS Sunday services only; call 01522 525621 for details

Hugh Segar (Sam) Scorer of Clarke Hall, Scorer and Bright 1962–63

ST MATTHEW
BIRMINGHAM

Maguire and Murray secured several commissions through the New Churches Reform Group, a multi-denominational group of architects and clergy interested in new church design, founded in 1957.

St Matthew's is their most complicated piece of geometry. Maguire first divorced the altar from a place under a central lantern, by lighting the church from seven stepped clerestories. These progressively rise in a circle from the low baptistry, round the rear of the congregation, to the sanctuary set forward of the longest wall. This brings the sanctuary and font physically close, as liturgists were beginning to demand, yet they are separately defined and at opposite ends of the processional route. The original structure was devised as an Archimedes spiral swirling into infinity. The roof structure on seven levels which was eventually built was a revision made on grounds of cost.

The cool quality of Maguire and Murray's St Paul, Bow Common (see page 534), is repeated in the bands of exposed grey brick and concrete walling, blue paviour flooring and simple bench seating. Maguire revelled in the use of simple and very beautiful practical objects, though he regretted that here the client rejected his proposed baldachino. Nevertheless, this is perhaps the firm's most satisfying interior.

LISTED grade II, 16 June 1997

ADDRESS Birdbrook Road, Perry Beeches, Birmingham

GETTING THERE train to Birmingham New Street, then bus; off B4138 north of city centre

ACCESS Sunday services and regular events; call 0121 360 2100 for information

Maguire and Murray 1962–64

WINTHORPE BRIDGE
NEWARK

The Winthorpe Bridge carries the Newark By-pass over the River Trent. It is a three-span continuous prestressed concrete bridge 158-metres long, with a central span of 79 metres over the river, formed of nine small box girders cast in situ on falsework. The abutment wingwalls are cantilevered, and are based on a concave cylindrical section, giving them a rare architectural elegance.

In addition to the fluted faces of the bridge the horizontal fascia along the top edge is also carefully detailed, formed by precast concrete units with a blue Shap granite aggregate finish.

The character of this bridge appears to be transitional between the 1950s and 1960s, having continuous box girders but a large number of small ones with no edge cantilever. It was listed, however, for its exceptional elegance and quality of finish. There is a fine view of the bridge from the train just north of Newark station.

LISTED grade II*, 29 May 1998
ADDRESS A1 near Newark, Nottinghamshire
GETTING THERE on A1 between Newark and South Muskham
ACCESS any time

R Travers Morgan and Partners, engineers 1962–64

CENTRAL BATHS
COVENTRY

This was one of England's most ambitious post-war swimming baths, with three pools and a cafeteria. Wartime bombing destroyed four of Coventry's five baths, and the chief architect, Donald Gibson, identified a central pool as a priority for the city in a World Service broadcast as early as 1942. The first plans date from 1956.

The 1944 Education Act recommended that children should be taught to swim, but it was only from 1960 that baths were built in large numbers. Coventry exemplifies a brief period of grandeur in their design. The 50-metre main pool is T-shaped – the first such to be planned – to include a diving area that projects into the garden to the south, where there are sunbathing terraces. On the north side is a great bank of 1174 seats, with changing rooms and slipper baths set beneath them. A teaching pool is set underneath the oversailing café, and a children's pool beyond that. The overall length of this hall is truly impressive, as is the great south wall of glass that lights it.

The white mosaic external finish has been overclad, and the building extended, but the sublime interior remains too special to be ignored. 'Coventry has been provided with one of the finest swimming pools in the world', claimed *Coventry New Architecture* in 1969.

LISTED grade II, 2 December 1997

ADDRESS Fairfax Street, Coventry

ACCESS open for sports daily; call 01203 838383 for information

Coventry City Architect's Department 1962–66

CHESTERFIELD COURT HOUSE
CHESTERFIELD

The Court House is remarkable for the consistently high quality of its materials, and its theatricality in a period noted for the sterility of civic building. Joe Allen, Professor of town planning at what is now Newcastle University, was invited in 1962 to replan Chesterfield's town centre, and to design its new magistrates' courts.

Allen was an 'enabler' rather than a designer, and the courts were conceived under his direction by a former student, Roy Keenleyside, who was killed in a car crash shortly after the building was completed.

The building is defined by its presence in a park, designed to be seen from all sides. It has a double fan-shaped plan, with three courtrooms in the larger, eastern fan, and offices in the smaller, western fan. The contrasting curved and straight sides are clearly differentiated, with white marble mullions and gables for the curved sides contrasted with grey Welsh and green Westmorland slate.

Expensive materials can also be found in the principal interiors. The courtrooms are panelled in rosewood and Norwegian quartz, with a grand imperial staircase in the full-height central entrance hall. This also contains an electrically operated glass screen which could separate adults from juveniles when different courts were sitting at the same time.

Listing saved the building from demolition, and instead there are proposals for its extension.

LISTED grade II, 10 August 1998
ADDRESS West Bars, Chesterfield, Derbyshire
ACCESS exterior only

J S Allen and Roy Keenleyside 1963–65

KEELE UNIVERSITY CHAPEL
NEWCASTLE-UNDER-LYME

The chapel is the one building of distinction at Britain's first post-war university, opened in 1950. That it is so substantial is due to the personal faith of its founders and the sponsorship of the Ecumenical Institute of the World Council of Churches, which resolved to build an experimental chapel shared by all denominations at its Birmingham meeting in 1959. Pace was commissioned following the success of his ecumenical chapel at Ibadan University, Nigeria (1951–54).

The Liturgical Movement sought to revive the simplicity of the early church before its division into different othodoxies. At Keele there are two drum-shaped chapels, and the sharing of one of these by the Anglicans and non-conformists was still novel in the mid-1960s. The other serves the Roman Catholics. These chapels form the twin end towers that are the building's most distinctive feature, and their internal voids are particularly dramatic. Behind them, a long hall with a gallery on one side can be used separately for a variety of worship, or for the university's ceremonial events.

The dark engineering brick of the building shows Pace becoming interested in industrial materials for his personal distillation of the arts-and-crafts idiom infused with the geometry of Le Corbusier. Keele is an interesting balance between his masterful use of timber, particularly for the barn-like main hall, and the stirrings of a more brutalist aesthetic.

LISTED grade II, 25 September 1998
ADDRESS near Newcastle-under-Lyme, Staffordshire
GETTING THERE train to Stoke on Trent, then bus
ACCESS open most days

George Gaze Pace 1964–65

MINERALS AND PHYSICAL METALLURGY BUILDING
BIRMINGHAM UNIVERSITY

The university work with which Arup Associates emerged from the engineering firm of Ove Arup and Partners in 1963 closely parallels that of Howell, Killick, Partridge and Amis. Both were early users of precast concrete, and here their work can be seen side by side.

For HKPA's warmth and vigour Dowson substitutes a supremely rational clarity. His sequence of four linked laboratories were designed to be extremely flexible internally and to provide a 'wall' at the edge of the campus, defining the greensward within. The sombre units were all cast off-site, save for the floor plates. But what made it truly special was its use of a tartan grid to incorporate the heavy servicing required. A column is placed at each corner of the square of the construction grid, meaning that there are four columns internally where the corners join, allowing space for services and ventilation between them. This is expressed on the elevations by little roof vents above each group of columns. The system is a simplification of Louis Kahn's Richards Medical Research Building at the University of Pennsylvania, and of Eero Saarinen's laboratories for Bell Telephones at Holmdel (both 1957–62).

Dowson's building constituted an important model for flexible deep planning in Britain, as is shown by the use of a similar grid at Ahrends, Burton and Koralek's Templeton College, Oxford (page 418).

LISTED grade II, 30 March 1993
ADDRESS Prichatts Road, Birmingham University
NEAREST STATION University
ACCESS exterior only

Philip Dowson and Arup Associates 1964–66

NEW STREET SIGNAL BOX
BIRMINGHAM

John Bicknell and Paul Hamilton had designed Harlow Town Station (see page 270) and many signal boxes for British Railways' Eastern and Midland Regions before beginning their own practice. This early independent work displays a tight control of design, and is tougher and more sophisticated than their in-house signal boxes, such as at Rugby.

With the electrification of the Euston line came automatically locking signals, requiring bigger signal boxes. Birmingham controls about 350 signals, and was the first multistorey box on a central city site.

The precise technical brief demanded exceptional sound insulation and very heavy floor loadings for the power plant. Sensitive electronic equipment had to be shielded by large areas of blank walls. The accommodation is laid out on five levels with various floor heights, around a central shaft projecting above the roof. The signal control room on the top floor is surrounded by a cantilevered roof with a deep fascia to shade the control console from the sun.

Hamilton felt that 'the prominent siting demanded a formal expression of its purpose', though he likened the completed building to a log house. The heavily textured precast panels were chosen because of the tight site and restricted access.

Subsequently an elevated road was built alongside, and it is now impossible to imagine the box in its original setting surrounded by buildings. The station itself is not listed – nor remotely listable.

THE MIDLANDS

LISTED grade II, 24 November 1995
ADDRESS Birmingham New Street station
ACCESS exterior only

Bicknell and Hamilton 1964–66

RC OUR LADY HELP OF CHRISTIANS
BIRMINGHAM

Richard Gilbert Scott joined his father Giles in partnership in 1953. This was the first church built to his own designs and to a central plan, having inherited the commission on the death of his uncle, Adrian Gilbert Scott, in 1962. Our Lady Help of Christians demonstrates the reforming ideas enshrined inthe promulgations of the Second Vatican Council of 1962–65 and the English Catholic Church's requirement for a forward altar from September 1964, by placing the celebrant in the centre of a T-shaped building. But its theatricality is astounding.

Scott wanted to give the church the sense of Gothic found in his father's works, but using a modern idiom. His choice was a fireworks display of 1960s shapes and materials. The exterior is dominated by a soaring ribbed tent of copper-coated concrete. Internally, the exposed concrete is juxtaposed with semi-abstract glass by Scott's friend John Chrestien, depicting the defeat of the Turkish Armada in 1571 which led Pope Pius V to found the Feast of Our Lady Help of Christians. His brilliant colours shine like neon against the rippling concrete shapes; more representational pieces dominate the Lady chapel and baptistry set between the arms of the T.

This is the ultimate in 1960s 'pop architecture' applied to a church, combining bravura and celebration.

LISTED grade II, 18 February 1999
ADDRESS East Meadway, Tile Cross, Birmingham
GETTING THERE train to Lea Hall; on B4128 east of city centre
ACCESS open regularly and for services; call 0121 784 7751 for more information

Sir Giles Gilbert Scott, Son and Partner 1966–67

BOOTS D90 HEADQUARTERS
NOTTINGHAM

D90 belongs to a clutch of prestigious headquarters buildings by American architects in England. SOM's Chicago office under Bruce Graham was selected to give Boots a sophisticated transatlantic image, complete with open-plan offices.

The SOM Chicago office under Graham developed independently from that in New York, and Mies' office – also in Chicago – exerted a greater influence. In 1957 Mies had designed offices for Bacardi Rum in Cuba. This unbuilt scheme was to have been a doughnut of offices set over a sunken service floor, which was treated as a platform and lit from a landscaped courtyard. This is the plan of D90 down to the deep eaves, but is executed here in the neatest steel.

YRM were more closely involved in the internal detailing. On one side a sleek executive suite has storey-high doors, on the other open-plan spaces have carrels or cubicles, flexible enclosed timber units supplied by an underfloor network of services set on a regimented 6-foot grid. Still more open was the typing pool. 'Would you let your daughter work in an open-plan office?' queried the *Observer Magazine*, a reminder of their rarity in 1968.

SOM and YRM were the outstanding transatlantic collaboration of the late 1960s. The listing has ensured that a linked new building, D90A, has been sensitively designed by Frank Duffy of DEGW.

LISTED grade II*, 28 August 1996
ADDRESS Thane Road, Nottingham
NEAREST STATIONS Nottingham or Beeston
ACCESS none

Skidmore, Owings and Merrill with YRM 1967–68

EXPRESS LIFT TOWER
NORTHAMPTON

This 127-metre landmark was built for the testing of lifts and their components, and for training staff in their installation and maintenance. Faults in lifts around the world could be simulated.

The tower contains three shafts. The high-speed lift shaft, which determined the overall shaft height, is for testing lifts at speeds of up to 7.5 metres per second. The tallest shaft contains a service lift and gives access to a laboratory above the fast lift. The third and shortest shaft contains four lifts for testing and training. There are engineers' rooms at the base, and a rooftop observation gallery. The building can be best appreciated as a skyscraper core without the attendant offices, resulting in a pure form.

The lifts are independent of the drum of the tower, which is an outer casing designed to produce the least wind resistance. It tapers parabolically from bottom to top, where its distinctive pierced shape provides added bracing. The lower parts were slip-formed in just three weeks by continuous pouring. Between it and the lift shafts is an impressive clear internal space for most of its height, occupied by only a staircase.

This was the only testing tower in Britain, and the largest of just two in Europe. Listing in 1997 saved the tower from demolition, but its future remains uncertain.

THE MIDLANDS

LISTED grade II, 30 October 1997
ENGINEER Michael Barclay Partnership
ADDRESS St James' Road, Northampton
ACCESS exterior only

Stimpson and Walton 1980–82

EASTERN ENGLAND

AMERICAN MILITARY CEMETERY
MADINGLEY

This is the only American Second World War cemetery in Britain, though there are 15 worldwide. It is very different from its subdued British counterpart at Runnymede (see page 432). It was built on high land given by the University of Cambridge, and is reminiscent of the many airfields which covered East Anglia. Each of the 3811 servicemen and women buried here in curved rows is marked by a marble cross or Star of David set in the smooth lawn. The landscaping is by the Olmsteds – like the architects, a major Boston firm.

Still more formal is the memorial to the 5127 airmen and sailors with no known grave. Their names are recorded on a long wall, interrupted by giant figures of a soldier, airman, sailor and coastguard, carved by English craftsmen. A canal makes an axis, leading to the memorial – part chapel, part museum to American endeavour. Outside, an incised map of Britain shows the larger stations where Americans were based. Inside, a giant relief, *The Mastery of the Atlantic – the Great Air Assault*, in polished Portland stone and French marble explains the principal American operations across Europe and the Atlantic. A mosaic depicting the Archangel trumpeting the Resurrection and the Last Judgment dominates the sanctuary, and continues across the entire ceiling, with ghostly aircraft escorted by angels on their final flight.

LISTED grade II*, 25 September 1998
GETTING THERE on A1303, nearly 5 kilometres west of Cambridge city centre
ACCESS open 8.00–18.00 summer; 8.00–17.00 winter

Perry Stuart and Hepburn, Kehoe and Dean 1944–54

BURLEIGH SCHOOL (NOW JUNIORS' BUILDING)

CHESHUNT

In 1944 the Ministry of Education recommended 'standardised construction' as the only means of coping with the backlog of school building exacerbated by the war, the expanding education programme and a baby boom. Hertfordshire additionally faced a massive influx from London, later compounded by the designation of new towns.

In West Sussex and Middlesex, C G Stillman promoted a standard classroom, which could be built in rows. But only Hertfordshire grasped the concept of a three-dimensional system in which every element would be designed to a grid of prefabricated parts composed to suit the individual site. It was masterminded by Stirrat Johnson-Marshall, appointed deputy architect in 1945, who assembled a team of idealistic young assistants with wartime experience of designing from first principles.

Because of the urgency, an existing system was adopted, from Hills of West Bromwich, who had devised a light-steel system on an 8-foot 3-inch grid, clad in precast concrete panels. Three bays equalled the ministry's recommended class size.

Cheshunt was the first of the new schools. The infants, by Mary Crowley, came first, where the grid system is apparent in the three projecting classrooms and linked cloakrooms. It was followed by David Medd and Bruce Martin's larger junior school, with a pitched-roof assembly hall. There is a Scandinavian quality to the massing, while the concrete panels have a pleasant blond finish.

LISTED grade II, 29 March 1988
ADDRESS Blindman's Lane, Cheshunt, Hertfordshire
GETTING THERE off A121, parallel to A10 west of town centre
ACCESS none

Hertfordshire County Council 1946–48

ESSENDON SCHOOL
ESSENDON

Essendon closely followed Cheshunt as the second of the prefabricated Hertfordshire schools. Like it, the assembly hall has a pitched roof, the corridors and kitchen areas are generously scaled, and the precast concrete panels have a pleasant yellow hue. The two predate the rest of the programme by nearly a year, while the Hills 8-foot 3-inch system was evaluated and refined. Bill Henderson and Dan Lacey were the job architects here.

Otherwise the schools could hardly be more different. Essendon is a real village school, originally with just three classrooms, two for juniors, a third set back for infants. A nursery was added in the late 1960s. It was a replacement for a school hit by a stray bomb, and its tiny scale and its position on an open hillside next to a wood give it a rare picturesqueness. The hall was originally also intended to serve as a village centre.

Tiny Essendon embodied the principles of the Hertfordshire programme. It was not intended as a design statement, but as an 'artifact to do the job', developed by architects and educationalists working together as a light and creative environment for small children to learn in. The tiny chairs and tables, the little sinks and low windowsills, are part of this holistic approach to design. Others likened it to a Swedish sanatorium, such is its gentle exhibition of health and freshness.

LISTED grade II, 30 March 1993
ADDRESS School Lane, Essendon, Hertfordshire
NEAREST STATION Welham Green; off B158 in village
ACCESS exterior only

Hertfordshire County Council 1947–48

BARCLAY SCHOOL
STEVENAGE

This was the first important secondary school to be built after the war. Although it was built using the Hills 8-foot 3-inch system being developed by Hertfordshire County Council, Eugene Rosenberg provided a more architectural character by using brick and stone as well as the customary concrete cladding. His proposed curved layout was modified by Yorke to form an 'H'-shaped, two-storey set of classrooms, with an assembly hall adjoining the entrance. A beautifully spacious vestibule is floored in Hornton stone and punctuated by open-tread staircases. There is also a mural by Kenneth Rowntree, and tiles by Peggy Angus.

Along the main classroom spine the upper-floor rooms are separated from corridor and cloakrooms by short spurs, so rooflights in the intervening wells can light the corridor on the floor below. This system was used again at Susan Lawrence School, London (see page 498), and at subsequent YRM schools. Part of the upper floor was completed only in 1951.

An important collaborator in Hertfordshire's enterprising building campaign was its chief education officer, John Newsom, an admirer of the pioneer educationalist and architectural idealist Henry Morris of Cambridgeshire. Morris had originally intended a Henry Moore sculpture, *The Family of Man*, for Impington Village College, but could not raise sufficient money for it. Newsom did, and it sits proudly against a curved stone screen by the entrance here.

LISTED grade II, 30 March 1993
ADDRESS Walkern Road, Stevenage, Hertfordshire
ACCESS none; groups only by special appointment with Mr Smith, on 01438 232 221

Yorke, Rosenberg and Mardall 1947–49, 1951

WINDMILL GREEN
NORFOLK

218

It is now hard to appreciate how primitive rural England still was in 1945, despite the revival of agriculture in the war. Piped water, mains electricity and sewers were rarities, and housing was urgently needed to keep farmworkers on the land.

The problem was grasped by the tradespeople and minor gentry of Loddon Rural District Council, south-east of Norwich. In 1945 they commissioned local architects Tayler and Green to build 163 houses. Herbert Tayler was the designer, David Green the committee man and services engineer. At Windmill Green they rejected the conventional council-house 'semi' in favour of terraces that respected the long lines of the open landscape. They had seen Ernst May's Frankfurt housing in 1930, and although subsequently Tayler considered pure modernism inappropriate for Norfolk, May's influence is still appreciable here. Because only poor-quality Fletton bricks were available the houses were colour-washed in a range of pinks, blues and creams – a local tradition, as were the pantiled roofs. Of equally lasting importance in the evolution of their work is Tayler's planning: each house is broad, and incorporates a walk-through passage and implement store leading to the back garden. Four bungalows were later added at the entrance to the green.

The scheme won the Ministry of Health Housing Medal for 1950 and was extensively featured in the 1949 Housing Manual.

EASTERN ENGLAND

LISTED grade II, 19 November 1998
ADDRESS Ditchingham, Norfolk
GETTING THERE train to Beccles; off A143, on north side of village, down Hollow Hill Road and Thwaite Road
ACCESS exterior only

Tayler and Green 1947–49, 1960, 1965

MORGAN'S JUNIOR SCHOOL
HERTFORD

Morgan's Walk School, as it was originally known, was among the first batch of 'mature' Hertfordshire schools, refined by experience at Cheshunt and Essendon (see pages 212 and 214). It is the closest of all the schools to the council offices, so was among the most published, and was visited by delegates from around the world.

Morgan's differed from Cheshunt and Essendon in being entirely flat roofed. Its massing is particularly satisfying, for it shows Bruce Martin, the architect, and his team exploiting the grid system to move away from the lines of classrooms still found at the earlier schools. Here the hall is set centrally, with radial spurs at each corner: one for the school's offices, two for the larger junior classrooms and one for the infants. The original junior classrooms have strongly geometric rooflights – an alternative to having a high ceiling with a clerestory on the corridor side. The infants' rooms are particularly distinctive for their projecting bays, creating a separate space for messy play and a characterful stepped profile.

The Hertfordshire schools were painted in strong colours to stimulate the children, and a range of primary colours was developed for the corridors, with slightly more muted shades for classrooms. At Morgan's Walk the Building Research Station advised on colours, which included red and blue external steelwork. These have gone, but much of Brenda Colvin's planting scheme survives.

LISTED grade II*, 6 May 1998
ADDRESS Morgan's Road, Hertford
ACCESS none

Hertfordshire County Council 1948–49

TEMPLEWOOD SCHOOL
WELWYN GARDEN CITY

Cheshunt and Essendon were followed a year later by ten more schools, and by another 22 in 1949–50. Changes can be seen in each annual programme, and Templewood's year featured vertical concrete cladding panels to allow more variety in window sizes. In A W Cleeve Barr's design room layouts became increasingly flexible. Classrooms spilled into the adjoining corridors, by means of folding screens on the junior side, to be used for modelling and painting as well as for hanging coats. A staggered plan allows for windows on two sides without the need for clerestories in high ceilings.

But why, given their common ingredients, should some Hertfordshire schools appear more attractive than others? And what makes Templewood unquestionably the finest of all? Partly it is its superlative position, its site dug out of a hillside next to a wood, with oaks and hornbeams left all around it. Partly it is the careful details, down to the little hexagonal seats and enclosing walls in the infants' playgrounds, and no less than three murals by Pat Tew in the entrance area and dining hall. Templewood was designed just before cuts in funding began to curtail separate dining and corridor areas, and its common spaces have a scale and richness never to be repeated. Above all, the staggered plan, particularly of the five junior classrooms set low against the hillside, is exceptionally picturesque.

LISTED grade II*, 30 March 1993
ADDRESS Pentley Park, Welwyn Garden City, Hertfordshire
ACCESS open for heritage open days and the school's anniversary, second weekend in September. Check press for details

Hertfordshire County Council 1949–50

THE LAWN
HARLOW

Harlow was the second new town to be designated after Stevenage, in 1947, but could be developed more quickly as there was no local opposition. Its master planner was Frederick Gibberd, who stamped his personality on the town over 35 years.

Gibberd seized the concept of 'mixed development', that there should be a variety of flats and houses to serve a community of families, single people and the elderly. He was also the co-author, with F R S Yorke, of *The Modern Flat* (1938), and felt that a neighbourhood should not wholly consist of suburban houses. The nine-storey Lawn was the first architectural statement in any new town, and its expense was justified amid controversy by the wish to preserve seven oak trees.

Gibberd likened the gently curved trapezoidal plan to a butterfly, and it gave all four flats on each floor south-facing living rooms and balconies. Larger flats were set in a long, three-storey ribbon block alongside. The tower is firmly Scandinavian in style, Gibberd eschewing exposed concrete in favour of patterned brick and render. It anticipates the style of the LCC's point blocks at Alton (see pages 678–680), but its form is more complex, and remained a one-off.

A few, more simply-massed tower blocks were built in Harlow, as focal points of the new neighbourhoods, but densities still remained less than 50 persons per acre.

LISTED grade II, 22 December 1998
ENGINEER T F Burns and Partners
ADDRESS Mark Hall Moors, Harlow
GETTING THERE train to Harlow Town (see page 270) or Harlow Mill; just west of junction between A11 and B183 on north-east side of town
ACCESS exteriors only

Frederick Gibberd 1950–51

DITCHINGHAM HOUSING
DITCHINGHAM

Specialised council housing for the elderly barely existed before the Second World War. Loddon first commissioned pensioners' bungalows from Tayler and Green in 1948, and usually sought to integrate them with family housing. An exception was Agnes Hood Terrace, the longest progeny of Tayler and Green's brief flirtation with curved terraces around 1951. Subsequently it was incorporated into a larger scheme of sheltered housing, the first of three such developments by Loddon RDC (see pages 234 and 298).

Scudamore Place is the least altered of all Tayler and Green's housing groups, and the corner to Thwaite Road is among their cleverest juxtapositions of contrasting volumes, with a warden's house and community hall. It also demonstrates their ever-growing armoury of decorative details. One gable is entirely covered in timber trellis, another has a date in raised brickwork, while others are patterned like Fair-Isle sweaters.

The rows of terraced bungalows are linked by crinkle-crankle walls, for though Tayler considered that 'the English garden like Gods in the front' he was less enamoured of their 'rural scruff' at the back, and sought to conceal this. By the late 1950s he had abandoned red brick for more neutral colours because they jarred less with the tenants' brilliantly hued annuals. A nice touch is the built-in garden seat by every front door.

LISTED grade II, 19 November 1998
ADDRESS Agnes Hood Terrace; Hollow Hill Road; Scudamore Place; Thwaite Road, Ditchingham, Norfolk
GETTING THERE train to Beccles; off A143, on the north side of the village next to Windmill Green
ACCESS exteriors only

Tayler and Green 1950–51; 1958–59, 1964

GREENFIELDS SCHOOL
SOUTH OXHEY

By 1950 the Hertfordshire schools programme was proven, amid enthusiastic publicity. Its begetter, Stirrat Johnson-Marshall, had moved on to the Ministry of Education, but the architects' department remained committed to the programme, persisting with refinements under his successor, William Tatton Brown.

Of greater impact were cuts in government budgets made in 1950 and more oppressively in 1951. Thereafter primary-school design concentrated on reducing non-teaching space, by eliminating corridors and separate dining halls. Henry Swain's experiments at Oxhey, within its existing 8-foot 3-inch system, coincides with the Ministry of Education's one-off at Limbrick Wood School, Coventry (see page 128).

A small school for some 240 children with two lines of classrooms, Greenfields' corridors are absorbed into the room space, so access is through the back of the room or around the outside. It meant, however, that very large rooms could be built, which could be divided organically into messy areas and quiet corners where children could work in small groups. Little patios with seating extend the working space outdoors.

The unexpected architectural bravura here is the large assembly hall, set aside from the classrooms, with a grandeur lacking in its contemporaries. It is fully glazed at either end, but with one side set low as a dining area, continuing the theme of open planning for a variety of activities.

LISTED grade II, 30 March 1993
ADDRESS Ellesborough Close, South Oxhey, Hertfordshire
NEAREST STATION Carpenders Park
ACCESS none

Hertfordshire County Council 1951–52

SMITHDON SCHOOL
HUNSTANTON

Hunstanton belongs, like St Crispin's School, Wokingham (see page 372), to the first flush of new ideas on secondary-modern education. Both schools experienced a long delay between design and realisation. There the similarity ends.

Alison was 21, Peter 26, when in 1950 they won a competition for Hunstanton school with a design of stupendous clarity, symmetry and modernity. It became an icon for architects and students throughout the 1950s. Nevertheless, its plan is grounded in the inter-war tradition of symmetrical layouts popular with municipal grammar schools, with a central hall set between two courtyards, around which are classrooms and laboratories. The unusual feature here is that most of the classrooms are set in pairs on the upper floors, reached by spindly steel staircases from a ground-floor gyratory of corridors and cloakrooms.

In 1949 Peter Smithson invested £4 in Philip Johnson's biography of Mies van der Rohe. The influence of the early phases of the Illinois Institute of Technology, particularly of its Minerals and Metals Research Building (1942–43) and Alumni Memorial Hall (1945) are unmistakable, though the Smithsons' corner detailing, an inset post between two 'I'-beams, is weightier and more finite. There is a surprising complexity in the projecting and receding rhythm of square glazing panels and opening toplights, and in the way the panels of brick in the end walls and freestanding gymnasium stand slightly proud: they are clearly only infilling.

Peter Smithson wrote in 1954 that Hunstanton would have 'two lives', bustling with noise by day, and a silent 'idea' that would live forever. The school was photographed empty, the anthesis of all their subsequent writing on 'inhabitation' or the personalisation of space. Emptiness brings out the startling quality of the unadorned finishes: exposed steel ceilings, exposed drainage from the sinks, a Braithwaite water tank. This triumphant

Alison and Peter Smithson 1951–54

SMITHDON SCHOOL

use of off-the-peg industrial components was married to a welded steel frame still novel in Britain, designed on the principle of plastic design that there is no single weak point.

Hunstanton has an ambiguous relationship with the term 'New Brutalism' coined by Alison in 1953. Whereas the term originally stood for truth to materials and found objects, as overtly demonstrated here, it was later appropriated by exponents of concrete expressionism, a style at odds with the Wittkower-inspired classical neutrality of the Smithsons' work.

Though given expansion joints, the direct glazing into the steel frame caused shattering as the building alternately overheated or chilled. Between 1984 and 1991 wooden subframes were introduced and black panels replaced the clear glazing to dado height. Though not then listed, a section was retained to show the original fenestration.

LISTED grade II*, 30 March 1993
ENGINEER Ove Arup and Partners
ADDRESS Downs Road, Hunstanton
GETTING THERE train to King's Lynn, then bus; on A149 on eastern edge of town
ACCESS exterior only

Alison and Peter Smithson 1951–54

CHURCH ROAD
BERGH APTON

Loddon RDC acquired land at Bergh Apton in the 1930s, and although Tayler and Green designed the entire scheme in May 1949 it had to be built in phases as Ministry of Housing grants became available.

The houses are grouped asymmetrically in short terraces around a green of mature trees, and Tayler and Green's plans include new planting and footpaths. Church Road demonstrates the evolution of their architecture, from the earlier, more austere bungalows at the front of the site, to the more elaborate buildings at the rear. Loddon's housing policy was for a ratio of three- and four-bedroomed houses and one-bedroomed bungalows in each scheme. The recurring pattern of one taller gable in each terrace, denoting the larger house, was derived by Tayler from an eighteenth-century silk mill and adjoining cottages at Ditchingham, long demolished. After 1951 he abandoned colour washing in favour of contrasting colours and patterns of brickwork, to save on maintenance costs and because better bricks were available. Sometimes, as here, just one house in a row would be colour-washed.

On the western side the houses and bungalows are linked by a crinkle-crankle wall similar to that at Gillingham (see page 246). This time it is the gable to the house, rather than the bungalow, which incorporates the date of construction, together with a 1961 Ministry of Housing award .

LISTED grade II, 19 November 1998
ADDRESS Bergh Apton, Norfolk
GETTING THERE train to Reedham (via ferry); off A146, at west end of village
ACCESS exteriors only

Tayler and Green 1951, 1956–57

ORCHARD CROFT
HARLOW

Harlow was unusual among the new towns in that Frederick Gibberd, for Harlow Development Corporation, attempted from the first to invest an urban character by means of carefully-placed point blocks across the neighbourhoods and town centre. But the rest of the housing remained low, and despite The Lawn (see page 224) Mark Hall North achieved the exceptionally low density of only 35 persons per acre.

The difficulty in new towns was always designing convincing three-storey town houses in a suburban setting. Orchard Croft succeeds because it marks the boundary between the local shopping centre, The Stow, and the open cricket field – a relatively urban location that is nevertheless visible from a long distance, where its distinguished crescent form can be best enjoyed. Gibberd said he developed the idea from the early-nineteenth-century Fortfield Terrace, Sidmouth.

The houses are set over ground-floor garages, which are themselves set back between the entrances to the upper floors. The terrace is thus dominated by the big first-floor living room windows, their concrete surrounds set against pale brickwork. The result is a very urbane blend of 1950s detailing within an early-nineteenth-century concept.

Orchard Croft was the old field name for the area, typical of Gibberd's desire to blend old and new here. The enclave, not then completed, won a Ministry of Housing award in 1953. Landscaping was by Sylvia Crowe.

LISTED grade II, 22 December 1998
ADDRESS 3–13 and 161–165 Markdyke Road, Harlow, Essex
ACCESS exteriors only

EASTERN ENGLAND

Frederick Gibberd 1952–54

THE 'COMET' FLIGHT TEST HANGAR
HATFIELD

The so-called Comet Hangar, with its integral block of offices, a fire station and control tower, was built to test and maintain the world's first jet-engined civil plane.

The De Havilland Aircraft Company moved to Hatfield in 1930 and established the town as a major engineering centre. In 1941–42 the firm developed the Goblin jet engine, which was used in American fighter planes. Its prime interest, however, was to build a jet passenger plane, which was seen as the future of the British aircraft industry in peacetime, particularly for the valuable export market. The Goblin and its successor, the Ghost, were Britain's only advantages over its American rivals. The Comet was designed from 1946 onwards, and the prototype flew in July 1949. The first commercial service was inaugurated in May 1952, after the Queen Mother and Duke of Edinburgh had been on test flights, amid jingoistic euphoria.

Disaster first struck in October 1952, when a Comet skidded on takeoff. Then, in 1953, one exploded in the sky over Calcutta, and in 1954 two more exploded climbing out of Ciampino Airport, Rome. Tests revealed fatigue to the thin aluminium shell, and provided a model for future aircraft design.

This dramatic story overshadows the successful use of aluminium for the hangar. It was built of a new strain-hardened alloy, HE, which was less prone to oxidisation than its predecessors. It was the world's largest permanent aluminium structure when it was built. Steel was in short supply, whereas aluminium was plentiful, and its ability to bridge large spans had been demonstrated by the Dome of Discovery at the Festival of Britain. The Comet hangar is 100 metres long and 14 metres high, with a clear span of 61 metres. It is composed of portal-framed trusses, with pin joints on welded steel bases that marked an increased sophistication over earlier aluminium structures. The side thrust is taken up by concrete prestressed tie beams. One end is entirely filled with the original folding doors.

James M Monro and Son 1952–54

THE 'COMET' FLIGHT TEST HANGAR

On its west side a more conventional steel-and-brick annexe was added in 1954. This includes the building's most distinctive feature, a five-storey tower topped by a control room, whose zigzag Festival-style balconies are repeated in the stepped profile of the fire station behind it.

The Comet Hangar directly influenced simpler hangars for the US Air Force and the British Admiralty. None of these, however, shares its combination of technical ingenuity, physical charm and historic interest.

Listing has prevented demolition, but its future remains uncertain.

LISTED grade II*, 21 September 1998
ENGINEER SMD Engineers Ltd
ADDRESS former British Aerospace site, Comet Way, Hatfield, Hertfordshire
ACCESS none at present

James M Monro and Son 1952–54

ALL SAINTS
BAWDESWELL

In 1944 an RAF Mosquito bomber, limping back to nearby Bexwell after a raid, crashed into Bawdeswell Church and set it ablaze. The crew were killed, and are commemorated in the replacement church.

With private houses, pubs and restoration work, Watson continued a gentle neo-classical tradition based on the local brickmaking and craftsmanship which also served Tayler and Green so well. This is his masterpiece, in the eighteenth-century style of New England churches, with a shingle spire and herringbone flint-and-brick walling. The tower batters towards its top to give a sense of greater height and refinement, while the spire was hoisted aloft in three prefabricated sections.

The traditional appearance belies a liturgical plan that was appropriate to its times. It is a simple basilica, with a long nave dominated by chandeliers and a round apse for a forward altar. Its fittings are similarly a reminder of the harmony between the communion and the word in eighteenth-century Anglicanism. Watson designed a traditional three-decker pulpit of limed oak, while the pews were produced to a Swedish anatomical formula for comfort. The font, under the rear choir gallery, is of Ancaster stone.

Watson's church superseded a modest early Victorian structure, which had itself replaced a fifteenth-century church whose tower collapsed in 1739. At last Bawdeswell has a church to be proud of.

LISTED grade II, 25 September 1998
GETTING THERE train to Norwich; on A1067 north-west of city
ACCESS open daily

James Fletcher Watson 1953–55

POPLAR MEADOW AND THE HAMLET, RUSHBROOKE
BURY ST EDMUNDS

Rushbrooke is a tiny estate village set in the hedgeless plain of the Suffolk 'beet belt'. John Weeks' modernistic response contrasts with Tayler and Green's housing in Norfolk.

Richard Llewelyn Davies had met Victor Rothschild at Cambridge in the 1930s. He and John Weeks went on to specialise in hospital design, but as early as 1950 Rothschild commissioned them to build estate cottages. The first houses, a linked pair and the village nurse's house at Poplar Meadow, established the idiom of white-painted brick with big monopitch roofs and black trimmings repeated when the core of the village was entirely rebuilt. All the houses have south-facing living rooms, a large walk-in store for tools, prams and bicycles and a first-floor playroom or store in what are otherwise bungalows. The style is reminiscent of contemporary Danish work such as Arne Jacobsen's Søholm, outside Copenhagen, and also closely related to designs subsequently developed by the Smithsons, Howells, James Stirling and other friends of Weeks for Habitat, the tenth CIAM conference, held in 1956.

The old village street, The Hamlet, is a larger informal grouping. Linking screen walls between the houses attempted to create a sense of enclosure around an old well house, and a clubroom provided a social centre at the end of the street. This was among the first social housing to be provided with car parking.

LISTED grade II, 22 December 1998
ADDRESS Rushbrooke, near Bury St Edmunds, Suffolk
GETTING THERE set between A45 and A134, south-east of town
ACCESS exteriors only

Llewelyn Davies and Weeks 1954–56, 1956–59, 1960–63

FORGE GROVE AND KENYON ROW
GILLINGHAM

The finest of all Tayler and Green's housing benefitted from the assistance of councillor Charles Hastings, chairman of the Housing Committee and land agent at Gillingham Hall. The proximity of the hall explains the site's exceptional mature landscaping, which frames Tayler and Green's composition. Landscaping was an integral part of their designs.

Early plans show two straight-angled walls linking the corner between the houses of Forge Grove and the two counterpoised bungalows that comprise Kenyon Row. As built, however, the end gables with their wavy bargeboards are complemented by a connecting crinkle-crankle wall. These curved brick walls were popular from the seventeenth-century onwards for sheltering fruit trees, and can be found in exceptional numbers in Suffolk. They became a popular Tayler and Green method of turning corners and hiding unsightly back gardens.

The incorporation of dates into the gable brickwork is a rarer local feature that became another Tayler and Green trademark, along with diaper patterns and alternating projecting headers. Tayler described these patterns as 'particularly cheap, and the men noticeably sing while building them'. They were fortunate that there were many local building firms who could meet their exacting standards. The rhythm of arched window openings and trellised porches to the houses is an early example of what was to become a recurring motif in their later work.

LISTED grade II, 19 November 1998

ADDRESS Gillingham, Norfolk

GETTING THERE train to Beccles; off A146, at entrance to village

ACCESS exteriors only

Tayler and Green 1955, 1957

82–125 KNIGHTSFIELD
WELWYN GARDEN CITY

Louis de Soissons of Peacock, Hodges and Robertson was appointed in 1920 as the first architect and town planner to Welwyn Garden City, which had been founded as a limited company the year before. He developed the new garden city with a more formal centrepiece than the prototype at Letchworth, and used a more consciously neo-Georgian idiom for the small houses that surrounded it.

Welwyn and Hatfield were jointly designated a new town in 1947, with de Soissons as Welwyn's planner. He expanded the town to the north and south-east, with a mixture of public and private housing. To encourage private house builders, who were using a variety of styles, he determined that a prominent group of houses and flats at the main intersection in the northernmost neighbourhood should continue the Georgian tradition.

Knightsfield is extraordinary for its consistent Regency detailing, with big first-floor balconies under prominent copper canopies. The bold massing hides a complex variety of differently-sized dwellings, with houses at the ends and three flats or maisonettes in each of the linked central units, which resemble three-storey town houses. The individual unit is thus subsumed in favour of the overall effect of four mirrored terraces set around a village green.

Listing was prompted by piecemeal window replacement, which was halted before it could undermine the group's consistent character.

LISTED grade II, 22 December 1998
ADDRESS Welwyn Garden City, Hertfordshire
GETTING THERE off A1000 at junction of Digswell Road, to north of centre
ACCESS exteriors only

EASTERN ENGLAND

Louis de Soissons, Peacock, Hodges and Robertson 1955–56

ST LUKE
LUTON

St Luke perfectly demonstrates how original thinking in church design has little to do with superficial architectural style. Nikolaus Pevsner dismissed it as 'startlingly out of touch with its age', but it may be that the diversity of functions contained under one roof and the ease of car access at two levels makes it more suited to contemporary needs than many overtly modern churches. The uniqueness of the plan is a tribute to Seely and Paget's range of imagination and their confidence, after many years of practice, in handling church buildings.

The building has a misleadingly domestic character from the road. The elevations are in an eighteenth-century Georgian brick style, and the cross on the roof ridge is the only external evidence of it being a church. The rectangular church itself is set to the rear, behind a main broad entrance and butterfly wings containing ancillary accommodation.

The church itself is on two levels. A Lady chapel forms a gallery to one side, where it can be used as an overflow space on special occasions, and is set behind a round-arched arcade. Otherwise the design is quietly neo-classical, dominated by pendant candelabra and an enormous altar painting by Norman Blamey, who specialised in religious subjects. Seely and Paget enjoyed incorporating murals in their churches and this is a particularly fine example.

LISTED grade II, 25 September 1998
ADDRESS High Road, Leagrave, Luton, Bedfordshire
NEAREST STATION Leagrave
ACCESS Sunday services; call 01582 572737 for more information

Hon. John Seely (Lord Mottistone) and Paul Paget 1955–56

CASTLE HILL UNITED REFORMED CHURCH
IPSWICH

Birkin Haward met the engineer Felix Samuely when working for Erich Mendelsohn on the Bexhill Pavilion in 1934–35. He subsequently became interested in thin slab roofs, which he used at his many schools around Ipswich, where he based his post-war practice.

Castle Hill Church is an early example of a folded slab, a dramatically high pitched roof engineered as a series of thin inverted 'V'-shaped wedges slung between two frames and post-tensioned. The apex is glazed. It is extended by upswept eaves to either side, which reduce the stresses in the main planes and which taper to just 102-millimetres thick. The saw-tooth profile of the vestibule, also produced by folded slabs, is a distinctive Haward device.

The interior is a high light hall, with a sanctuary at one end and a stage at the other, which can be used for a variety of functions. The side walls are formed of precast diamond-shaped blocks in three patterns, inset with glass, and which are also used to form the cross over the altar. They were to have been filled with stained glass, but for economy clear glass was sprayed with oil paint and varnished. The Compton organ comes from a demolished cinema in Clacton.

The church is the centrepiece of the Castle Hill estate, where Haward also designed the primary school.

EASTERN ENGLAND

LISTED grade II, 25 September 1998
ENGINEER Felix Samuely
ADDRESS Dryden Road, Ipswich
ACCESS Sunday services only

Johns, Slater and Haward 1955–57

CLOCK TOWER AND RAISED POOL
STEVENAGE

Stevenage was the first new town to be designated, in November 1946. Leonard Vincent's clock tower, ostensibly commemorating the opening of the town centre by The Queen in April 1959, serves effectively as a monument to the whole new town programme. It incorporates a memorial to Lewis Silkin, the Minister of Town and Country Planning who adopted the recommendations of the Barlow Commission (1938–43) and the Reith Committee (1945) that London's overcrowding be eased by satellite towns, along the lines of the 'garden cities' promoted by Ebenezer Howard as early as 1898. Satellite towns were also crucial to Patrick Abercrombie's influential stratagem, The Greater London Plan, published in 1944. Silkin was not always so welcome in Stevenage: signs on the railway station appeared renaming the old market town 'Silkingrad'.

Stevenage was England's first pedestrian-only new town centre, modelled on the Lijnbaan in Rotterdam. The clock tower is its centrepiece, an elegant, open concrete frame with black granite cladding. On the east face is a map in painted ceramic tiles showing Stevenage and the principal occupations of its residents. A later panel commemorates the Stevenage Development Corporation (1946–80).

The pool has recently been modified to include an inner pool and fountain. Nearby is Franta Belsky's separately listed sculpture, *Joy-ride*, a mother and child symbolic of the new town.

LISTED grade II, 22 December 1998
ADDRESS Town Square, Stevenage, Hertfordshire
ACCESS any reasonable time

Stevenage Development Corporation 1957–59

ST ANDREW AND ST GEORGE
STEVENAGE

This church was built as St George's, the 'Mother Church' of the new town. It now serves a parish of 10,000, and its undercroft has since 1977 been adapted as the town museum.

At Seely and Paget's first church, St Faith's, Lee-on-the-Solent, Seely perfected a theory that the most stable form of structure was the catenary arch – the form that a chain naturally takes when draped over a rail – and developed this in reinforced concrete. At Stevenage such arches were precast, prestressed and set in pairs, extending outwards to give the effect of flying buttresses and appearing internally as pointed arches at their intersection. They permitted large clerestories which fill the church with light. Also built of prestressed columns is the adjoining open campanile, with tuned metal rods instead of bells.

The church has taken on a harmonious mellow quality as fittings have been added over the years. Seely and Paget's favourite artist, Brian Thomas, produced murals for the basement Lady chapel which since the creation of the museum have framed the high altar. Above it is a gloriously colourful east window added by him in 1966. The organ, side chapels and vestry are enclosed in aformosia wood, which fits well with the blond timber of the original furnishings and the nave altar devised from fittings brought from St Andrew's, demolished in the early 1990s.

LISTED grade II, 25 September 1998

ADDRESS St George's Way, Stevenage

ACCESS open Monday, Thursday, Saturday and Sunday mornings, and Friday lunchtimes for services; call 01438 351631 for further details

Hon. John Seely (Lord Mottistone) and Paul Paget 1957–60

CORPUS CHRISTI, SIDNEY SUSSEX, WOLFSON AND GIRTON BOATHOUSE
CAMBRIDGE

This little boathouse, originally shared by just Corpus Christi and Sidney Sussex colleges, was the first boathouse built at Cambridge since 1930. It reacted against the jauntily vulgar Queen Anne-style still in vogue between the wars. Roberts' simple design, built of unrendered brick and tiny in scale, provided a new model for boathouses.

The boathouse consists of a ground-floor store and workshop with a small pavilion and changing rooms on top. From a first-floor balcony outside these changing rooms two spiral staircases wind their way to water level, their duality reflecting the original shared occupancy of the premises. It was also the first boathouse to be shared by two colleges. Shared boathouses are now more common, and this is now used by four colleges, as denoted by the four flagpoles which have subsequently been erected. Extensions have been added to either side without destroying the elegant symmetry of the original composition.

The influence of this building can be seen in the number of boathouses that followed its winning formula. That shared by Selwyn, King's, Churchill and the Leys School is a bigger variant in Cambridge, and similar too is that built for Emanuel School at Barnes in 1960 by Lawrence King, which was the first post-war boathouse on the Thames.

LISTED grade II, 2 December 1997
ADDRESS Sidney Sussex, Wolfson and Girton Boathouse, Cutter Ferry Lane, Cambridge
ACCESS exterior only (best from across the River Cam)

David Roberts 1958

ST JOHN
HATFIELD

This small church is made to seem larger by its massive pitched roof and prominent site. There is a strong resemblance to Frank Lloyd Wright's Unitarian church at Shorewood Hills, Wisconsin, designed in 1947.

Peter Bosanquet's church was planned for a congregation of 200 and a choir of up to 50 seated in a rear gallery. It is set on a steep slope and, to make the most dramatic impact, it is orientated with the sanctuary at the west end. Its climax is the curved gable wall at the sanctuary end.

The altar, pulpit, font and lectern are more closely grouped than is usual in older churches, an early form of liturgical thinking that tried to give equal emphasis to the important elements of a church, and which was revived from the later 1960s. What really impresses, however, is the exposed timber, both in the roof and in the fittings. Timber roof trusses with exposed stainless-steel connections are supported on reinforced-concrete columns and on the gable walls, whose curve braces them against the wind. Designs for a 24-metre campanile, compared by *The Builder* to a fire station, were exhibited at the Royal Academy but never built. The church is the centrepiece of South Hatfield, a suburb developed by Brett, Boyd and Bosanquet with elegantly designed terraces by themselves and by Tayler and Green.

LISTED grade II, 25 September 1998
ADDRESS Hilltop, Hatfield, Hertfordshire
ACCESS regular services; call 01707 262072 for details

Brett, Boyd and Bosanquet 1958–60

1A–37 HIGHSETT
CAMBRIDGE

Highsett is among the most architecturally refined of Eric Lyons's mature works for Span, and his best outside London. There are three phases, but only the first is listed. Lyons, encouraged by Leslie Martin, originally proposed a 15-storey tower for part of the site, which was refused planning permission in 1958 and substituted by houses.

The remaining part of the original scheme is a true quadrangle, in collegiate fashion and with a similar fortress quality. On three sides the ground floor is partially open – the two upper storeys are supported on pilotis – so you can peer from the street right through the block to the shrubberies beyond. Living rooms in the flats have a dual aspect, so the residents enjoy similar views. The fourth side has maisonettes set over garages, making the overall planform far more complex than is usual with Span housing. Only the slightly later South Row, Lewisham (page 716), is more ambitious. Lyons believed that flat-roofed buildings fitted more naturally into his lushly planted landscapes, but – as at the earlier Parkleys, Richmond – tile-hung walls give the comfort of traditional materials. Here tile-hanging is contrasted with a sophisticated dark brick, while the block's structural cross walls have been concealed to give a greater horizontality and fluidity of design. Like all Span schemes, Highsett is a cunning integration of architecture, landscaping and careful management.

EASTERN ENGLAND

LISTED grade II, 22 December 1998
ADDRESS Hills Road, Cambridge
ACCESS exterior from street only

Span Developments Ltd 1958–60

RC OUR LADY OF FATIMA
HARLOW

Gerard Goalen was working for the Harlow Development Corporation when in 1953 he was asked to design the town's first and largest Catholic church.

The incumbent, Father Francis Burgess, asked that it be planned for 500 parishioners to sit as close to the altar as possible. The sanctuary was to be large, and the altar freestanding. This was a very radical brief for 1953, but Goalen had studied under F X Velarde at Liverpool and was aware of continental developments. Had the church been built then, it would have been the first in Britain inspired by the Liturgical Movement; but it took until 1958 to secure funding.

The church is a T-plan with the sanctuary set at the junction of the three equal arms; the congregation is thus split into three sections. On the fourth wall are the organ and a large figure of Christ by Daphne Hardy Henrion. Otherwise the church is dominated by the brilliant colours and loud patterns of its fused slab glass, designed and made by monks from Buckfast Abbey led by Dom Charles Norris. Goalen was an expert in modern French glass, and Norris's was the first English approximation on a large scale.

Alarmingly, the fixing of the glass has spalled and become unsafe. Listing has failed to secure hoped-for repair grants, and the church is currently closed.

LISTED grade II, 20 December 2000
ADDRESS Howard Way and First/Mandela Avenue, Harlow
NEAREST STATION Harlow Town
ACCESS exterior only at present

EASTERN ENGLAND

Gerard Goalen 1958–60

ARTS FACULTY BUILDINGS
CAMBRIDGE

The squalor of the science sites prompted the arts faculties to carefully plan their new precinct, on a site selected in 1950. A limited competition was held in 1952 between Sir Hugh Casson and Robert Atkinson. Casson's was the first large post-war university plan, and led to his major Birmingham commission. But at Sidgwick Avenue it proved impossible to secure all the land required, and even a revised scheme of 1963 was quickly abandoned in favour of a more piecemeal programme, one that included James Stirling's later History Faculty.

Casson and Conder provided an urbane integrated environment of refined buildings, walkways and lawns that is Cambridge's best effort at a public campus. It is good to meander through. The centrepiece is a three-sided cloistral building housing the English and language departments, with their respective libraries. The higher building to the west is largely for economists. At the entrance to the site are the more public halls, including the Lady Mitchell Hall, completed in 1964 only after much controversy and many revisions. A simpler taller block of lecture theatres and low departmental buildings provide a modest foil to the east.

Casson and Conder's low-key work has become integrated into the Cambridge scene in a way Stirling's work never has, but it has its own problems of inflexibility, and radical internal alterations have recently been implemented.

LISTED grade II, 30 March 1993
ADDRESS Cambridge University, Sidgwick Avenue, Cambridge
ACCESS exteriors only

Casson, Conder and Partners 1958–64

WESTCLIFF LIBRARY
SOUTHEND

Westcliff Library is an early example of a district library designed to a deliberately domestic scale to encourage people to come inside and enjoy books. It is thus unassuming, light and friendly, with deep eaves to keep out the sun, and a high central clerestory that gives an even light across the building.

The County Borough of Southend had recognised the need for a library to serve the growing suburb of Westcliff in the 1930s. The site was 'fortuitously supplied by enemy action', as the opening brochure puts it. The design was made in 1956.

The building has always combined adult and children's lending facilities with some reference material in a space made deliberately open plan. This has enabled the library to adapt well to modern needs, with new shelving for videos and audio books, and computer terminals. The children's section was originally by the entrance, but has been moved to the far end to allow better supervision, and a low window gives good light for the smallest readers. A curved bench, originally built to screen the newspaper tables, now provides respite for weary parents, who can also sit in the pleasant rear garden.

The kidney-shaped issue desk is original. The staff particularly enjoy the building, admiring its flexibility and the generous rear work room.

LISTED grade II, 24 April 1998
ADDRESS London Road, Westcliff-on-Sea, Southend, Essex
GETTING THERE train to Westcliff; on A13 in town centre
ACCESS open 9.30–17.30, except Wednesdays and Sundays; call 01702 341961 for more information

Patrick Burridge, borough architect 1959–60

HARLOW TOWN STATION
HARLOW

In the late 1950s Eastern Region developed as the most design-conscious and creative of the four railway architecture departments. Harlow, a rebuilding of Burnt Mill station to serve the new town, is the greatest manifestation of what the designer Paul Hamilton describes as a pent-up urge to build, after years producing standard plans for the LCC, whence he and his collaborator John Bicknell were headhunted by the region's chief assistant, Roger Walters.

The land was unstable, so Hamilton's team decided to use as little of it as possible, placing the waiting room on the bridge and making a feature out of the lifts which then principally served parcel traffic. This concept had been pioneered by Western Region in 1956–58 at Banbury.

Hamilton was concerned that the station's chunky detailing and robust finishes should be able to withstand knocks and expect little maintenance. Its distinctive image is a series of thick horizontal concrete and timber slabs, covering the glazed booking hall, brick offices and stairs from the platforms, which rise to the covered bridge building and are crowned by the lift towers. It is tempting to draw references to Hamilton's favoured Frank Lloyd Wright, though *The Architects' Journal* considered this 'facile and misleading'. Bicknell and Hamilton later set up in private practice and designed Birmingham's New Street Signal Box (see page 200).

Listing has saved the building from proposed demolition.

LISTED grade II, 25 November 1995
ADDRESS Station Approach, Harlow

British Railways Eastern Region 1959–60

GARRET HOSTEL BRIDGE
CAMBRIDGE

A new bridge across the River Cam was built to replace William Chadwell Mylne's cast-iron Gothic bridge of 1837. It had to be higher than its predecessor and it had to withstand occasional car traffic. Its steep camber serves as a brake to speeding cyclists.

The project was sponsored by the Trusted family, supporters of the adjoining Trinity Hall. The construction was another family project, being engineered by Guy Morgan and Partners, and designed by Guy's son Timothy, who was then studying at the Cambridge School of Architecture. Timothy's death shortly after the bridge was completed gives this precocious undergraduate work a particular piquancy.

The bridge is an elegant two-hinged arch of prestressed concrete, 24 metres in span, with a keel-shaped underside. The concrete portal frame is supported on a concrete hinge at one end and steel rollers at the other, a structure that minimises the depth of the deck to just 533 millimetres at the crown. Embedded within, nevertheless, are two water mains and two ducts for electric cables. The abutments appear more weighty by being concealed in York stone, with which the bridge is also paved. The handrails are of polished bronze.

A simple job simply done, but done with a flourish worthy of its historic setting – it is the sixth bridge on the site since records began in 1455.

EASTERN ENGLAND

LISTED grade II, 29 May 1998
ADDRESS Garret Hostel Lane, Cambridge
ACCESS any reasonable time

Guy Morgan and Partners 1960

KEELSON
CAMBRIDGE

Keelson was commissioned by Dr Olga Kennard and her husband, and is one of the best-known examples of Danish design in England. It makes the optimum use of a very long, narrow site by adopting a courtyard plan. Its simple, understated elegance is largely the result of its extremely slender timber frame, which is infilled with white-painted brickwork and large areas of glass.

The entrance is from the north-west, its door set beneath a projecting canopy that also forms a carport. A simple, open-planned idiom is continued through the house. Behind a central courtyard is a fully glazed garden elevation, where the main rooms are placed. Rooms for the Kennards' two children give on to the protected courtyard. Quarry tiles are used throughout, and the house has a sense of quiet sophistication coupled with practical domesticity.

Dr Kennard is a leading figure at the Cambridge Crystallographic Data Centre, and was the force behind the centre's major new building, comissioned from Sørensen in 1992.

LISTED grade II, 15 July 1998
ADDRESS Hills Avenue, Cambridge
ACCESS exterior only

Eric Sørensen 1960–61

BROOKE HOUSE
BASILDON

The new towns found it difficult to inject life into their central areas outside shopping hours. Many experimented with flats to complement the shops, just as the prototype Lijnbaan in Rotterdam had done in the 1950s, but only at Basildon was a block of exceptional quality produced.

Moreover, Brooke House is not set in a back street, but forms a vital vertical node at the junction of the two main shopping parades, facing a sunken square. Its bold yet subtly profiled and extremely tall pilotis make the building stand out forcefully.

The flats, on 14 floors and with six to a floor, were aimed at professionals without families. Their structure is based around four concrete boxes of great strength, which contain the kitchen, bathroom and duct units, and these are carried down on to the piled foundations via the pilotis. This means that the entrance hall can be a virtually free-standing glass box set between them. In the foyer is a sculpture by F E McWilliam, given to Basildon in 1959 by Harold Lever. This elegant glass detailing is continued upwards in the ranks of canted windows that enliven the façade. An open parapet completes the composition.

This is a building of glistening force and personality that deserves to be better known.

LISTED grade II, 22 December 1998
ADDRESS East Square, Basildon, Essex
ENGINEER Ove Arup and Partners
ACCESS exterior only

Basildon Development Corporation with Basil Spence 1960–62

HARVEY COURT
CAMBRIDGE

Harvey Court rethinks the traditional Cambridge quadrangle. Developed from a project by Wilson for King's on a more urban site, it is a hostel separated from its parent college, with a breakfast room but no dining facilities. Like Stirling's similarly equipped Florey Building, Oxford, it is designed to a rigorous idea, and remains controversial.

The top-lit breakfast room is on the ground floor, with a south-facing lounge leading on to beautiful grounds. These rooms are floored over to form a raised brick courtyard, reached up steps from two sides. Around this are three storeys of bedsitters, arranged in a stepped section akin to that then being developed by Martin and Patrick Hodgkinson (who assisted here) at the Brunswick Centre, London. Groups of rooms are linked by staircases, which project between the brick piers that dominate the outward elevations, although there are also broad internal corridors for students to congregate.

Leslie Martin most often worked in collaboration with a 'studio' of sympathetic younger architects. Many recurrent themes were first realised here: the strict orthogonal planning, the use of brick, the similarities with post-war Aalto and particularly his Säynätsalo Town Hall and – here – Baker House at the Massachusetts Institute of Technology. Above all there is a logic and coolness that is nevertheless belied by an underlying romance in its sculptural elevations and quirky plan.

LISTED grade II*, 30 March 1993
ADDRESS Gonville and Caius College, West Road, Cambridge
ACCESS exteriors by application to the lodge on 01223 332400

Sir Leslie Martin and Colin St John Wilson 1960–62

EASTERN ENGLAND

WATER GARDENS
HARLOW

Harlow is the most consistently planned of the post-war new towns, a naturally picturesque site developed by Gibberd and the landscape architect Sylvia Crowe over three decades. The centrepiece was a Civic Square at the town's highest point. In 1952 Gibberd developed the idea as a terraced garden looking south across the town to Rye Hill. Detailed designs were made by Gerry Perrin, an architect with the Development Corporation, who also chose the materials. There were two canals in the top and middle terraces, the retaining wall between them set with seven fountain jets in the form of lions'-head gargoyles by William Mitchell. Below were a chequerboard of seven smaller pools and squares surrounded by clipped hedges.

Mitchell specialised in sculptural concrete, combined here with broken blue tiles to create a Mexican feel. The framework of terraces and steps also became a showcase for the Harlow Arts Trust's exceptional sculpture collection. Pieces included *Boar*, an early work by Elisabeth Frink, a copy of Rodin's *Eve*, and Henry Moore's *Bronze Cross*, bought from the artist specially for the site.

In 2000 Harlow District Council announced the redevelopment of its town hall and water gardens. The gardens were listed, but the DETR immediately granted consent for them to be rebuilt lower down the slope. The sculptures and lions' heads will be resited in the new scheme.

LISTED grade II, 5 October 2001
DEMOLISHED early 2002
ADDRESS Water Gardens, Civic Square, Harlow, Essex

Frederick Gibberd and Gerry Perrin 1960–63

CHURCHILL COLLEGE
CAMBRIDGE

A trust was founded in 1958 to establish a men's college in Winston Churchill's honour devoted to science and engineering. With 42 acres and sponsorship from industry and the trade unions, it was intended for over 500 students. The two-stage competition among 21 firms, invited by the trustees and Sir Leslie Martin, was the most influential of the era; younger competitors, including the Smithsons, Howell and Killick, realised elements of their designs in subsequent commissions.

Sheppard adopted a traditional approach in gathering the residential accommodation around staircases in small courtyards, which gave on to larger quadrangles. A central spine houses Cambridge's largest dining hall, common rooms and a bar. A chapel was included in the original brief but was subsequently rejected; an ecumenical building was added at the far end of the site in 1967–68. The first element of the design, 20 flats for married students were built there too, and served also as offices and common rooms until permanent accommodation was completed.

Churchill's scale and quality are conservatively majestic. Though harried by the trustees, Sheppard succeeded in creating a language of concrete and brick based on Le Corbusier's Maisons Jaoul which gave a sculptural form to repetitive blocks. Stirling and Gowan had adopted the idiom at Ham Common, but this was its first large-scale manifestation and was widely imitated.

EASTERN ENGLAND

LISTED grade II, 30 March 1993
ADDRESS Storeys Way, Cambridge
ACCESS exteriors by application to the lodge on 01223 336168

Richard Sheppard, Robson and Partners 1960–68

BARSTABLE SCHOOL
BASILDON

Barclay School, Stevenage (see page 216), was YRM's first school. This is one of their last, built as they began to concentrate on larger commercial and civic schemes following their successful building of Gatwick Airport (1958–63). It demonstrates the tougher aesthetic that appeared in the firm's work thereafter, particularly in the hands of a talented younger generation led by Brian Henderson and David Allford, who worked here.

Barstable was built as a grammar school but is now a bustling comprehensive for 11–16-year-olds. It is notable for the tall, board-marked concrete columns which stand forward and rigorously articulate its main teaching block. The concrete frame is contrasted with infill panels of dark-bluish brick. This three-storey block, housing administrative offices and classrooms for mathematics, English, home economics and humanities, forms a strong contrast with a long, lower block set at right angles. This contains a large assembly hall, with a folded plate concrete roof, and a swimming pool.

Windows have been replaced and the concrete painted following repair work. The school has also been greatly extended with the building of new facilities for science and technology in separate blocks. The original building retains its former vigour, but it is now part of a larger complex that has the feel of a small township.

LISTED grade II, 30 March 1993
ADDRESS Timberlog Lane, Barstable East, Basildon, Essex
GETTING THERE train to Basildon or Pitsea; south of A1321
ACCESS none

Yorke, Rosenberg and Mardall 1961–62

44 WEST COMMON WAY
HARPENDEN

Povl Ahm was working for Ove Arup on the Sydney Opera House when he persuaded Jørn Utzon to design him a house. As built, it closely follows Utzon's concept, except that an intermediate truss was introduced to prevent the concrete beams that support the gently pitched roof from being too deep. These smooth, precast beams – exposed the length of the fully glazed garden front – contrast with the house's cool brickwork.

The main house sits along one side of the sloping site. Although it is only one-storey high, its hall and car port are at a slightly lower level to the living room, and further steps rise to the dining and kitchen area beyond. This sense of progression is an important feature, as is its consistency of finish, with Swedish Hogamass white tiles throughout the house and extending on to the terrace beyond. The joinery details follow those of the houses at Fredensborg which Utzon was then designing.

In 1972–74 the house was extended by Ulrick Plesner with Christopher Beaver Associates. Plesner's wing presents a blank brick frontage to the road. It provides separate children's accommodation which has no through link to the main house. He was an architect with Arup Associates at the time, and his work is entirely sympathetic with Utzon's. The combined result is a distinguished and beautifully detailed modern house, in the idiom of an internationally important architect who built relatively little.

EASTERN ENGLAND

LISTED grade II, 15 July 1998
ADDRESS Harpenden
ACCESS wall only visible from street

Povl Ahm 1961–63

2 AND 2A GRANTCHESTER ROAD

CAMBRIDGE

No. 2a was built for Dr and Mrs Peter Squire, while No. 2 was Colin St John Wilson's own house and studio. The two houses have a similar plan, with living rooms projecting to the rear, but the Squires have a single-storey living room with a bedroom above, while Wilson's is double height and there is an open-well staircase. His house, moreover, is hidden behind an office wing that forms a continuous street façade with No. 2a. Colin Rowe called its colonnade 'the smallest monument in Cambridge'. They are the first houses to be built of ferroconcrete blocks, which give them their feeling of rigorous austerity. They are also perfect for displaying art and sculpture.

Inside Wilson's house one is overwhelmed by the rigour of the 4-foot-4-inch module, set in a tartan grid that extends to the pattern of the paved rear patio. Its intellectual, mathematical quality seems appropriate to its present use as the Wittgenstein Institute. But the planning is exciting, particularly in the double-height spaces of the living room, staircase and office entrance, whence separate stairs rise to a first-floor drawing office across the front of the building. Wilson's own office formed a bridge between house and studio. The house must always have been intended as a semi-public space, for displaying works of art and giving parties, but it is also capable of absolute privacy.

LISTED grade II, 13 April 2000
NEAREST STATION Cambridge
ACCESS exterior only

Colin St John Wilson 1961–64

JOHN LEWIS WAREHOUSE
STEVENAGE

John Lewis chose Stevenage for its main distribution depot for its proximity to the A1. YRM had been involved with the new town since 1945, but here Rosenberg invited the Spanish architect and engineer Félix Candela to collaborate on the structural design. They had met in Mexico, though Candela's work had become fashionable in England since he had lectured here in 1957. He had escaped Franco's Spain in 1939 for Mexico, where he developed folding plates and hyperbolic paraboloid shells as a cheap and architectural means of bridging large spans. This is his only work in Europe.

The 142-metre-long building is entirely roofed with hyperbolic paraboloids of board-marked reinforced concrete, 127 millimetres thick, supported on square columns. Each unit resembles an inside-out umbrella, or warped parallelogram, and is tilted to create a string of north-facing rooflights between each of the 11 rows of 15 shells. Candela had already used the system for his High Life Clothing Factory in Mexico City and Tulancingo Wool Mill (both 1955) and the Texas Instrument Factory, Dallas, designed with O'Neil Ford. Ford himself had repeated the design for Texas Instruments in Bedford (1960, with Oscar Faber). At Stevenage, 15 half-shells project over the loading bays, and these may be unique.

All 23 John Lewis stores are supplied from Stevenage. The adjoining office building, a typically understated YRM design, is not included in the listing.

LISTED grade II, 24 November 1995
ADDRESS Gunnel's Wood Road, Stevenage, Hertfordshire
ACCESS none

Yorke, Rosenberg and Mardall 1962–63

29A LOOM LANE

RADLETT

George Marsh was one of Richard Seifert's first partners, and designed Centre Point (see page 546). Here he enjoyed an unaccustomed freedom in designing a house for himself. The Marshs had previously lived in a Kensington flat with exceptionally high ceilings, and elements here reflect its influence – particularly the decision to make the principal rooms open plan on a single level. The site slopes steeply from the road, on which the house turns its back. Thus, though it is entered at road level, the principal rooms give on to a south–facing balcony over a playroom and sauna. As soon as the house was completed, the Marshs added a wing for their parents.

The complex room heights are made possible by two hyperbolic paraboloid timber roofs, supported on a light steel frame at three points, with the 'granny flat' under a third. The hypa form was also chosen as it could be constructed first, allowing the builders to work under cover, and its overhangs prevent solar gain through the large windows. The eclectic assemblage of materials include brick, York stone paving and grey and gold mosaic reminiscent of that at Centre Point.

Like Rodney Gordon's Turnpoint (see page 452), Loom Lane points to similarities between concrete and timber construction; here links with office design continue in Marsh's careful attention to maintenance issues and heating.

EASTERN ENGLAND

LISTED grade II, 18 February 1999
ADDRESS Radlett, Hertfordshire
ACCESS none

George Marsh 1962–65

NEW HALL
CAMBRIDGE

New Hall was founded in 1954 as Cambridge's third women's college, in recognition that an 11:1 male/female ratio was no longer acceptable. However, fundraising lagged behind that for new male colleges, and though Peter Chamberlin was appointed architect in 1959 following an invited competition, only subsequent grants from the Wolfson and Nuffield Foundations made building possible.

At the core of the college are the dining room, common rooms and library, in bold white brick and concrete set around a courtyard. The abiding image is of the domed first-floor dining hall set sentinel over a reflective pool. Its double sprayed-concrete skin, resembling a half-peeled orange, is testimony to the new possibilities of precision precasting, each section craned into position around a central plug. Inside the hall, breakfast still arrives from the kitchen below via a dumb waiter set into the middle of the floor. Common rooms cluster round at ground-floor level, and these spaces and the adjoining wide corridors have been enhanced by the college's important collection of works by women artists.

Less dramatic, but in some ways a more satisfying composition, is the tall, narrow library on the opposite side of the courtyard. Its two galleries are reached via a soaring central staircase. Beyond, the residential Orchard Court was built immediately afterwards, its variety of single and shared rooms reflected in the busy patterning of its façades. Chamberlin also intended an entrance and chapel on the western side of the site, but these were never built, for lack of funds.

New Hall's bold forms were at first deemed inappropriate for cosy Cambridge. It remains assertive, yet its clean white masses make a tranquil environment in which to study, and it gave a progressive institution the strong architectural identity it sought. New Hall demonstrates Chamberlin's fascination with new structural methods at this piv-

Chamberlin, Powell and Bon 1962–66

otal point in the firm's career, and is like nothing else in the firm's oeuvre. It was a unique opportunity for them to design interiors on a broad scale, with an attention to quality finishes that they could only hint at in their public commissions.

Since the building's listing, extensions have been made in a lighter, subordinate idiom, and the college has finally gained the distinguished entrance it deserves.

LISTED grade II*, 30 March 1993
ADDRESS Buckingham Road, Cambridge
GETTING THERE on A1307 north-west of city centre
ACCESS by application on 01223 762215

Chamberlin, Powell and Bon 1962–66

DAVY PLACE
LODDON

In 1962 Nikolaus Pevsner called Tayler and Green's incorporation of traditional details 'post-modern', before that epithet achieved popular currency. This is the most distinctive of their later works for Loddon RDC. It replaced some run-down cottages in a narrow defile formed from old gravel workings, and an old brick garden wall survives. The ingredients of a prominent warden's house and adjoining community hall, with rows of terraced bungalows, are repeated from Scudamore Place, but the contrasting levels are unusual for Norfolk.

The treatment of the gable ends and fretted barge boards is particularly elaborate here, one alternating bricks with the bottoms of wine bottles set in cement, others incorporating local flint pebbles.

Tayler and Green designed 709 houses, flats and bungalows for Loddon RDC between 1945 and 1973. They won more housing awards than any other authority, and the piquancy and sense of place found in their work is matched nowhere else. Their retirement coincided with the absorption of the local authority into the larger South Norfolk District Council, which in the 1990s has developed an enlightened policy for the conservation of the most distinctive elevations through design guidelines.

LISTED grade II, 19 November 1998
ADDRESS High Bungay Road and Low Bungay Road, Loddon, Norfolk
GETTING THERE train to Reedham (via ferry); off A146, south of village centre
ACCESS exterior only

Tayler and Green 1963

LONG WALL
NEWMAN'S GREEN

Long Wall was devised by Philip Dowson and Peter Foggo as a weekend house for a doctor and his wife. It takes its name from the brick wall which runs through and beyond the house, giving privacy at the front and sheltering a large terrace at the rear. On one side is the garage, on the other a simple open-planned house. The wall serves to highlight the entrance and to provide a logical position for the chimney. Otherwise this is a lightweight timber structure with long beams carried on timber posts, which rest on a low brick wall. Three sides of the perimeter are glazed, giving an open pavilion reminiscent of Mies, while the materials and the deep overhanging eaves suggest Frank Lloyd Wright. A brick terrace carries the floor level from inside to outside.

Dowson wrote that 'we wanted to establish a relationship between the hearth and the horizon and let the spaces develop, each with their own function and influence in graduated steps between these extremes.' But for the strong, sheltering eaves the house would appear diminutive in the big Suffolk landscape that surrounds it.

Dowson and Foggo were among the founders of Arup Associates, the architectural practice linked to the engineer Ove Arup and Partners. In 1995–96 the house was beautifully restored by Hugh Pilkington in consultation with Sir Philip Dowson.

EASTERN ENGLAND

LISTED grade II, 28 February 1997
ADDRESS Newman's Green, Acton, Suffolk
NEAREST STATION Sudbury; down tiny lane off B1115
ACCESS none

Arup Associates, Philip Dowson and Peter Foggo 1963

FERRUM HOUSE
HARPENDEN

John Bonnington was a partner in one of Basil Spence's three practices specialising in civic commissions, when he designed this neat little house for himself. It is one of the very first steel-framed houses in England, and is maintained in immaculate condition.

It is the principal first floor which is steel framed, and its black outline is complemented by yellow brick crosswalls on the ancillary lower floor. The influence of Mies van der Rohe can be clearly felt in the precision of the planning, using a 9-inch brick module and a 3-foot grid. Storey-high windows in aluminium frames fit naturally into this grid. An addition in similar style was made in the 1970s for the Bonningtons' growing family.

The interior is equally sophisticated, with Swedish white-glass mosaic floors and sitka-spruce boarded ceilings. There is considerable use of timber, with large hardwood sliding doors and partitions and much built-in furniture.

LISTED grade II, 15 July 1998
ADDRESS Grange Court Road, Harpenden, Hertfordshire
ACCESS exterior visible from street only

John S Bonnington 1963

WILLIAM STONE BUILDING
CAMBRIDGE

A massive legacy from an American centenarian enabled the building of Cambridge's first tower of student accommodation. A double cluster of rooms and staircases was originally proposed by Martin and Wilson, a development of their earlier Harvey Court (see page 278), but an eight-storey tower was preferred as a means of preserving Peterhouse's extensive parkland. The plan, however, seems to derive from these earlier schemes.

Each floor has three undergraduate bed-sitters and a fellow's 'set' of three rooms, which can be divided by sliding partitions into two separate units if required. The staggered profile of south-facing windows, with views to the river, is the building's distinctive image. As in the architects' earlier collaborations there are affinities with Alvar Aalto here, with his stepped blocks of flats for Bremen (unbuilt) and Tapiola (1961). The three-step brick rear elevation and service tower are more reminiscent of Louis Kahn. A basement storage area is shielded by the earth bank in front of the tower.

At eight storeys, this was the first Oxbridge college building to have a lift. Unlike at Harvey Court there were ample funds for high-quality interior fittings, chosen by the architects. Indeed the only economy was the choice of load-bearing brickwork, for this is one of the first 1960s blocks to show that cellular buildings could be built high without reinforcement, anticipating the residential towers at Essex University.

EASTERN ENGLAND

LISTED grade II, 30 March 1993
ADDRESS Peterhouse, Trumpington Street, Cambridge
ACCESS exterior only by application at the lodge, 01223 338202

Sir Leslie Martin and Colin St John Wilson 1963–64

LECKHAMPTON HOUSE
CAMBRIDGE

Two linked blocks were built behind Leckhampton House, a Victorian villa set in grounds so hidden that they have a dream-like quality. It was the first accommodation in Cambridge designed solely for research fellows and graduates, who are provided with large study bedrooms and a few sets over a shared ground-floor common room and library.

Dowson and Arup Associates had in 1962 built two blocks at Somerville College, Oxford, for undergraduates and graduates respectively. Leckhampton is a refinement of ideas on precasting first explored there, to a simpler, refined plan. Like HKPA, Dowson was concerned that dirt-laden water from glass surfaces should not discharge over the concrete and cause streaks. His solution was to set the glass behind the frame, which serves as a screen and which gives some privacy to the larger windows. The resulting impression is of a lattice 'kit of parts', here set over solid brick piers and walls which link the two blocks to each other and the original house. It can also be compared with the slightly earlier and far larger Point Royal, Bracknell (see page 398).

The echelon layout gave every room a view of the mature gardens. Perhaps it is this setting, or the fact that it is for graduates, but here is one block divorced from its parent college which is remarkably successful.

LISTED grade II, 30 March 1993
ENGINEER Ove Arup and Partners
ADDRESS Corpus Christi College, off Grange Road, Cambridge
ACCESS none

Philip Dowson of Arup Associates 1963–64

3 CHURCH WALK
ALDEBURGH

In 1957, H T (Jim) Cadbury-Brown designed an opera house in Aldeburgh for Benjamin Britten. It was never built, but Cadbury-Brown was given first option on the site. He designed two houses there, one for Britten's assistant, Imogen Holst, the larger one for himself and his wife Betty, who did the detailing.

The house is concealed in a wild garden, but gaps in the screen walls and enveloping creeper allow views of Aldeburgh church. House and walls are all of pinkish brick. It is long and low, with an entrance courtyard – filled with big-leafed plants – formed by the projecting bedroom to the rear. The land falls to the south, so while the roof remains a constant height, steps in the living room lead down to what Betty termed her 'passion pit'. Light falls into the depths of the house from projecting 'light scoops' in the living area, over the kitchen sink and beds, and in the corridor that runs along one side of the house; a corresponding axis runs through the kitchen on the other.

The carefully directed light is one reason this house is so special; the other is Betty's detailing, from the tiled floors to the kitchen cupboards. Particularly elegant are her full-height doors, a leitmotif of the 1960s she justified because 'we are tall people, we could do it'.

LISTED grade II, 4 December 2000
NEAREST STATION Saxmundham, then bus
ACCESS none

EASTERN ENGLAND

H T and Elizabeth Cadbury-Brown 1963–64

NEW NORTH COURT
CAMBRIDGE

The local architect David Roberts began working in a light-brick idiom around Cambridge in the mid 1950s, beginning at his own Magdalene College. By the early 1960s his work had become more consciously modern, with the support of Sir Leslie Martin, who as a fellow of Jesus College secured the commission here.

New North Court replaced a house by Sir Alfred Waterhouse, who also designed the adjoining range. Its open, boomerang plan, built in two phases, bounds the college's gardens and sports grounds. Otherwise it closely follows the form of 'The Beehives' at St John's College, Oxford, by Michael Powers (see page 380).

Where Powers conceived a three-deep honeycomb of hexagons, New North Court is formed of linked cubes, set at right-angles to the line of the block. Alternating central cubes contain staircases and service rooms, with four study bedrooms set in the corner of each landing. Each has a projecting fully glazed window at its apex, and the reflection of scuttling clouds send a translucent shimmer down the block. Each room also has a private balcony. The textures of light brick and blue soffits now appear quite conservative compared with Martin's contemporary Harvey Court (see page 278) but New North Court was admired from the first for the quality of its undergraduate accommodation, and for gently updating the character of the college.

LISTED grade II, 30 March 1993
ENGINEER Peter Dann
ADDRESS Jesus College, Jesus Lane, Cambridge
ACCESS exteriors only, afternoons, by application to the lodge, 01223 339339

David Roberts and Geoffrey Clarke 1963–65

COCKAIGNE HOUSING GROUP
HATFIELD

The Ryde was a new concept in low-budget private housing. In 1962 Michael Baily, transport correspondent of *The Times*, advertised for people to join a co-operative housing venture. This became Cockaigne, named from William Morris's *News from Nowhere* 'to work out afresh the real needs of the family of today and the type of structure which would best answer them'. Hatfield Development Corporation offered land on a long-term repayment deal.

Baily was impressed by the MHLG's 'adaptable house' at the Ideal Home Exhibition, partly designed by Peter Randall and David Parkes. They and Peter Phippen subsequently decided on single-storey 'L'-shaped units as a way of building high-density, self-contained housing. The patio or courtyard house was first conceived in 1920s Germany by Hugo Häring, and by Meyer and Hilberseimer at the Bauhaus, but this is its leading English manifestation.

Cockaigne is a staggered broken terrace of long narrow single-storey two-, three- or four-bedroom dwellings, partly lit by internal courtyards. Exposed timbers span the concrete block crosswalls. Randall described the rigorous construction as 'earthy, economic and pragmatic', indebted to Le Corbusier and early Habitat shops. There are private and shared gardens, a tennis court, community centre and lodgings for visitors. Collectively managed, it remains a popular home with architects, and inspired subsequent Phippen Randall and Parkes schemes elsewhere.

LISTED grade II, 22 December 1998
ADDRESS The Ryde, Hatfield, Hertfordshire
ACCESS exteriors only

Phippen Randall and Parkes 1963–66

103 MAIN STREET, CALDECOTE
CAMBRIDGE

John Meunier designed this house when he was a junior lecturer at Cambridge University, and it is his first significant building. It was made possible by a university mortgage scheme specially designed for faculty members with no savings. An extremely austere and modest house, it makes a feature of its cheap Fletton brickwork.

Meunier's students recall that he saw everything in terms of the cube and the square, and here the plan is of two intersecting squares. The larger, higher one contains the open-plan living, dining and kitchen areas, while the lower one has an enclosed study and bedroooms. The intersection is the bathroom and service core. The two squares are set on a raised brick plinth, also square, which forms two terraces.

The façades follow a sequence from the completely blank north face to the totally glazed south face of the higher block. Inside, the Fletton brick is left exposed, and contrasted with Columbian pine ceilings and built-in cupboards. Meunier describes it as 'an English Brutalist version of a Frank Lloyd Wright Usonian house', but this understates the classicism of its proportions and severe logic. In this it anticipates Meunier's subsequent and better-known work with Barry Gasson, which culminated in the Burrell Museum, Glasgow. He has since stated that a house should be noble and elevating rather than comfortable.

LISTED grade II, 12 July 2002
NEAREST STATION Cambridge
ACCESS none

John Meunier 1964

HISTORY FACULTY
CAMBRIDGE

Few post-war buildings have inspired as animated a debate as James Stirling's History Faculty, a building either loved or hated. In 1980 falling tiles from its façades led the University to consider its demolition; instead most were replaced with brickwork – hence the humble grading for what has subsequently come to be regarded as among Stirling's most important works.

It occupies a pivotal place in his oeuvre, in which his early synthesis of Le Corbusier's Maisons Jaoul with the nineteenth-century red-brick tradition of industrial England is first tempered by a symmetry inspired by the drawings of Sant'Elia. Comparisons can also be made with the work of Louis Kahn, whom Stirling knew through his teaching at Yale and whose ideas in the 1960s evolved in a similar fashion. For the postmodernists he was an early classicist; now he can also be seen as among the pioneers of deconstruction. The History Faculty demonstrates both qualities.

In December 1962 Stirling and James Gowan were invited to participate in a limited competition of 15 invitees for a new History Faculty building at Cambridge. The design was substantially or entirely made by Stirling, and in December 1963 the partnership split so that Gowan could pursue his own design work elsewhere. The Faculty admired the concept of making the centrepiece of the building its large library, around which are ranged – in ascending order as the building narrows – common rooms, seminar rooms and tutors' rooms. Stirling wrote that 'the room shapes are stacked to become the total building form', the glass roof of the library allowing an even light and being buttressed by the rooms that form an L around it. For him, 'Cambridge refers to 19th century public reading rooms with glass lantern roofs'. Internally the finishes were kept deliberately simple, and white; the impact comes from the sense of clear space, disappointingly rare in modern university architecture, and exposed roof structure.

EASTERN ENGLAND

James Stirling 1964–68

After the building was designed the University could not acquire all the necessary land, and so it was turned through 90 degrees. This had a notorious effect on the complex and then innovative ventilation system of louvres and blinds. In summer it is hot. As controversial was the way it deliberately eschewed any compromise with Casson and Conder's adjoining arts buildings (Sidgwick Avenue, page 266). Today it has to compete with Sir Norman Foster's Law Faculty (1996) alongside, yet it still feels rebarbatively modern. For John Summerson, writing in 1983 when the building's fortunes were at their lowest ebb, it was 'a redoubtable, daunting monument; enigmatic; a crystal fort with a shiny brick rampart; something of a factory, something of a conservatory.' That analysis still holds good.

Listing was prompted by proposals to remove external ramps in order to deter skateboarders.

LISTED grade II, 13 April 2000
ADDRESS off West Road, Cambridge
NEAREST STATION Cambridge
ACCESS exteriors only

James Stirling 1964–68

SPRING HOUSE (CORNFORD HOUSE)
CAMBRIDGE

This house was commissioned by Christopher Cornford, painter and Dean of the Royal College of Art. His brief was for an inward-looking house which would be suitable for displaying works of art and for entertaining, together with a secluded studio. The result is an exciting sequence of spaces surrounding a double-height living space, with a studio wing – entered separately – that flanks the entrance forecourt. This massing of the house around this forecourt and the interplay of monopitched roofs are reminiscent of Aalto, and in particular of his Säynäsalo Town Hall (1950–52).

Inside, the small house has a more rigorous geometry. As at Wilson's Grantchester Road houses (see page 288), there is a module, this time of 1.8 metres. There is a strong diagonal axis from the hearth in one corner to a cut-away glazed section in the other, an outdoor patio with stairs to a first-floor verandah that links the indoor and outdoor worlds. This cut-out corner is at the apex of the gallery which overlooks the living room on two sides, and which gives access to the three bedrooms. Under it are the kitchen and dining areas. The strongly braced timber gallery, the open roof, and the timber internal partitions – more simply detailed than any Aalto equivalent – give the house its great character and very considerable beauty.

LISTED grade II, 13 April 2000
ADDRESS Conduit Head Road, Cambridge
NEAREST STATION Cambridge
ACCESS exterior only

Colin St John Wilson (assistant M J Long) 1965–67

WILLIS CORROON
IPSWICH

Willis Corroon was the first building of the 1970s to be listed, in 1991, a reflection of its seminal position in the development of the 'high tech' idiom still active today. Nothing in this building seems dated.

And yet its balance of technical innovation and a brief for advanced social facilities could perhaps only have been built in the early 1970s, and for exceptional clients. In 1970 Willis Faber and Dumas, insurance brokers, decided to relocate their administrative staff from London and Southend to a single location, and commissioned Foster Associates from an invited shortlist.

The four-storey, deep-plan building was a response to the location, and to Norman Foster's careful analysis of the firm's working practice, which suggested the open plan. The sinuous wall hugging the surrounding roads maximised the contorted plot.

Every element of the shell and servicing was considered from first principles. Most attention focuses on the building's continuous glass sheath, fixed between internal glass fins using patch fixings with a 50-millimetre tolerance. Rainwater runs into a gully in the pavement. Dark by day, at night the building comes to life, when the lighted interior shines through. The glass is also responsible for the building's one 'heritage' feature, its reflection of the seventeenth-century Quaker Meeting House next door.

The interior is truly spectacular. A concrete frame, its internal columns a mighty 14 metres apart, and an advanced sprinkler system enabled the offices to open directly off paired escalators that run straight up through the building. The innovative raised service floor gave a complete flexibility that has enabled the building to easily absorb the revolution in computer technology. The deep plan and dark external glass make this a low-energy builidng, while the fluorescent yellow and green decoration reflect predominant colours within the lighting system.

Foster Associates 1972–75

WILLIS CORROON

The highlight of the building today is the top-floor restaurant and its surrounding roof garden. There are no expansion joints in the structure, and a turf roof provides insulation as well as a recreational facility, culminating in a parapet hedge.

Behind the entrance hall was originally a swimming pool. Listing was prompted by a proposal to infill this for more office space, and instead a suspended floor has been laid, with the outline of the pool still visible below glass slabs. The building has subsequently pioneered the strategy of management guidelines, which identify those elements crucial to the building's architectural integrity and those working areas where its inherent flexibility should prevail.

LISTED grade I, 25 April 1991

ADDRESS 16 Friars Street, Ipswich

ACCESS group tours and heritage open days; call 01473 223000 for details

Foster Associates 1972–75

SOUTH-WESTERN ENGLAND

YELLOW BUS GARAGE
BOURNEMOUTH

As trams and trolleybuses were replaced by buses in the 1940s, so larger garages were required for the more numerous and larger vehicles. Their need for uninterrupted spans strained the limited steel resources available, but could be readily met by shell concrete construction. Reinforced concrete, as little as 50 millimetres thick, has great tensile strength when cast as a cylinder or conoid, and was widely used in Germany from the 1920s. In England the earliest surviving shell is at Wythenshawe Bus Garage, Manchester (see page 20).

Originally two garages were planned in Mallard Road, to be divided by a central office range, but only one was constructed. Even so it was the largest shell roof of its day, at 91 metres long by 46 metres wide, and giving an uninterrupted space of 4180 square metres. There are nine halfcylinders supported on an edge beam, and it seems to have been the first shell roof in England to also be prestressed. The resulting wavy roof is most distinctive, and is complemented by a curvaceous concrete canopy and patterned brickwork and these reinforce the building's Festival of Britain image. Slits above the entrance doors are surviving evidence that the garage was originally built to take trolleybuses as well as motor buses, which also determined its height of 5.8 metres. Adjoining the garage is the wash house, slightly later but similarly jaunty.

LISTED grade II, 17 August 1999
ENGINEER Alfred Goldstein
ADDRESS Mallard Road, Charminster, Bournemouth
GETTING THERE train to Bournemouth; off A3060
ACCESS none

Jackson and Greenen 1950–51

MEDLYCOTT BUILDING, SHERBORNE SCHOOL
SHERBORNE

Sherborne School has medieval origins, but its present form is the product of an energetic Victorian headmaster, the Rev. H B Harper. His architects responded to the sublime site, formerly the abbey cloisters, with a mixture of Gothic and Tudor styles that was continued into the twentieth century by Sir Reginald Blomfield.

Amazingly, Sherborne suffered bomb damage. By the 1950s, too, it needed more space – a response to the need for better-organised teaching as well as increasing rolls. A block was built with four classrooms, on two floors either side of a central staircase. Two entrances (one on either side) eased congestion between lessons.

Their style was the seventeenth-century vernacular, perhaps more associated with the picturesque area around Lacock, Wiltshire, where it was popularised by Oswald's father, Harold Brakspear. Medlycott looks diminutive, yet its classrooms are surprisingly light and comfortable for large groups. It is named after Sir Hubert Medlycott, a governor of the school for 44 years.

Brakspear also restored R H Carpenter's 'Big School' or assembly hall of 1879, and added a war memorial as part of a new entrance. He remodelled the interior with a stage and large gallery.

Medlycott was listed long before a 'thirty-year rule' was formalised, because it is a prominent element in the quadrangle of buildings, called Great Court, that is the focus of the school.

LISTED grade II, 4 October 1973
ADDRESS Abbey Road, Sherborne, Dorset
NEAREST STATION Sherborne
ACCESS none

Oswald S Brakspear 1954–55

CHURCH OF THE ASCENSION
PLYMOUTH

Robert Potter trained under W H Randoll Blacking, who was himself a pupil of Sir Ninian Comper, the most intellectual force in English church architecture in the early twentieth century. Potter was profoundly influenced by Comper's St Philip's, Cosham (1937), whose rectangular plan and freestanding baldacchino inspired similar features at the Church of the Ascension.

Other Potter and Hare characteristics first came to the fore here. The firm specialised in combining modern materials with local stone, a reminder of their parallel career as restorers of historic buildings and one which enriches the 'contemporary' styling of the angled walls, tapered tower and butterfly roof. The placing of the choir in a rear gallery, rather than in stalls between the celebrant and the congregation, was first explored in England in the 1930s, but Potter refined the idea by setting his gallery in front of a full-height baptistry so that sound could filter down from front and back.

Potter also enjoyed collaborating with artists. Jacob Epstein was originally commissioned to design glass roundels for the east end, but died after making only a few sketches, and Geoffrey Clarke substituted more abstract designs. The baldacchino is decorated with paintings by Robert Medley, but most striking of all is the deep red in which the concrete ceiling is painted, and which unifies the many disparate elements.

LISTED grade II, 25 September 1998
ADDRESS The Lawns, Crownhill, Plymouth, Devon
ENGINEER E W H Gifford and Partners
GETTING THERE train to Plymouth; next to A386, north from city centre
ACCESS regular services, by appointment on 01752 783617

Potter and Hare 1956–57

MARY HARRIS MEMORIAL CHAPEL OF THE HOLY TRINITY
EXETER

It was rare for a post-war university to be given a freestanding Anglican chapel, but this was the bequest of its architect Vincent Harris in memory of his mother. Harris, pre-eminent designer of public buildings, was appointed architect to the university college at Exeter in 1931, but his master plan was only partly realised. The chapel is his swansong.

A perspective of its design was exhibited as early as 1943, and shows a symmetrical composition at the centre of a formal axis facing the city, with a central outside pulpit much as was built. The axis was sidelined in William Holford's more picturesque replanning of the hilltop university site in 1953, and the chapel's neo-Georgian character was softened by two pairs of tall Elizabethan bay windows – such as Harris had used on his nearby laboratories of the 1930s. One of his smallest and most perfect buildings, the chapel is the more pleasurable for being domestic in its detailing.

The interior has a tranquil austerity, its oak pews set in collegiate fashion facing whitened walls, gently lit by the clear-glazed bay windows. The only colour is in the ceiling, a muted mural of abstract geometric shapes by Thomas Monnington, who had just completed two still larger compositions for Harris's Bristol council house.

LISTED grade II, 29 March 1988
ADDRESS Queen's Drive, Exeter University
GETTING THERE train to Exeter St David's or Central stations; then an uphill walk or bus to university
ACCESS open most days

E Vincent Harris 1956–58

SOUTH-WESTERN ENGLAND

DEVON COUNTY HALL
EXETER

Devon County Hall is reassuringly undramatic, yet bears the strong and very personal imprint of Donald McMorran's authorship in its detailing. The massing of the three- and four-storey blocks is reminiscent of his contemporary work at Cripps Hall, Nottingham (see page 156).

McMorran's buildings stand in the grounds of two earlier houses, one of which, Belair, is listed in its own right and houses members' rooms. The council chamber and committee rooms occupy the adjoining range at the back of the site, its superior status and greater architectural complexity denoted by a broad bell tower. The council chamber is entered through a groin-vaulted porte-cochère which leads into an arcaded entrance hall. This space, with walls of polished Purbeck marble, echoes the staircase hall at Edwin Lutyens' Castle Drogo. The Ionic columns of the staircase landing are the only explicitly classical elements in the entire building. The offices are arranged around long courtyards, their spine corridors developed as cloistered walks on the ground floor.

McMorran's mannerisms – including the round-arched arcading and the blockiness of features such as the bell tower, contrasted with large areas of blank walling – display a confident use of classicism on a large scale rarely found in post-war architecture. Devon County Hall confirms McMorran as an underrated master of an undervalued genre.

LISTED grade II*, 24 April 1998
ADDRESS Topsham Road, Exeter
GETTING THERE train to Exeter; on B3182 to south-east of city centre
ACCESS exteriors only

Donald McMorran 1957–64

ST GEORGE
POOLE

St George's is a development of the ideas found in the firm's earlier Church of the Ascension, Plymouth (see page 332), within a more complex plan and on a rather larger scale.

Here the material is principally brick, but again stone and concrete are used to give variety, and the canted tower is also reminiscent of the earlier church. The scheme was initiated by the Mothers' Union, and therefore Potter designed an unusually large Lady chapel within the single space. There are also short transepts to give the semblance of a crossing, and the altar is placed here. It is thus one of the earliest central altars to be erected for the Church of England. The west end more closely follows that of the Ascension church, with a choir gallery set in front of the baptistry and font in Potter's preferred manner. Here, however, the bright colour is not in the ceiling, but in the green piers of granolithic concrete at either side of the main spaces.

LISTED grade II, 25 September 1998
ENGINEER E W H Gifford and Partners
ADDRESS Worgret Road, Oakdale, Poole, Dorset
GETTING THERE train to Poole or Parkstone; close to A3049
ACCESS Sunday services; by appointment on 01202 675419

Potter and Hare 1959–60

ST AUSTELL PUBLIC LIBRARY
ST AUSTELL

St Austell's little branch library is striking for its combination of granite rubble walling and blue patent glazing within a neat steel frame. It is this juxtaposition of old and new materials which gives the building its singular character.

The library was designed as the first phase of a new civic centre, close to the railway station. It was originally planned to house 12,000 books, with the lending library on the main floor and a reference collection in the small gallery above. This is reached via a central flight of stairs, which with their aluminium balustrading resonate musically when ascended. The steel frame is strongly expressed and its elegance, coupled with the light flooding through the continuous clerestory rooflights, makes the building seem bigger than it really is. A small extension was subsequently added to one side, which also uses the rubble walling and the strong cornice line.

St Austell Library exemplifies the quality of architecture being designed by the Cornwall County Architects' Department under F Kenneth Hicklin around 1960. It is less well known than the contemporary Saltash Library, a diminutive version of Le Corbusier's Palais de Justice at Chandigarh, but has a greater coherence and attention to detail.

LISTED grade II, 24 April 1998
ADDRESS Carylan Road, St Austell, Cornwall
ACCESS open Monday, Wednesday to Friday, 9.30–17.00; Tuesday, 9.30–19.00; Saturday, 9.30–16.00; call 01726 73348 for details

Cornwall County Architects' Department 1959–60

SEVERN BRIDGE AND WYE BRIDGE
AVON

This was the first bridge in the world to use the revolutionary concept of the streamlined deck and inclined hangers, and was an early example of a fully welded steel deck.

A road bridge over the River Severn was seen in the 1930s as a means of regenerating South Wales industry and the project was revived after the war. In 1947 the Ministry of Transport built a wind tunnel to test the aerodynamics of suspension bridges, which first defined the vertical and torsional stresses to which they are subject. This research informed the truss girder road bridge built over the River Forth in 1958.

For Sir Gilbert Roberts's Severn Bridge, for Freeman Fox and Partners, a more refined steel-plated box structure was developed. Its stability depended on the aerodynamic shape of an extremely shallow deck only 3-metres deep, compared with the 8-metre trusses of the Forth Bridge. The Severn Bridge uses an inclined suspender system to reduce vertical motion, to which a shallow deck construction would be liable. The towers, more than 122-metres high, are remarkable for their low tonnage of steel.

The M48 continues across the Bleachey peninsula on a viaduct, whence a cable-stayed bridge carries it into Wales over the River Wye. Both have a similar aerodynamically shaped deck to the Severn Bridge. Though strengthened in 1985–91, the handsome forms of the Severn and Wye bridges remain as testaments to British engineering at its most innovative.

LISTED Severn Bridge and Aust Viaduct, grade I, Wye Bridge and Bleachey Viaduct, grade II; 29 May 1998
ENGINEER Mott, Hay and Anderson
GETTING THERE train to Pilning or Chepstow

SOUTH-WESTERN ENGLAND

Freeman Fox and Partners 1961–66

ST ALDATE
GLOUCESTER

The sale in 1927 of the city-centre St Aldate's church, originally a Saxon foundation, was used to fund a new parish in the suburbs. Only in 1958 was it resolved to build a permanent church here, and Potter and Hare were recommended by the diocese.

The model for St Aldate's was St Agnes, Fontaine-les-Gres in northern France (1956), seen by Potter and Hare with the New Churches Research Group. Their design was finalised in 1961. It is dominated by a sweeping hyperbolic paraboloid roof of timber, which contrasts with fine brickwork and large areas of glass more typical of the firm. The experimental roof structure was perfected by Gifford with students from Southampton University. Equally dramatic is the needle-like concrete spirelet over the sharp prow at the west end.

Potter considered that the roof gave the church's angular plan its 'thrust'. It is a fan-shaped auditorium, unusual in being wider at the east end than at the west because of two side chapels, one now part of the vestry. A western choir gallery is a favourite Potter and Hare feature. It was their first interior with a mature liturgical plan, and has an unexpected intimacy. Potter wanted to line the lower walls with slate, but the congregation requested Iroko hardwood and clear glazing, features that have been copied in more recent timber screens and furnishings.

LISTED grade II, 9 December 1999
ENGINEER E W H Gifford and Partners
ADDRESS Finlay Road, Gloucester
GETTING THERE train to Gloucester; on the A38 south-east of city centre
ACCESS open most mornings

SOUTH-WESTERN ENGLAND

Potter and Hare 1962–64

GOD
SO LOVED THE WORLD
THAT HE GAVE HIS ONLY SON
THAT EVERYONE WHO HAS FAITH IN HIM
MAY NOT PERISH
BUT HAVE ETERNAL LIFE

CORNWALL COUNTY HALL
TRURO

The County Hall is a tribute to Cornwall's unashamedly modernist public-building pro-gramme of the early 1960s. A hillside outside Truro is a supremely appropriate location for a version of Le Corbusier's Sainte-Marie de La Tourette clad in precast granite aggregate panels. County Hall hides its large scale on a prominent site by its muted colouring; the articulation of its surfaces into a rhythm of smaller elements; and the way in which this heavy structure seems effortlessly carried on open colonnades of pilotis.

Closer inspection reveals a building of greater subtlety. It is built around a square terraced courtyard, beautifully landscaped by Geoffrey Jellicoe with local plants and with a sculpture by Barbara Hepworth. Jellicoe also insisted on local granite for the building and pool surrounds. The deeper-plan council chamber is cantilevered out on the east side over the entrance and exhibition hall, and is expressed as a solid wall on the courtyard side. The main staircase is at a higher level to the north, and the entrance is denoted by aluminium mullions rather than concrete.

The interior is lively, light and spacious, with the reception and communication areas devised as interrelating spaces around a staircase and exhibition hall. The council chamber has natural lighting only from behind the chairman's rostrum, and along with the Grenville and Trelawney committee rooms it retains contemporary furniture and fittings.

SOUTH-WESTERN ENGLAND

LISTED grade II, 24 April 1998
ENGINEER Felix Samuely and Partners
ADDRESS Treyew Road, Truro, Cornwall
ACCESS exterior and public spaces only

Cornwall County Architect's Department 1962–66

TAUNTON DEANE CREMATORIUM
TAUNTON

Potter and Hare were originally placed second in the competition for this outstanding crematorium, assessed by Sir Edward Maufe, but secured the commission. It features their characteristic blend of local rubble walling, concrete and copper roofs, but the planning is more organic than was possible in their earlier churches. The separation of the distinct elements produces a close harmony with the mature surrounding landscape. The principal components are a high, light chapel, with the crematory next to it, and a separate memorial chapel to the east.

The chapel is notable for the combination of rough walling with glass and works of art. The north wall has tall strip windows with stained glass in muted greens and blues deeply recessed and set in rough-textured aluminium frames. They were designed by the sculptor Geoffrey Clarke, who also produced the textured aluminium altar cross and candlesticks.

The memorial chapel is as dark as the main chapel is light, a conical building lit only at clerestory level and with another cross by Clarke.

Potter and Hare enjoyed a long collaboration with artists of the highest quality, and first worked with Clarke at the Church of the Ascension in Plymouth (see page 332). This is a more truly equal partnership between architects, artist and landscaping, the whole being greater than the sum of its well-crafted parts.

LISTED grade II, 25 September 1998
ENGINEER E W H Gifford and Partners
ADDRESS Wellington New Road, Taunton
GETTING THERE train to Taunton; south-west of town on A38
ACCESS exterior and chapels (weekdays)

Potter and Hare 1963

ALL SAINTS
CLIFTON

All Saints was a prominent Anglo-Catholic foundation that demonstrated the best in Victorian church architecture. An incendiary caused great damage in 1940, but it could have – should have – been restored. Instead, Randoll Blacking was appointed to rebuild the church, only to die while his expensive scheme was being debated. Eventually only G F Bodley's 1900 narthex and F C Eden's elegant sacristy of 1928 were retained.

Potter's resolution of this mess is simple yet stunning. He linked the surviving fragments by means of a glazed cloister, entered through Street's stumpy, uncompleted tower, and built a smaller, square church to the side. The old church faced south, but the replacement is properly orientated eastwards. The altar stands beneath a ciborium designed by Blacking in 1952, with a piscina by John Skelton. The dominating feature, however, is the brilliant Perspex glass designed by John Piper, which fills the west end and the large south window over the choir gallery – a characteristic feature of Potter's work. On the north side Bodley's narthex became a chapel and is filled with glass by Christopher Webb, one window depicting the old church.

The church's assemblage of elements from throughout the twentieth century places it among the most exhilarating of post-war church recreations. It is across the road from Clifton Cathedral, and it is instructive to compare their contrasting forms of Catholicism.

LISTED grade II, 1963–67
ADDRESS Pembroke Road, Clifton, Bristol
NEAREST STATION Bristol Temple Meads
ACCESS open daily, 7.00–18.00, and for Sunday evensong. Closed Wednesday afternoons

Robert Potter 1963–65, to tower of 1872 by G E Street

THE STANTON GUILDHOUSE
STANTON

The Stanton Guildhouse was the personal vision of Mary Osborn (1906–96), a devout Christian and pacifist inspired by Mahatma Gandhi. She had met Gandhi in 1931, when she was working among the unemployed of London's East End, and he encouraged her spinning lessons. She later inherited a spinning wheel left by him in London.

During the war Osborn moved to the Cotswolds, and her spinning and woodworking classes maintained something of the area's crafts tradition at a time of technical change. She believed that there was a basic spirituality behind the simplest of tasks, and sought to create a semi-religious community which would be supported by craftwork and teaching.

A local architect, experienced in restoring old buildings, produced a design of concrete block faced in stone, with a stone slate roof. It was mainly built by volunteers, yet the quality of workmanship is high. There is a central guildroom, with a weaving room, pottery workshop and dining room in the wings. Upstairs are dormitories, and it is hoped that in future the Guildhouse will develop as a holiday centre for city children.

Stanton is close to Chipping Camden, which became a centre for crafts and rural conservation in the 1900s. The Guildhouse, with its honest joinery and simple idealism, symbolises the continuation of this tradition.

LISTED grade II, 11 June 1999
ADDRESS Stanton, Gloucestershire
NEAREST STATION Evesham; Stanton is close to the A46
ACCESS by written appointment

Iorwerth Williams 1963–73

CREEKVEAN

FEOCK

Creekvean was built as a holiday and sailing home for Marcus and René Brumwell, founders of the Design Research Unit and Su Rogers's parents. An exceptional building, especially for its date, it is a large but well-concealed house on a very steep site overlooking an arm of Falmouth Harbour. It is the first major work by Richard and Su Rogers, with Norman and Wendy Foster. While it demonstrates the influence of Frank Lloyd Wright on Rogers following his studies at Yale, its use of neoprene and split planning portend later developments in his work.

The plan unfolds from an entrance drawbridge that divides the house in two. Grassed steps lead down to the river, while the bedroom wing has a turfed roof. The 'daytime' rooms form a low tower, complete with a vertiginous staircase to the rooftop. Once inside, spectacular views down Pill Creak are revealed by the full-height glazing, which pushes neoprene technology to its limits. A thin, suspended concrete floor slab is pierced to provide links between the upper sitting area and downstairs living room, where the cooker and sink are built into an elegant freestanding steel unit. A top-lit gallery leads to the bedrooms.

Despite the forticrete block construction and uncompromisingly modern detailing, Creekvean also has the intimacy found in local vernacular buildings, coupled with the free-flowing spaciousness of the Modern Movement.

LISTED grade II, 15 July 1998; upgraded to grade II*,
9 May 2002
ADDRESS Feock, Cornwall
NEAREST STATION Falmouth Town
ACCESS none

Team 4 (Richard and Su Rogers, Norman and Wendy Foster) 1964–67

SHELDON BUSH LEAD SHOT TOWER
BRISTOL

Although its form was dictated by a precise industrial purpose, Bristol's lead shot tower demonstrates the widespread post-war ambition to create cultural landmarks. This is the context in which its simple, admissibly phallic, design should be enjoyed.

In 1782, the story goes, a dream showed William Watts how to make lead shot by dropping molten lead mixed with arsenic through perforations in a piece of metal. When dropped from a great height into a vat of cold water it falls into perfect spherical beads. Watts built two extra storeys on to his house to achieve an adequate fall. His technique is still used for making shot, though Watt sold his patent to set himself up as a builder, only to go bust in the Napoleonic wars.

Watts's original tower in Redcliffe was demolished for road widening in 1968. Its replacement a mile away was built to the same principle, but using reinforced concrete and with a more aerodynamic shape. It is 42 metres high, with a gallery at the top and a pit at the base, set on a prominent site next to the harbour. There were once six shot towers in England, but today that in Chester, built in 1799 and long listed, is the only other surviving reminder of Watts' extraordinary premonition.

SOUTH-WESTERN ENGLAND

LISTED grade II, 24 November 1995
ADDRESS Temple Back, Bristol
NEAREST STATION Bristol Temple Meads
ACCESS exterior only

E N Underwood and Partners, engineer 1968–69

RC CATHEDRAL CHURCH OF SS PETER AND PAUL
CLIFTON

A new cathedral in Clifton was commissioned in 1965 to supersede the Pro-Cathedral of the 1830s. It is an outstanding work from one of Britain's largest post-war architectural practices, most of whose buildings are in Wales. It also claims to be the first cathedral in the world to accord completely with the liturgical guidelines issued by the Vatican in November 1963 that required the celebrant to face the congregation. It is more successful than Liverpool Metropolitan Cathedral (see pages 100–102) because it places the top-lit sanctuary to one side, in front of a fan of seating for the congregation. The celebrant can thus face everyone at once. The entrance, over a basement car park, is to the side, so that one enters alongside a screen wall of coloured glass by Henry Haig that leads first to the baptistry, which shields first views of the main worship space. William Mitchell carved the low-relief Stations of the Cross in wet concrete, with just $1^{1}/_{2}$ hours to complete each one.

Built in a remarkably short time to a low budget (£600,000), the rough wigwam-like exterior does not prepare one for the quality of the interior. There, Clifton achieves a rare integration of materials and spatial quality, combining serenity and simplicity with crafts-manship in the concrete detailing.

Listing followed a grant from English Heritage for repairs to the roof.

SOUTH-WESTERN ENGLAND

LISTED grade II*, 20 December 2002
ARCHITECTS IN CHARGE Ronald Weeks, E S Jennett and Antoni Poremba
ADDRESS Pembroke Road, Clifton, Bristol
NEAREST STATION Bristol Temple Meads
ACCESS open daily

Sir Percy Thomas Partnership 1969–73

RIGG SIDE
GOODLEIGH

Rigg Side is Aldington's most important house outside his adopted Buckinghamshire. While it has strong affinities with his earlier houses in that county, it is also a personal response to a very different landscape and vernacular tradition. Here is a modern interpretation of the traditional Devon long house, with a carport at one end of its low rectangular shell instead of an animal byre.

The brief was refined over a year of meetings between Craig and the clients, Mr and Mrs Anderton, respectively a pharmacist and Aldington's father's long-time secretary. How to plan a living area for a meticulously tidy wife, and for an untidy husband who did not want to be shut away in a separate office? Aldington devised an office set in a low-walled pod between the kitchen and living room areas, between two levels, the latter with a clear-glazed gable end giving long views across the fields. The square office pod is countered by a circular bathroom at the junction between the open living areas and the more conventional bedroom wing.

The house's timber frame was prefabricated in Oxford, where Aldington could supervise its immaculate detailing. The house also features many complicated built-in cupboards and fittings, typical of Aldington's timber work, while making room for the Anderton's old-fashioned furniture. The ensemble is remarkably harmonious.

LISTED grade II*, 24 July 1998
ADDRESS Goodleigh, Devon
NEAREST STATION Barnstaple
ACCESS none

Peter Aldington and John Craig 1970–71

W D AND H O WILLS HEAD OFFICE
HARTCLIFFE, BRISTOL

The slick American image created by SOM and YRM for Boots' headquarters offices at Nottingham (see page 204) seemed just right for the British arm of Anglo-American Tobacco, based in Bristol. The two practices were commissioned in 1969 to design head-quarters offices and an adjoining factory in the outskirts of Bristol. The factory was demolished in 1999, but the office building survives.

It is perhaps more human in feel than earlier corporate office buildings. This may be partly because it is built of Cor-ten steel, rich in manganese and vanadium, which rapidly oxidises to a warm rust finish; but important too is the landscaping, by Kenneth Booth. For the building sits on a broad podium astride a lake, from which rises a narrower, five-storey office building. The podium roof itself is landscaped, its grid of paviours, gravel and planters mirroring the sophisticated, clean proportions of the architecture.

The offices were required to be calm, flexible, neutral spaces, while below them the podium housed computers, servicing, a canteen, bank and shops. An escalator joins it to a bus stop, an open-sided version of Mies's Farnsworth House. Here, then, was the total working environment, a late-twentieth-century version of the company village hidden in its own valley and lacking only housing for its workers.

Listing was secured as demolition of the offices was about to begin.

LISTED grade II, 11 April 2000
ADDRESS Imperial Park, Whitchurch Lane, Hartcliffe, Bristol
NEAREST STATIONS Parson Street; Bristol Temple Meads then bus
ACCESS none at present; future uncertain

Skidmore, Owings and Merrill, with Yorke, Rosenberg and Mardall 1970–75

FOOTBRIDGE OVER THE RIVER CHERWELL
OXFORD

This little portal-frame footbridge crosses the tail of the Parson's Pleasure weir, and now forms part of the Marston cycle track. It has claim to be the first prestressed fixed-arch bridge in the world, and was certainly first statically indeterminate prestressed concrete bridge in Britain.

Most of the bridge was formed on site. The only precast elements were the pre-stressed concrete planks forming the walking surface, and these have subsequently been replaced by an in-situ concrete slab.

Due to the difficulties of securing a building licence, the engineer, Albert Goldstein, designed the parapets in aluminium rather than steel.

LISTED grade II, 29 May 1998
ADDRESS South Parks Road, Oxford
ENGINEER Alfred Goldstein
ACCESS any reasonable time

R Travers Morgan and Partners, engineer 1949

RHINEFIELD BRIDGE

BROCKENHURST

Rhinefield Bridge was one of a number of little bridges built in the New Forest during the late 1940s, and carries a minor road over a stream. The bridge, by E W H Gifford for Hampshire County Council was the first of the series to be constructed of precast, post-tensioned units using the Freyssinet system and stressed together transversely. Its slight vertical curvature made the longitudinal cables straighter, which reduced friction and produced a very attractive little bridge which sits harmoniously in the landscape. The Freyssinet system of pre-stressing, first patented in England in 1938, reduced the amount of steel required at a time of shortages and licensing.

Gifford went on to enjoy a successful career in private practice, working extensively, for example, with the local church architects Potter and Hare.

LISTED grade II, 29 May 1998
ADDRESS near Brockenhurst, Hampshire
GETTING THERE train to Sway; south of A35
ACCESS open

E W H Gifford for Hampshire County Council 1949–50

NUFFIELD COLLEGE
OXFORD

William Morris, Lord Nuffield, the Oxford car manufacturer turned philanthropist and edu-cator, in 1937 conceived a postgraduate college in his name. It was to be co-educational and academically innovative, but traditional in design. The architect chosen by the university first produced a dramatic neo-Byzantine scheme – not surprisingly since Austen St Barbe Harrison had worked almost exclusively in Macedonia and Palestine. This is his only building in England, conceived with Thomas Barnes and Robert Hubbard, two young assistants.

Nuffield's desire for a building in a more local vernacular won out – then the war intervened and Harrison's design subsequently became more austere. The style of hon-eyed stone gables and roofs is more in the Cotswold-revival idiom of Chipping Camden than Oxford, while the distinguished tower – in fact a bookstack – adds a tall Scandinavian note to the skyline. Its set backs and spire are also reminiscent of Lutyens' St Jude's, Hampstead Garden Suburb, London (1915).

The college consists of two quadrangles, each with a pool. The principal internal spaces are imposing: the hall with its marble floor and red-panelled oak roof, and the chapel – set in the roofspace – with glass by John Piper and Patrick Reyntiens.

LISTED grade II, 30 March 1993
ADDRESS New Road, Oxford
ACCESS by application to the lodge, 01865 278500

Harrison, Barnes and Hubbard 1949–57

ST CRISPIN'S SCHOOL
WOKINGHAM

In 1948 Stirrat Johnson-Marshall, the impresario of Hertfordshire's schools' programme, was head-hunted by the Ministry of Education to co-ordinate its architects' department. He immediately set up a Development Group to expand the lessons of prefabrication into new areas.

Lightweight secondary schools were a difficulty because their size demanded several storeys. St Crispin's was the first of five secondary schools built under Johnson-Marshall, designed as early as 1949–50 by Mary Crowley and David Medd recruited from Hertfordshire, and Michael Ventris, decoder of the Minoan cypher Linear B.

The architects used a hot-rolled steel system developed to the Ministry's 3-foot 4-inch module with Hills of West Bromwich, and other builders and artists who had similarly collaborated at Hertfordshire were also brought in. Most innovative was the deliberately informal planning, particularly of the single-storey art and technical areas, which sought a distinctive character for the new 'secondary moderns' introduced by the 1944 Education Act. St Crispin's dispersed plan, punctuated by a three-storey classroom tower, offered a more popular model than the LCC's comprehensive slabs developed in these years. Bright colours, new materials and murals by Fred Millett, long gone, enhanced the impression of lightness from within. The distinctive concrete cladding and loose plan were repeated in subsequent Ministry of Education schemes at Worthing and Belper, but these have been demolished, leaving St Crispin's as the sole model for a generation of school building across England.

LISTED grade II, 30 March 1993
ADDRESS London Road, Wokingham, Berkshire
ACCESS exterior only

SOUTHERN ENGLAND

Ministry of Education Architect's and Building Branch 1951–53

ST JOHN THE EVANGELIST
NEWBURY

A lone German bomber in May 1943 destroyed William Butterfield's Tractarian church of 1859–60. Dykes Bower's rebuilding reflects and enhances many elements of Butterfield's bombastic work, at a time when Victorian architecture was unfashionable and church polychromy regularly painted over.

Dykes Bower's narrow red and grey bricks were handmade locally, and have a quality which is lacking in the materials of its predecessor. The saddleback tower is developed not only from this Butterfield church but also from its contemporary St Alban's, Holborn. It is loftier and more powerful than Butterfield's, as is the body of the church, which takes the monumentality of Albi Cathedral as its cue – a popular inspiration in the nineteenth century but rarely adopted with such sophisticated might as here.

The interior is made to seem still taller by the painted ceiling which incorporates built-in lighting. The east end has abstract glass by Goddard and Gibbs made up from Victorian fragments, and a painted tester over the altar. It needs little decoration beyond that supplied by the architecture itself.

Dykes Bower was a follower of F C Eden, whose few works included a mission church for St John's in the 1930s. Dykes Bower himself built only four new churches, which confirm his belief in an unbroken continuity between past and present, and is best known for his additions to St Edmundsbury Cathedral.

LISTED grade II, 29 March 1988
ADDRESS St John's Road, Newbury, Berkshire
ACCESS open daily

Stephen Dykes Bower 1955–57

WOODSIDE SCHOOL
AMERSHAM

Stirrat Johnson-Marshall's Development Group at the Ministry of Education produced a series of one-off model schools, handling every element of research, design and contracting. Most of their early work adapted the success of the Hertfordshire programme (see page 372) to new problems, such as secondary schools, and to new materials. For Buckinghamshire, which successfully fought a lone campaign for traditional construction through the 1960s, ex-Hertfordshire architects including Mary Crowley and her husband David Medd proved that the child-centred Hertfordshire school could be built equally cheaply of brick.

Brick demanded thick expensive cross walls to support the roof. By keeping them to a minimum Crowley and Medd were able to pair classrooms by age group and introduce a greater degree of flexiblility, with larger areas for sinks and pets. It is a forerunner of later, still more open-planned schools such as their Eveline Lowe School, Southwark (1966). A courtyard with a pond encourages gardening and nature activities. Woodside also pioneered a range of furniture, and the long narrow sinks are backed with tiles depicting fish, hedgehogs and snails by Dorothy Annan.

Woodside was the first Ministry of Education school built specifically for 7–11 year olds. While small additions and some modernisation have been necessary, the former library has been preserved as a 'heritage room', with original flooring, lighting and fixed window benches.

LISTED grade II, 30 March 1993
ADDRESS Mitchell Walk, Amersham, Buckinghamshire
ACCESS none

Ministry of Education Architect's and Building Branch 1956–57

PROVOST'S LODGINGS, QUEEN'S COLLEGE
OXFORD

Erith's brief was for a house combining dining and reception rooms for college functions with private accommodation for the Provost's family. A through passage links the lane to the north and the college to the south. Like Erith's houses in Aubrey Walk, London, the Provost's Lodgings assumes a different character on each elevation. Here the garden front is to the east; to the south he retained an abutting brewhouse as garages; and to the west is a driveway. The garden elevation has the simplicity of a Georgian vicarage, although a central belvedere, lighting a first-floor lobby, is visible from here and from no other direction.

Equally austere but very different is the frontage to Queen's Lane. It is one of Erith's boldest compositions, and is deliberately both more formal and has few windows because it stands on the busy street. The ground floor is rusticated, with a central door under a broad fanlight and band, flanked by two empty niches and, at a distance, two tiny barred windows. Over it is another niche, two narrow windows and a cornice. And that is all. While the planning and toplighting of the upper floor owes something to Soane and to Burlington's Chiswick Villa, this façade has more direct references to early Palladio, and in particular to his Palazzo Thiene, Vicenza, of 1542.

LISTED grade II, 30 March 1993
ADDRESS Queen's College, Queen's Lane, Oxford
ACCESS exterior only

Raymond Erith 1958–60

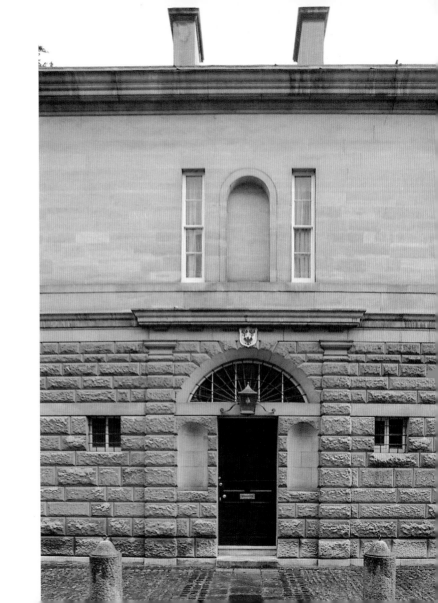

THE BEEHIVES, ST JOHN'S COLLEGE
OXFORD

The Architects' Co-Partnership was commissioned in 1957 on the recommendation of the architect and historian John Summerson, after the college rejected a traditional design by its honorary fellow, Edward Maufe. ACP's brief was for a building 'which would not be disturbing' to its historic surroundings, and a series of sketches developed into the distinctive sequence of linked hexagons finally chosen unanimously by the college fellows. It was the first truly modern design to be erected in Oxford, just as Cambridge University reached the forefront of architectural thinking.

Michael Powers' design is a honeycomb, three hexagons deep, with the centre units filled by three top-lit staircases and two bathroom units. The undergraduate study-bedrooms are arranged off half-landings, giving three floors overlooking the President's Garden and two facing the quad, raised over a semi-basement bicycle store. The building is an early example of the use of Portland Roach, a stone with holes left by fossils which became popular in the 1960s, though hitherto it had been thought to be unsound. Otherwise it is firmly of its times: Powers wrote of Oxford's 'spiky skyline, in which suddenly to insert a flat-roofed, flat-faced building – it was 1957! – would have been wrong'. ACP were subsequently commissioned to landscape North Quad, and their York stone and concrete paving gives a dignified plinth to this jaunty little building.

SOUTHERN ENGLAND

LISTED grade II, 30 March 1993
ADDRESS North Quad, St John's College, Oxford
ACCESS by application to the lodge on 01865 277300

Architects' Co-Partnership 1958–60

QUEEN ELIZABETH II COURT
WINCHESTER

Cowles-Voysey, son of C F A Voysey, was commissioned in the 1930s to build new offices, an art school and a library for Hampshire County Council. After the war only offices were required and the scheme was entirely redesigned by Brandon-Jones, who produced a quadrangle, with one committee room – the Wellington Room – projecting towards the medieval gateway opposite.

The scheme was inspired by Brandon-Jones's studies of Philip Webb and the early-twentieth-century Dutch architects A J Kropholler and Hendrik Berlage. Brandon-Jones was instrumental in the post-war reappraisal of Webb and W R Lethaby through his teaching at the Architectural Association, while the Dutch influence suggests what might have been had Winchester been colonised by more recent Anglo-Saxons. The Purbeck stone plinth and the use of small tiles in the roof eaves are deft local touches, while the dormers closely follow Webb prototypes. At first impression neo-Georgian, close study reveals a deeper understanding of vernacular traditions. The Hampshire Hog weather vane is by Laurence Bradshaw and the fountain basin in the central courtyard by Darsie Rawlins, who also designed the internal oak-leaf cornices.

The Arthurian influence is more profound internally, with lean neo-Saxon stone columns in the entrance halls. The coats of arms and a Festival of Britain-style map of Hampshire in the Wellington Room were created by the art school staff. The building makes a sensitive yet strong addition to a historic setting.

SOUTHERN ENGLAND

LISTED grade II, 24 April 1998
ADDRESS County Hall, Upper High Street, Winchester, Hampshire
ACCESS exterior only

Cowles-Voysey, Brandon-Jones, Broadbent and Ashton 1959–60

COLLEGE OF MARITIME STUDIES
WARSASH

Richard Sheppard and Geoffrey Robson early specialised in college buildings for local education authorities, producing neat, well-planned buildings on low budgets. Warsash trains officers for the Merchant Navy, from 17-year-old cadets to senior personnel. As originally designed the buildings were intensely hierarchical, and this is still evident in the duplication of some facilities.

'Moyana' is the social centre of the college, with dining and common rooms in a long line on the edge of a slope leading to the Hamble River. They are separated by partitions, which can be opened up to create a large hall with a stage. The quality of materials gives this building its distinction: its lowest part is faced in brick headers set at angles, reminiscent of Alvar Aalto, while inside the timber floors and curved ceilings are emphasised by long clerestories.

'Shackleton', alongside, houses the cadets. The original dormitories have been subdivided into single and double rooms, set around three staircases. The larger windows on the first floor denote tutors' suites, while the fourth floor has common rooms, with balconies for watching ships. It has the same neat detailing and attention to materials as its neighbour.

There are three later buildings by the firm at Warsash; two more on an adjoining site were demolished after they were rejected for listing.

LISTED grade II, 30 March 1993
ADDRESS Southampton Institute of Higher Education, Newtown Road, Warsash, Hampshire
GETTING THERE train to Swanwick; south of A3024
ACCESS none

SOUTHERN ENGLAND

Richard Sheppard, Robson and Partners 1959–61

LADY MARGARET HALL
OXFORD

Lady Margaret Hall was founded in 1878, the year girls were first admitted for examination at Oxford. Erith inherited a tangle of Queen Anne-style buildings, mostly by Reginald Blomfield, and these influenced the style and materials with which he completed the entrance quadrangle. First came the library, a double-height space with Diocletian attic windows, set over an arcaded ground floor which housed the book stack. The overall form is an Oxbridge convention of the later seventeenth century; its greater height and lack of moulding more reminiscent of Hawksmoor's demolished Christ's Hospital Writing Schools (1692–95). The interior is remarkable for its use of timber: wooden Tuscan columns support the gallery, and gentle settlement and the patina of dark varnish suggest a venerable age. All the furniture was also designed by Erith.

For the western entrance block Erith proposed 'a rest from windows'. The result is convincingly Palladian, a white pedimented portico in an almost blind brick wall that closes the end of Norham Gardens.

LISTED grade II, 30 March 1993

ADDRESS Norham Gardens, Oxford

ACCESS by application to the lodge, 01865 274300

Raymond Erith 1959–61, 1963–66

PAST FIELD
HENLEY-ON-THAMES

Past Field was built for Dr Salmon, a local GP, and his wife, a professional singer, who still live in the house and are still close friends with Patrick Gwynne. The site was a south-facing field, and Gwynne devised the overhanging eaves as an 'umbrella' to compensate for the treeless foreground, though the garden is now richly planted. All the main rooms were set facing south and, to catch the sun and to provide a sense of enclosure, a boomerang plan was adopted. The high living room, with excellent acoustics for Mrs Salmon, was placed on one side of the entrance, the bedrooms on the other. On the north front the roof has a low pitch, so that ceilings are sloped and shaped in Gwynne's inimitable manner.

Gwynne designed the house to be extended at either end, and in 1966 the master bedroom suite and a family room were added. This last was subsequently converted by Gwynne into a new kitchen, the old one becoming the dining room.

The house demonstrates Gwynne's attention to detail, his unity of interior and exterior form and surface by his idiosyncratic use of traditional materials in novel shapes and juxtapositions. He succeeded in giving a new house on an open site an immediate character, one less formal than his London houses.

LISTED grade II, 15 July 1998
ADDRESS Henley-on-Thames, Oxfordshire
GETTING THERE on south side of town
ACCESS none

Patrick Gwynne 1960, 1966

STAIRCASES 16–18, BRASENOSE COLLEGE
OXFORD

Powell and Moya were masterful at squeezing modern additions into historic Oxford and Cambridge college complexes. Here began 20 years of great commissions, on a 18-metre wide back yard. In it they contrived 32 study bedrooms, with a five-storey block on the widest part and a single-storey range behind. Linked by raised courtyards and the taller building bisected by ground-floor passageways, the plan is a skilful subversion of the Oxford staircase tradition.

That this was combined with some of the most forcefully modern architecture of its time in Britain is a still greater achievement, especially given Oxford's previous architectural conservatism. Early drawings show a balanced composition of solid stone wall and window grid. The final version has a sculptural sense rare in Powell and Moya's work, which may be due to the assistance of Richard Burton, who worked here before founding Ahrends, Burton and Koralek (Peter Ahrends designed some of the furniture). The materials are traditional – Portland Whitbed and Roach stone contrasted with large lead panels most suggestive of ABK; their clean-cut strength enforces the modernity of the design. The geometry, too, is striking, from the chamfered, battered plinth, to the slight angle given each tread of the tight timber staircases tucked off the passageways. It is Powell and Moya's most tactile work.

LISTED grade II*, 30 March 1993
ADDRESS Brasenose College, Oxford
ACCESS exteriors by application to the lodge, 01865 277830

Powell and Moya 1960–61

SPENCE HOUSE
BEAULIEU

Basil Spence built this house as a holiday home when he was working extensively at Southampton University, and he was at the height of his creative powers. Although it is a very small house, the individual elements appear large in scale. 'Powerful and resourceful', as Sir Nikolaus Pevsner described it, it is also efficiently and imaginatively planned. The use of large areas of glass and cedar cladding are very appropriate to its location high above one of England's most important yachting centres. The principal rooms are on the upper floor, to enjoy the best of the dramatic views, and are reached via an outside stair. Bedrooms lead directly off a large open-plan living room lined entirely in timber and warmed by a giant stove. The effect is reminiscent of a sedate ocean-going schooner.

Spence also built a small studio in the woods behind the house, also listed. The landscaping was by his regular collaborator Sylvia Crowe.

LISTED grade II, 10 December 1997
ADDRESS Dock Lane, Beaulieu River, Hampshire
GETTING THERE train to Beaulieu Road; south of B3054
ACCESS none

Basil Spence 1961

ST CATHERINE'S COLLEGE
OXFORD

St Catherine's is the quintessence of cool architecture in post-war modernism, a demonstration to English architects of how it should be done by an international virtuoso. In Alan Bullock, the commissioning Master, Jacobsen had a perfect client, even if budgetary limitations rarely perceived in Oxbridge forced economies on the size and equipment of the 260 study bedrooms. It was the first new Oxford college built at a single go since Keble in 1868, and makes the contemporary, English-designed Churchill College, Cambridge (see page 282), look rather insular.

Every detail is Jacobsen's; from the cutlery to the landscaping, the latter's studied textures and shades of green now swamping the grey brick and concrete, his deeply considered but unemotional vision is omnipresent. The complexity of low courtyards created by hedges and walls complements the simplicity of the plan: two long ranges of study bedrooms flank separate central buildings for the library, an auditorium and an L-shaped end block for the dining hall and common rooms. Their formal symmetry contributes to the coolness, while their long low form seems to spring naturally from the surrounding water meadows. The study bedrooms are highly, even excessively, glazed while the dining hall emphasises its restraint by being entirely top-lit. Only the bell tower attempts a more sculptural statement.

A refurbishment and further extensions are being planned by Stephen Hodder.

LISTED grade I, 30 March 1993
ADDRESS Manor Road, Oxford
ACCESS accessible most afternoons; call 01865 271700 for details

SOUTHERN ENGLAND

Arne Jacobsen 1960–66

ASKETT GREEN
PRINCES RISBOROUGH

Peter Aldington was one of the first architects to blend local vernacular traditions with the austerity of the modern movement, anticipating the greater humanism desired of housing from the 1970s. Because it was ahead of its time, his work is sometimes hard to appreciate. This is his first house, designed while he was working at the London County Council for mountaineering friends Michael and Celia White.

Askett Green was conceived as a rural cottage hugging the lane, built of brick and with small windows. The interior was made partially open-plan, because the Whites 'liked giving parties'. Michael White is an expert on timber, and thick timber screens and fitted cupboards are a feature of the house, and particularly of the fitted kitchen, into which every modern appliance is cunningly stowed.

As the house neared completion the Whites went to Nigeria for two years, and the newly-wed Aldingtons moved in. The experience prompted them to build their own house, Turn End (see page 410). (see page 410) Aldington says that Askett Green 'established the philosophy of an architecture born of materials and structure that informed the practice's subsequent work'.

LISTED grade II, 8 July 1999
ADDRESS Askett, Princes Risborough, Buckinghamshire
GETTING THERE train to Monks Risborough
ACCESS exterior only

Peter Aldington 1961–62

POINT ROYAL
BRACKNELL

Despite the example set by The Lawn, Harlow (see page 224), few new towns experimented with tall flats, leading to accusations of wasted land. The exception was Bracknell, where the planner Sir Lancelot Keay conceived an 18-storey block in answer to a land shortage.

The flats, designed by Philip Dowson for Arup Associates, were intended for single professionals and form part of a mixed development. Their design was determined by surrounding mature trees, here to the extent that an underground car park was provided by scooping out the grassy mound on which the block sits. Pedestrian bridges lead to the entrance. The slightly concave, hexagonal floor plan was chosen as requiring fewer internal walls than a rectangular block, while giving each flat a dual aspect. Kitchens and bathrooms, at the centre, are rectangular.

Much of the building was precast, using a panel system developed by Dowson at Oxford and Cambridge. Every room has access to a terrace, enclosed by the peripheral frame of precast mullions, which also takes part of the floor load. This projecting grid of columns and floor slabs provides a modular geometry and powerful brise-soleil for the block. Although alterations were made to the windows and balconies in 1992, Point Royal is so boldly modelled that it was still an obvious candidate for listing.

LISTED grade II, 22 December 1998
ENGINEER Derek Sugden, Ove Arup and Partners
ADDRESS The Green, Easthampstead, Bracknell
GETTING THERE train to Bracknell; west of A322
ACCESS exterior only

Arup Associates 1961–64

ST CROSS LIBRARIES
OXFORD

After his appointment as Cambridge's professor of architecture in 1957 Leslie Martin's chief architectural work was as a consultant. His buildings were often designed with a younger associate, and it is particularly difficult to detach his cool style from Wilson's. Wilson had met Alvar Aalto at Cambridge in 1958 and been profoundly influenced by him; the concept of a raised courtyard of public spaces reached from an off-centre staircase is derived from Säynätsalo Town Hall (1949–52). Here the design is more interlocked and the courtyard more tightly planned, while being much larger than the original. The overall massing and concentration of fine brickwork makes this one of Oxford's finest modern corners. Funding was supplied by the Rockefeller and Gulbenkian foundations.

There are three libraries, reached at different levels off the staircase, the centrepiece of the design. In ascending order and increasing size, they serve the Institute of Statistics, the English and law faculties. Below are shared lecture theatres and seminar rooms, reached down an internal stair of equally handsome proportions. Each reading room is square and top lit, with galleries and peripheral carrels.

The building impresses for the effortless way in which such large libraries have been engineered. The architect Geoffrey Robson likened the staircase to ascending an Aztec temple.

LISTED grade II*, 30 March 1993
ADDRESS Manor Road, Oxford
ENGINEER Ove Arup and Partners
ACCESS exterior only

Sir Leslie Martin and Colin St John Wilson 1961–64

SOUTHERN ENGLAND

WOLFSON AND RAYNE BUILDINGS
ST ANNE'S COLLEGE, OXFORD

St Anne's began as a society for women students living at home or in lodgings, and became a college only in 1952. It then rapidly outgrew the other women's institutions. In 1961 Howell, Killick and Partridge designed a necklace of six linked buildings that could be erected as funding permitted. In practice just two were built, funded by bequests from Sir Isaac Wolfson and Max Rayne. That the scheme was never completed matters little; the convex curved blocks with their concave covered link sit well in a mature setting of nine-teenth-century houses and trees.

The curves were intended to make the short corridors seem less institutional, and to give interesting shapes to the 45 study bedrooms within each block. The cigar-shaped core of each unit contains staircases, kitchens and bathrooms, and two common rooms. But it is the façades which are most memorable, with storey-high precast panels and canted, projecting bay window units. This pioneering use of butt-jointed, crisply finished panels became HKPA's trademark. It is the idiom in which they designed the Alton West estate for the LCC (see pages 678–689), which won them second place in the Churchill College, Cambridge, competition of 1959, and which attracted progressive university institutions – first at Birmingham (see page 174) and then here. Similarly distinctive work at Oxford, Cambridge and Reading was to follow.

LISTED grade II, 30 March 1993
ADDRESS St Anne's College, Woodstock Road, Oxford
ACCESS by appointment with the lodge, 01865 274800

Howell, Killick, Partridge and Amis 1962–64, 1966–68

15–17 BLACKHALL ROAD
OXFORD

Michael Powers had already designed the Beehives for St John's College (see page 380), and was invited back to design three fellows' houses on a site adjoining the main college. The Architects' Co-Partnership came to prominence with the Brynmawr Rubber Factory in Wales (1948–52) followed by a series of schools; examples of their domestic work are few.

Largely hidden behind high walls, the houses consist of one mirrored pair, and one smaller detached house. Like Ahrends, Burton and Koralek's extension to Keble College just across the road (see page 426), they adopt pale brick and concrete as a counter to their largely red-brick Victorian surroundings. Here the brick is almost white, with bands of concrete where floor slabs and ring beams are exposed. No. 16 has a small rear extension, added sympathetically by Cluttons in 1973.

The interiors are most impressive, with fashionable exposed brickwork and built-in timber fittings. The top-lit semi-circular stairwells are particularly dramatic. Perhaps it is because fellows are expected to have relatively few possessions, save for books, that these houses make such strong architectural statements without the need for personal embellishments.

LISTED grade II, 15 July 1998
ACCESS none

Architects' Co-Partnership 1963

SYNAGOGUE AND AMPHITHEATRE, CARMEL COLLEGE
WALLINGFORD

Carmel College, now acquired by a charitable Jewish trust, was founded as England's only Jewish public school in 1948 by Rabbi Dr Kopul Rosen. In 1953 it moved to an estate by the Thames at Mongewell, and was developed around a Victorian mansion. Thomas Hancock, a Reading architect, produced a masterplan around 1960, though it was not strictly followed. With John Toovey he designed a series of classrooms, a swimming pool, music block and dining hall. Yorke, Rosenberg and Mardall designed two dormitories.

The synagogue is the centrepiece of Hancock's development. It is wedge-shaped, with glass on three sides. The roof is supported by four wooden beams which curve upwards from the entrance to the 15-metre-high east wall. Flanking it are concrete panels filled with dalle de verre by Nechemiah Azaz, an Israeli sculptor who was then working with Eugene Rosenberg on his Belfast synagogue. Azaz also made glass for the low entrance wall, and a sculpture of the Burning Bush alongside. Carmel and Belfast were Britain's most heroic post-war synagogues, but Belfast has been converted to offices.

A contrast to the height of the synagogue is the sunken amphitheatre behind it. It is a small outdoor theatre of concrete and engineering brick.

LISTED grade II, 9 December 1999
ENGINEER Anthony Hunt
ADDRESS Carmel College, Mongewell, Wallingford, Oxfordshire
GETTING THERE train to Goring and Streatley; at junction of A4074 and B4009
ACCESS future uncertain

Thomas Hancock 1963, 1965

NEW HOUSE
SHIPTON-UNDER-WYCHWOOD

This is one of the most magical post-war houses, by virtue of its hidden setting and its sur-prisingly successful relationship with the Japanese water garden in which it sits. The entrance, across stepping stones over raked gravel, is conceived as a means of trans-portation to another sense of place and time, which the house fulfills.

It was built for the barrister Milton Grundy as a weekend retreat. It comprises a series of five juxtaposed parallelograms giving on to different aspects of the water gar-den, with a long central kitchen running between the living and sleeping ends. The three identical bedroom pavilions have a rotated symmetry and are separated by glazed links. Cotswold stone and pitched roofs were a requirement of the planners and Stout and Litch-field found themselves turning from an initial Corbusian scheme, breaking up the house's components and discovering the use of parallelograms to achieve the slightly canted roofs reminiscent of old farm buildings. Inside is still more simple, with exposed timber posts and trusses.

For the architects, Shipton marked 'a simple reaction against the rigidity of struc-ture, breaking down scale, accepting that you could put a roof on – that you didn't have to stick to right angles.'

This was Stout and Litchfield's first major independent work and remains the best-known. It set the pattern for the many houses they built subsequently.

LISTED grade II, 15 July 1998
ADDRESS Shipton-under-Wychwood, Oxfordshire
NEAREST STATION Shipton; off A361
ACCESS none

Stout and Litchfield 1964

THE TURN, MIDDLE TURN AND TURN END
HADDENHAM

Turn End is Peter Aldington's answer to Frank Lloyd Wright's Taliesin, built by himself and his wife, Margaret, as their home, with a studio and large garden. The two smaller houses gathered around the entrance forecourt helped the young couple's precarious finances. The loose-knit, single-storey group, with big pantiled roofs and high dormers, has the rambling quality of Wright's house, but the aesthetic is a more complex mix of modern and vernacular sources.

The site is a very particular one, at the heart of a big village noted for its high walls of kneaded chalk and straw, called wychert. Two of these walls sit happily here amid painted concrete block walls, lacquered timber and Eames furniture. Big joinery details, every possible seat, cupboard and appliance built in, are a feature of Aldington houses, and particularly of Aldington kitchens. The difference here is the complexity of the plan and the enclosure of rendered walls, which give privacy between the houses and a still tranquillity where everything has its special place. At Turn End there are also folding windows, opening on to an internal courtyard and pool arranged with the same careful disposition as the house itself. To the rear the garden extends through a curving glade to a series of further articulated garden rooms, some the result of later land purchases and each retaining an individual character.

SOUTHERN ENGLAND

LISTED grade II, 15 July 1998
ADDRESS Haddenham, Buckinghamshire
ACCESS garden regularly open for charity; see architectural or local press

Peter Aldington 1964–67

CLAYTON HOUSE
PRESTWOOD

While still living at Askett Green in 1964, Aldington was commissioned to build a house for Howard and Liz Quilter, successful offal merchants. It was the job which enabled him to set up in private practice, and the first where Craig was involved. There is a greater opulence here than in his earlier work, although the cost was a relatively modest £25,000. For once there is no setting in which to relate the house, and the result is a rare example of the influence of Frank Lloyd Wright in England, in which enclosed volumes in brick and open-plan spaces of timber – stained black externally – are carefully delineated.

A low wing at the entrance provided independent accommodation for the Quilters' four children. The adult area, at right angles, has a first-floor living room, bedroom and study, reached by a circular stair from the dining area. Large windows open on to a garden pool similar to that at Turn End, and on to a balcony that has the only views of open country. The first-floor suite is among Aldington's most luxurious. The harmony of the timber frame, partitions and flooring is exceptional.

In 1992 Paul Collinge, Aldington's partner from 1980 until 1985, added a swimming pool. It is so discretely placed and sympathetically detailed that it does not detract from the listability of the main house.

LISTED grade II, 8 July 1999
ADDRESS Green Lane, Prestwood, Buckinghamshire
NEAREST STATION Great Missenden
ACCESS none

Peter Aldington and John Craig 1965–66

CHRIST CHURCH PICTURE GALLERY
OXFORD

Disappointingly few art galleries were built or extended in the immediate post-war years. Christ Church was one of the first examples of what has become a quintessential building type of recent decades, and it exemplifies the problems faced by many galleries when accommodation has to be squeezed on to a tight site. Most of Powell and Moya's building is buried beneath the deanery garden and roofed in grass.

The architects designed two top-lit galleries for displaying the college's collection of Italian and Flemish paintings and a sequence of smaller spaces for showing and storing its large collection of drawings. Conservation requirements mean that these can be exhibited for only short periods at a time, in artificial light.

Entry is through a semi-basement at the back of James Wyatt's Canterbury Quad, and a ramp leads down into the sequence of cool cellars. The universally sophisticated detailing and generous materials give the spaces a monastic purity which suits the collection perfectly.

Powell and Moya also designed residential accommodation at Christ Church, and their Blue Boar Quad (1965–68) develops the styling of their Brasenose staircases into a long perimeter block.

LISTED grade II*, 24 April 1998
ADDRESS Oriel Square, Oxford
ACCESS open 14.00–17.00 most days

Powell and Moya 1965–68

WYNDHAM COURT
SOUTHAMPTON

Lyons Israel Ellis worked extensively for Southampton City Council in the 1960s, building its catering college as well as several housing schemes. Wyndham Court was a particularly sensitive site, being next to the railway station and close to E Berry Webber's dominating civic centre of 1929–39. The latter dictated a low-rise design, and the choice of a complementary white concrete. Wyndham Court was targeted at professionals, with rents well above those for normal council housing, and brought a population back to the city centre.

There are two floors of flats and four floors of two-storey maisonettes raised above ground level. This layout is best seen on the south-facing Blechynden Terrace. It is, however, at the bottom of a slope, and the Commercial Road elevation substitutes a row of shops for the open ground floor while eliminating one storey of flats. The plan consists of a private courtyard development, with a spur to the east separated by a public right of way set under pilotis. There is a basement garage under Lyons Israel Ellis's landscaped courtyard.

Just before the proposal to list was announced it was discovered that the block was being reglazed with uPVC windows, but such is the strength of its composition that it could withstand such a change with its quality unsullied.

SOUTHERN ENGLAND

LISTED grade II, 22 December 1998
ADDRESS Commercial Road and Blechynden Terrace, Southampton
ACCESS exterior only

Lyons Israel Ellis for Southampton City Council 1966–69

TEMPLETON COLLEGE
KENNINGTON

England's first three business schools were founded in 1965. Oxford's first director, Norman Leyland, had commissioned Powell and Moya at Brasenose College, Oxford (see page 390), where Richard Burton had been job architect. Now he requested a phased scheme of teaching facilities and superior accommodation for middle managers on six-month secondments. Burton set the classrooms around an atrium library, placed centrally to encourage the managers to use it. Separate blocks contain the bedrooms, arranged on a scissor plan and each with a study area for informal discussion groups. The building has a 'tartan' grid, each square 'unit' supported independently, enabling services and partitions to pass between columns at junctions and extensions to be added rapidly.

Leyland wanted his building to be 'maintenance free'. Burton chose zinc as the principal facing, after problems with lead at Brasenose. The elevations are less formal than Powell and Moya's work. Because of the nearby ring road, the bedroom windows face an internal courtyard, their sloping profile an early version of the firm's better-known additions to Keble College (see page 426). There is also a close interplay between the buildings and James Hope's landscaping, with unexpected vistas between blocks and bridges over the courtyard stream. The entrance is designed around a central tree, with a narrow rill running between the steps.

Only the earliest phases and the library extension are listed.

LISTED grade II, 15 April 1999
ADDRESS Kennington Lane, Kennington, near Oxford
GETTING THERE train to Oxford; off A423 south-west of city
ACCESS exterior by appointment on 01865 735422

Ahrends, Burton and Koralek 1967–69, 1974, 1985

SOUTHERN ENGLAND

GARDEN BUILDING, ST HILDA'S
OXFORD

St Hilda's is a women's college, and the Smithsons sought a design that would be recognisable as a 'girls' place'. It is a square building, with big windows set behind a timber screen to cut down glare and suggest greater security which the Smithsons described as 'a kind of yashmak'. The dressing areas in each bedroom were designed to hide a 'cascade of washing powder and stockings', and provided sound insulation from the central core of service rooms and corridors. Not only is the building extremely practical, it is also exquisitely detailed with thick timber joinery inside and out.

This is the Smithsons' only university building. It is also the only one of their works to incorporate services as a 'pod' between living and circulation space, a feature of their 1959–60 Churchill College design and one explored in their 'House of the Future' in 1956 and 'Appliance House' projects of 1958. There are similarities with *The Economist* offices (see pages 634–636) on a small scale, but the Garden Building reflects their growing concern to treat façades as a series of skins. It shows a gentler approach to architecture, which they saw increasingly as a framework for their users to personalise. This increased interest in domesticity is paralleled in the work of their international colleagues within Team 10, such as Aldo van Eyck.

LISTED grade II, 12 November 1999
ADDRESS St Hilda's College, Cowley Place, Oxford
ACCESS exterior only by application to the lodge; college normally open afternoons during term; call 01865 276884 for more information

Alison and Peter Smithson 1968–70

JULIUS GOTTLIEB BOATHOUSE, CARMEL COLLEGE
WALLINGFORD

Carmel College was largely developed as a Jewish boarding school by Thomas Hancock, who designed the synagogue (see page 406). This building by Sir Basil Spence, assisted by his son John, is very different. Their brief was for a memorial to Julius Gottlieb, a wood designer and patron of the arts, whose son was a school governor.

It is a building of two parts. The lower section is a boathouse, set sideways into the riverbank. Its roof serves as a sculpture terrace to the higher end, which is an exhibition hall under a concrete pyramid. The gallery was intended for exhibitions of industrial design as well as for artwork by students and touring professionals. Concrete gargoyles feed rainwater to pools below, and the few windows are denoted by incised wedges of primary colour. Inside the concrete is board-marked, and there is a large enclosed area for sculpture and other free-standing exhibits. Even the holders for gallery spotlights are of shuttered concrete, showing a remarkable consistency of vision.

The striking form of the gallery and boathouse are perhaps the ultimate expression of Spence's increasing interest in geometry through the later 1960s. This trend was developed at the University of Sussex (see pages 448–450). But this is one of his least known and most sculptural works.

LISTED grade II*, 9 December 1999
ADDRESS former Carmel College, Mongewell, Wallingford, Oxfordshire
GETTING THERE train to Goring and Streatley; at junction of A4074 and B4009
ACCESS future uncertain at time of writing

Sir Basil Spence, Bonnington and Collins 1969–70

BLACKWELL'S MUSIC SHOP AND WADHAM COLLEGE HOUSING
OXFORD

Blackwell's Music Shop was opened in November 1970 by Sir Adrian Boult. Isi Metzstein and Andy MacMillan of Gillespie, Kidd and Coia were consultant architects to Wadham College, who owned a garage on the site. By building the depth of the block they were able to create a sizeable shop, with student accommodation above. Additionally, a quadrangle for Fellows was tucked behind the adjoining King's Arms Public House.

The street frontage is a pastiche in concrete of the jettied buildings found along Holywell Street. The two-stage roof with a clerestory and the set-back splays to the shopfront are particularly distinctive. MacMillan claims that they had 'a style for every job' and that they were inspired by the medieval form of Holywell Street. The firm fitted out the interior with bookshelves, and two lightwells bring natural light down into the basement trading space. From a terrace in Wadham College behind you can see right down into the depths of the shop. The single-storey Fellows' Court is lined in zinc sheeting and is deliberately minimal in design.

Metzstein and MacMillan also remodelled the King's Arms, and willingly admit to spending many happy hours there. It is ironic then, that proposals to expand the pub's restaurant into the bookshop should have prompted the listing. It is hoped that a more sympathetic conversion will result.

LISTED grade II, 4 December 2000
ADDRESS 38 Holywell Street, Oxford (accommodation for Wadham College to rear)
NEAREST STATION Oxford
ACCESS exterior; shop interior when conversion completed

Gillespie, Kidd and Coia 1969–70

DE BREYNE AND HAYWARD BUILDINGS
OXFORD

ABK was commissioned in 1969 to build study bedrooms, two flats and a common room following Casson and Conder's master plan for expanding Keble College on its island site. The difficulty was to design a building that could stand up to Butterfield's apotheosis of high Victorian brutalism. Their solution was a snake-like building, which falls in height as it uncoils down Blackhall Road. It is ABK's first use of a curve, later to become one of their hallmarks, and its honey-coloured brick and angled black glass offer a sophisticated coolness juxtaposed against Butterfield's fireworks. The solution to the tight site is reminiscent of Powell and Moya's twisting buildings at Oxford and Cambridge – beginning at Brasenose College, Oxford (see page 390) on which members of ABK worked – but is more sinuous and romantic in its treatment.

The pairs of rooms set across the block, reached by staircases linked by a sunken glazed walkway, are a refinement of those at Templeton College. The black glass and enclosed aspect limit solar gain through the sloping fenestration. The firm also fitted out the common room that curves across the lawn in front of Butterfield's work.

Listing was hastened when a new block by Rick Mather threatened the tip of the snake's tail on Blackhall Road. It did not prevent its demolition.

LISTED grade II*, 4 October 1999
ADDRESS Keble College, Blackhall Road, Oxford
ACCESS exteriors only by aplication to the lodge, weekdays 14.00–17.00; call 01865 272727. Much of the building can be seen from the street

Ahrends, Burton and Koralek 1971–73, 1975–76

SOUTH-EASTERN ENGLAND

ST JOHN THE EVANGELIST
ST LEONARDS-ON-SEA

Goodhart-Rendel accepted every tenet of Gothic architecture except the pointed arch. His rebuilding of St John's is a much closer synthesis of Gothic than his other post-war churches, however, for here he had to incorporate Arthur Blomfield's baptistry and tower of 1883–84, which survived the destruction of the rest of the church in 1943.

The nave and transepts were rebuilt first, and display both round arches in the lower arcades and pointed arches defining the bays above. The pale nave windows by a Mr Ledger and the colourful baptistry angels by a Miss Thompson repeat themes from the previous church. The interior's most powerful feature is the double chancel arch, designed to give added support to the concrete vault and to carry the organ, as shown in a drawing by Goodhart-Rendel in the south transept. The present organ was brought from St Catherine's College, Cambridge, in 1974 and occupies the north transept. An intended north chapel was never built. The eagle lectern, choir stalls and bishop's chair, together with fittings in the Lady chapel, were salvaged from the old church and painted in muted pastel shades.

Externally the old and new work mesh together particularly successfully, with Goodhart-Rendel demonstrating his love of diaper brickwork patterning. The stepping of the transepts and vestry rooms on the falling site is particularly masterful.

LISTED grade II*, 25 September 1998
ADDRESS Brittany Road, St Leonards-on-Sea, East Sussex
ACCESS open Wednesday morning and Sunday

H S Goodhart-Rendel 1950–52, 1955–57

AIR FORCES MEMORIAL
ENGLEFIELD GREEN

Runnymede encapsulates the mid-20th century's sentimental attitude to English history, making it the perfect location for a monument to the 20,000 airmen and women who died in the Second World War but who have no known grave. It has a similarity to the neo-Georgian public school or mess hall that is movingly appropriate, and a humility that contrasts with the American Cemetery at Madingley (see page 210).

Maufe's simple detailing is in contrast to his sublime use of a dramatic setting. You first cross a greensward of lawn into a cloister, where wall tablets are inscribed with the names of the dead. Their rippling effect is impressive. On the furthest side a tower, embellished only by Vernon Hill's figures of Justice, Victory and Courage, forms a 'shrine'. Its limed oak fittings are familiar from Maufe's churches. There, suddenly, you can see right across the Thames, from Windsor to London. The etched angels on the picture windows are by John Hutton, who executed a similar commission for Coventry Cathedral. On sunny days you can climb the tower, a progression of tranquil spaces with seats and plaques to aid the pervasive spirit of contemplation. There are also two distinctively 1950s-style 'look outs', set at a curve off the cloister at either side.

The Heathrow flight path overhead is an apposite modern tribute.

LISTED grade II*, 25 September 1998
ENGINEER Bylander and Waddell
ADDRESS Cooper's Hill, Englefield Green, Surrey
GETTING THERE train to Egham; signposted off A328
ACCESS March to October 9.00–18.00 weekdays, 10.00–18.00 weekends; November to February 9.00–16.00 weekdays, 10.00–16.00 weekends; closed Christmas Day and Boxing Day. Call 01784 4333239 for more information

Edward Maufe 1952–53

ST MARY
WILLINGDON

Maufe brought to this diminutive church the most distinctive elements of his personal style, and it is one of his most charming designs. It replaced a church of 1908 which was destroyed in the Second World War.

St Mary's hugs a low rise overlooking Hampden Park, its glistening white-painted brick the first clue to its authorship. The big-roofed nave has a barn-like quality, from which emerge a narrow bell-turret and a broad stubby tower over the chancel – an endearing massing amid Eastbourne's suburban estates. The clock, a memorial to the Reverend Donald Carpenter who supervised the church's rebuilding during his long ministry (1952–73), is an appropriate addition.

Inside is quintessential Maufe. The pointed concrete arches, dividing the church into bays and defining narrow aisles, are refined from those at St Thomas, Hanwell (1934), and subsequent churches. The cushion capitals and their corresponding stepped window section, particularly noticeable in the squint between the chancel and the little Lady chapel, is also a Maufe signature, copied from his favourite Stockholm buildings, Ivar Tengbom's Högalid church (1917–23) and Ragnar Östberg's city hall (1902–23). The same mouldings appear in his contemporary restoration of Gray's Inn Chapel, London. The limed oak fittings are also characteristic, combining with the grey-white render and blue ceilings to provide a space that is at once highly sculptured yet tranquil, and virtually unaltered.

LISTED grade II, 28 September 1998
ADDRESS Decoy Drive, Hampden Park, Willingdon, Eastbourne, East Sussex
GETTING THERE train to Hampden Park; east of A2021 towards station
ACCESS open daylight hours

Edward Maufe 1952–53

ROYAL OAK MOTEL
NEWINGREEN

The Royal Oak is an early nineteenth-century inn on the A20 outside Folkestone. Next to it Louis Erdi was commissioned to build what was then called an 'auto hotel', comprising ten garages and twelve bedrooms set in an alternating line along a huddled Z-shaped range. At either end, under higher sloping roofs, were larger suites with living rooms for families. It was the first of a series of motels and hotels around England built by Erdi for a local entrepreneur, Graham Lyon, and established his specialism in the field. Newingreen was aimed principally at European travellers visiting England, and the public house was converted into a restaurant for their needs.

The little building was strongly picturesque, for all its simplicity. Its rough elm weatherboarding, contrasted with irregularly coursed stonework at either end, hinted at romantic countryside far from Kent suburbia. The boxed-out windows and thin steel posts of the covered way that sheltered the line of entrance doors were more clearly in the style of the Festival of Britain. In 1975 cars were banished from the main building and the garages converted into extra bedrooms.

Although it was rapidly spotlisted when it was threatened with redevelopment in January 2000, it remained derelict and in February 2001 permission was granted for its demolition.

LISTED grade II, January 2000
DEMOLISHED 2001

Louis Erdi 1952–54

23 ST GEORGE'S STREET
CANTERBURY

Shops are among the most ephemeral of building types and it is remarkable that so much of the exterior of this shop survives. It was built for a family firm of butchers and grocers, David Greig's, who are commemorated by an engraved inscription at the end of the arcade on to Canterbury Lane, and replaced a shop destroyed in the Blitz. They conceived it as a challenge to the self-service stores then beginning to appear.

The double-height shop is backed by a higher range, which originally contained cold stores, offices and two flats. The building can be best enjoyed from narrow Canterbury Lane, where columns clad in pink and grey-green mosaic support a folded concrete slab roof and shield a lower arcade lined with varnished plywood advertising panels. The roof was exposed internally, and this feature was restored in 1999. A large thistle motif has gone from the corner. The shop was originally intended to overlook a square, and so was treated as a lower pavilion, masking the original Woolworth's being rebuilt next door, and with deliberate emphasis given to both elevations.

A yard with garages and a dispatch room at the rear of the building have been replaced with a new block that repeats the triangular motifs of the main building in its windows and roofline.

LISTED grade II, 24 November 1995
ENGINEER Ove Arup and Partners
ADDRESS Canterbury (formerly David Greig's, now part of Woolworth's)
NEAREST STATION Canterbury East
ACCESS open Monday to Friday, 9.00–17.30, but exteriors chiefly of interest

Robert Paine and Partners 1953–54

ST LEONARD
ST LEONARDS-ON-SEA

James Burton, the developer of St Leonards-on-Sea, built a simple Gothic chapel here in 1831–34, which was destroyed by a rocket in 1944. The War Damages Commission insisted that the church be rebuilt on the same site, despite subsidence problems from the surrounding cliffs.

There are strong similarities with Scott's RC Church of SS Mary and Joseph, Lansbury (see page 500), in its parabolic or catenary arches, and in the blue-stone dado with its continuous wave motif. Scott probably worked on both schemes simultaneously, after an initial proposal for St Leonard's with his brother Sir Giles Scott was deemed too expensive. The principal difference is that here the brothers Scott stressed a single axis, facing the sea, which is dominated by the tower added in 1960–61.

The internal iconography of the sea was determined by the incumbent, Canon Griffiths. The marble sanctuary floor is decorated with loaves and fishes, the images of locally-caught skate and herring combining forcefully with the reference to the first Christian communion. The pulpit is a prow of a fishing boat, made for Griffiths in Ein Gev, Galilee, and transported by the Prince Line Shipping Company, who gave a binnacle as a lectern. In the 1970s the gallery was extended and the area underneath it enclosed as a hall.

The church has had to be shored against the moving cliff and its future is uncertain.

LISTED grade II, 25 September 1998

ADDRESS Undercliff, St Leonards-on-Sea, East Sussex

ACCESS open most days in summer, but future uncertain; call 01424 422189 for more information

Adrian Gilbert Scott 1953–56, 1960–61

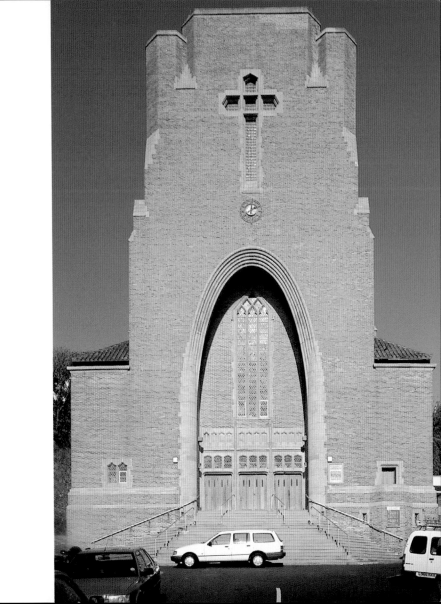

THE BEACH HOUSE
PETT

Michael Pattrick built this house as a holiday home for his friends Richard and Phoebe Merrick, members of a prominent local family with an interest in modern design. It is set high on pilotis to give views of the sea across the high sea wall built at Pett Level following floods in 1953. The ground floor is of concrete, with a small blue-painted entrance and more recent galley kitchen, but most of it is left open as a car port. The rest is a pre-stressed timber frame designed to withstand gales and clad in dark-stained timber.

Inside, the first floor has four tiny bedrooms with built-in bunks and bookshelves. At the top is the living area, with wonderful views down the coastline, and a balcony that leads on to external timber stairs down to the beach. This upper room is particularly nautical in feel: streamlined, compact and with varnished timber floors, cabinets and stairhead.

This is a magical house, intended as a beach house for a family who lived nearby, but adapted with minimal intervention for longer-term living. It is rare to find a seaside house that communes so closely with its setting and which embodies so many romantic notions of summer living.

Listing was prompted by proposals to infill the ground floor.

LISTED grade II, 26 November 2001
ADDRESS The Beach House, Pett Level Road, Pett, East Sussex
NEAREST STATION Winchelsea
ACCESS exterior only

Michael Pattrick 1959–60

SORRELL HOUSE
CHICHESTER

Around 1960 fashionable and sophisticated young architects came to recognise the possibilities of timber as a flexible and lightweight building material ideally suited to small houses.

This weekend cottage is a supreme example, a tiny building just four bays wide and entirely hidden by trees. It is erected on stilts to give the accommodation views over the countryside, and to allow the storage of boats and bicycles underneath. Access is thus by a distinctive timber staircase, which leads to a verandah from which the rooms can be entered separately. There is a continuous wall of windows overlooking the sea.

Some of the details are nautically inspired by the use of a shipbuilder as contractor, others were simply and carefully detailed by the architects. The whole gives the impression of being created from a kit of parts, a conceit rarely realised elsewhere. The building's diminutive scale is a remarkable contrast to Foggo and Thomas's renowned large-scale office buildings done later as partners in the firm of Arup Associates, but the attention to detail is the same in all their work.

Since listing, an addition has been made in similar style.

LISTED grade II*, 15 July 1998
ADDRESS Bosham Hoe, near Chichester, West Sussex
NEAREST STATION Bosham
ACCESS none

Peter Foggo and David Thomas 1960

GERALD ASKEW WILDFOWL RESERVE
FRAMFIELD

Gerald Askew began his wildfowl collection in 1960 and by 1966, when it was opened to the public, it was the largest private holding of its kind in England. The farmhouse was enlarged over 12 years and buildings added to the grounds. In 1960–61 an east wing for a new drawing room was made, to the same height as the original house but only one-storey high, with vertical areas of flintwork on the front elevation and rendered niches marking the junction with the earlier house. A continuous timber entablature unites the old and new parts on the same building line. A Venetian window is the most distinctive feature.

Erith also made a first-floor octagonal room with Tuscan columns. In 1969–71 a west wing was added, to form the 'bird room' picture gallery, with stone fireplaces based on those by Palladio at the Villa Barbaro, Maser. In 1962 Erith built a car lodge or *barchessa* – with Tuscan columns supporting a big tiled roof – and in 1965 added fat brick gatepiers to a deliberately skewed plan. Further gatepiers, of vermiculated flintwork, were built in 1967.

Although long listed as an eighteenth-century house, Erith's alterations and additions give Bentley Farm greater distinction. Askew's collection is now in the care of East Sussex County Council.

LISTED grade II, 26 November 1953/15 July 1998/7 February 2002
ADDRESS Bentley Farm, Harvey's Lane, near Framfield, East Sussex
GETTING THERE train to Uckfield; south of Uckfield off A22
ACCESS open daily from Easter to 31 October, 10.30–16.30; November, February, March, weekends only; closed December and January. Call 01825 840573 for more details

Raymond Erith 1960–71

UNIVERSITY OF SUSSEX
FALMER

The seven new universities built in England in the 1960s were the culmination of public patronage of higher education in the post-war years, and offered exceptional opportunities for architects to create new campus communities. A prototype, founded at Keele in 1950, challenged traditional course structures but produced unplanned, unfocused architecture. Its successors, including East Anglia, York and Essex, were not to repeat its mistakes.

Sussex was the first of the seven, and under its first Vice Chancellor, John Fulton, developed an architecture and image appropriate to its modern image, based on course structures that bridged the traditional boundaries between academic disciplines. Brighton Council offered a picturesque site at Stanmer Hall, on the Downs, and subsequent universities were to repeat its campus model. Spence was appointed architect in 1959 and produced his most powerful work here. Combining local brick and flints with bold concrete segmental arches Spence developed a style reminiscent of Le Corbusier's Maisons Jaoul, on a grander scale but nevertheless respectful of the line of the surrounding Downs. His masterstroke was first to design a courtyard building, Falmer House (1960–62), which would be an inward-facing centre for both study and recreation while the rest of the campus was constructed. He likened it to the Colosseum in Rome: 'a magnificent ruin', with gaps in the exposed brick construction. At Sussex there are open terraces within the framework of the upper storeys, allowing views through to the countryside. Ivon Hitchens donated a mural to the canteen.

Spence designed all the most prestigious buildings at Sussex, which were set around the pedestrian greensward of Fulton Court. To the east buildings for physics (1960–66), chemistry (1963–65) and engineering and applied sciences (1964–66) repeated the brick-and-concrete idiom with a long covered arcade, from which steps rise to lecture theatres behind. To the north is the more amorphous Arts Building (1962–68),

Basil Spence and Partners 1960 onwards

a series of semi-open courtyards, where much of Sylvia Crowe's landscaping survives. The Arts Building marked a first attempt to express inter-disciplinary teaching by means of a homogenous building. The west side is dominated by the library (1962–71, and subsequently extended), while to the south-west is the Gardner Arts Centre of 1968–69, a series of galleries and bars wrapped round an auditorium. Close to Falmer House a second focus was given to the campus by the non-denominational meeting house (1965–67), shaped like an oast house.

At Sussex, despite later accretions, the sense of a small village in the Downs has never been diluted, and it remains the best place to enjoy the sense of opportunity and optimism that were among the brightest features of the 1960s.

LISTED Falmer House grade I; other buildings in Fulton Court grade II*, 30 March 1993
ADDRESS Falmer, Brighton
ACCESS exteriors only; plus Gardner Arts Centre open 10.00–19.00; Sundays and evening events, open one hour before performances; call 01273 685861 for information

Basil Spence and Partners 1960 onwards

TURNPOINT
WALTON-ON-THAMES

Rodney Gordon was the design architect of the Owen Luder Partnership, headhunted from the LCC after designing the Michael Faraday Memorial, Southwark (see page 712). After years of designing for committees, Gordon found speculative work invigorating, for he had complete freedom so long as he maximised plot ratios and kept down costs. Eros House, Catford (1961–63), was followed by the Tricorn Centre, Portsmouth (1963–67) and Treaty Centre, Gateshead (1964–67).

Meanwhile Gordon designed himself a house. The contrast between his gargantuan office structures and tiny timber Turnpoint, fitting naturally into a woodland setting, could not be greater. Gordon explains that at Eros House he was detailing pine shuttering for concrete, and his interest in the two materials became interrelated. Turnpoint's skeleton is formed of steel channels, including the stilts that raise the house more than one metre above the ground. Preliminary excavation allowed for car parking under the house. The constructionalist aesthetic is continued in the way that the walls and eaves are extended with chains to carry rainwater to the ground. All the windows were double-glazed, with a blind set between the two layers of glass; most are of the same size, so they are a unit like the steelwork and boarding that gave the house its proportions.

In 1996 spotlisting was prompted by an application to demolish the house. It has subsequently found sympathetic new owners.

LISTED grade II, 6 December 1996
ADDRESS Onslow Road, Burwood Park, Walton-on-Thames, Surrey
ACCESS none

Rodney Gordon 1961–62

CHICHESTER FESTIVAL THEATRE
CHICHESTER

Retired councillor Leslie Evershed-Martin conceived the idea of a theatre and festival for Chichester in 1959, after seeing Tyrone Guthrie's Shakespeare Festival Theatre at Stratford, Ontario, on television. The concept was identical: a thrust stage, summer seasons starring famous actors, and seating for 1400. At Guthrie's suggestion, Sir Laurence Olivier was invited to be the first director. There is a strong comparison with the open stage at the National Theatre, to which Olivier was appointed director in 1962.

New theories on theatre design and on how Shakespeare's plays were originally staged abounded in equal profusion in the late 1950s. Here they were combined in the apron stage, symbolically of Canadian maple, a Juliet balcony and minstrel gallery.

Evershed-Martin's concept was for a 'tent in the park', bringing a Glyndebourne atmosphere to a summer theatre festival. Powell and Moya, typically, initially refused the job, then could not resist having a go. The hexagonal plan was theirs; the amphitheatre seating which swells out over the foyer was taken from Greek models. The projecting staircases anchor the ring beam that supports the roof. It was largely built by voluntary donations, and originally had no backstage workshops or rehearsal spaces. The finishes reflect its cheapness, its £105,000 costs comparing favourably with Nottingham Playhouse (see pages 178–180), which was designed first but completed later.

LISTED grade II*, 12 June 1998
ADDRESS Oaklands Park, Chichester
ACCESS regular seasons; group tours on 01243 811363

Powell and Moya 1961–62

Chichester Festival Theatre
Box Office
Administration

Minerva Studio Theatre
Theatre Restaurant
Theatre Society Offices
Theatre Shop

BIRD'S EYE
WALTON-ON-THAMES

Bird's Eye was one of the first companies to move its offices out of London, bringing staff on to a single site handy for railway and airport connections. It wanted a four-storey building, and although planning permission was only granted for three storeys the design optimistically envisaged future permission; instead a small addition was made to the side, via a glazed link.

Most memorable is the image created by the anodised aluminium curtain walling, with projecting half-hexagon panels that set up a rhythm along the façades. Its rippling silver-blue surfaces are as clean and crisp as the company's products, an early example of the 1960s predilection for geometric op-art shapes. Their form is repeated in the arches of the bush-hammered concrete on the ground floor and is reflected in the pool which runs the length of the building. The sculpture of flying birds is by John McCarthy.

The building has two floors of offices over a directors' suite, set around two internal courtyards with pools, which are beautifully landscaped, by Philip Hicks. One is Japanese in feel, the other has concrete sculpture by Allen Collins. The second-floor canteen was, appropriately, one of the first in Britain to serve only pre-packaged meals.

LISTED grade II, 24 November 1995
ENGINEER Bylander, Waddell and Partners
ADDRESS Station Avenue, Walton-on-Thames, Surrey
ACCESS exterior only

SOUTH-EASTERN ENGLAND

Burnet, Tait and Partners 1961–62, 1967–68

CONGRESS THEATRE
EASTBOURNE

Eastbourne Borough Council wanted a large auditorium for opera, ballet and conferences to complement its two Victorian theatres and Winter Gardens. Few halls respond successfully to a mixed brief, because of conflicting staging and acoustic requirements. The Congress Theatre is an exception.

The compromise is a square hall for a massive 1680 people, with two tiers of balconies and side slips, and a giant stage with full flying facilities. The slips and the windows behind them can be curtained off when not required for daytime conferences, and then the theatre assumes a traditional plan. The floor can be lowered to make an orchestra pit or raised for an apron stage. The acoustics were designed for speech, but the overhanging galleries sufficiently enhance the base frequencies to make it adequate for music.

Outside the Congress comes to life at night, when light pours from the great foyer which runs under and around the auditorium. Its curtain-wall frontage is an early use of butyl rubber gaskets to hold the glazing, while to the rear a more 'contemporary' patterning of coloured brick, cut brick, tile, concrete facings and slate hangings lessens its massive bulk.

The Westwood brothers were specialist shop and restaurant designers who turned to theatre work following their successful refronting of the bombed Queen's Theatre in London.

LISTED grade II*, 12 June 1998
ADDRESS Carlisle Road, Eastbourne, East Sussex
ACCESS regular events; call 01323 415529 for information

Bryan and Norman Westwood 1961–63

SWANSCOMBE FOOTBRIDGE
DARTFORD

This is a particularly elegant bridge, closing the notch which the cutting of the road makes in the skyline. It is a three-hinged concrete arch spanning almost 49 metres, with a pre-stressing tendon through it, and was novel in England for its date. This was John Bergg's first bridge for Kent County Council, and although he went on to design other bridges – in Kent and notably for the Shoreham bypass in Sussex – he never bettered this simple but inspired response to the beautiful setting of the North Downs.

Motorways and trunk roads need over twice as many bridges per mile as older roads, and some 3000 were built in the 1950s and 1960s. Swanscombe has had many imitators, but its picturesque refinement remains exceptional.

LISTED grade II, 29 May 1998
ENGINEER John Bergg
ADDRESS A2 at Swanscombe Park, near Dartford
GETTING THERE train to Swanscombe; on A2 adjoining Swanscombe Park
ACCESS any reasonable time

Kent County Council 1963–64

FORMER GILLETT HOUSE
CHICHESTER

This former hostel for theological students was ABK's first English commission, passed on by Philip Powell, for whom they had previously worked. The brief was for 35 study bedrooms, three staff flats, a library and a lecture room, which ABK set in four blocks around a courtyard, bridged at first-floor level over covered ways leading from the adjoining chapel to the main college buildings on Westgate. Gillett House also had its own tiny chapel on the first floor.

The building is largely built of local brick, but with hefty concrete bridges and baffles. In addition to a window each room has a skylight – under which desks and bookcases were originally set – to give extra light while maintaining privacy. The library at the rear was also top lit. It is the most brutalist of ABK's buildings in its honest use of brick, concrete and tiles, and in its Corbusian waterspouts. The *Architectural Review* described it as a young architect's building, but it demonstrates the precise, three-dimensional geometry that became the firm's signature.

The theological college was closed in 1994 and Gillett House was threatened with demolition. Listing has ensured its preservation, though in its conversion to a nursing home part of the courtyard has been infilled with aluminium glazing and alterations have been made to the interior.

LISTED grade II, 31 January 1996
ADDRESS Chichester Theological College, now Marriott House nursing home, Avenue de Chartres, Chichester, West Sussex
ACCESS limited exterior by appointment on 01243 536652

Ahrends, Burton and Koralek 1963–65

WHITE FOX LODGE
RYE

Sidney Horniblow was a successful advertising manager who bought 69 acres at Udimore on which to build a home for his collection of modern art and antique furniture. He proposed a 'neo-Georgian bungalow' but Schwerdt persuaded him to look at the work of Frank Lloyd Wright while he was working in the USA.

The final design makes understated references to Wright's houses of the 1930s, as well as to early de Stijl designs and Mies van der Rohe's 'design for a brick country house' of 1924. These are particularly seen in its overhanging timber eaves and projecting brick walls. They serve to integrate the house with its beautifully preserved garden by Sylvia Crowe, and there are long views across the South Downs. This relationship is developed further by the house's pinwheel plan, set round a small hallway, which overlooks a courtyard and fountain sculpture. Each of the four wings serves a different function. The internal finishes are simple but carefully crafted, with special attention given to the full-height doors and fitted cupboards.

Listing was requested by Mrs Joan Horniblow before her death, and as the house had never been published its discovery was a revelation. John Schwerdt trained in Brighton and worked extensively around Lewes; this was his most ambitious work, undertaken for an exceptional client.

LISTED grade II, 25 March 1999
ADDRESS Udimore, near Rye, East Sussex
NEAREST STATION Winchelsea
ACCESS none

John Schwerdt and Partners 1964–65

CHURCH OF THE RESURRECTION, WEST MALLING ABBEY
WEST MALLING

The convent of St Mary's Abbey, founded c.1090, was revived in 1892, and in 1916 an Anglican Benedictine community moved here. The site is extraordinarily emotive, for the twelfth-century west front and south transept survive, and were landscaped in the eighteenth century as the setting for a Gothick house.

Maguire and Murray first rebuilt the fifteenth-century cloister, with a meeting room for the nuns. For the new church they allowed themselves a greater freedom of form and materials, because although it sits on the site of the old crossing and is joined to the south transept it appears freestanding. The boldly geometrical building, a rectangle rising to a cylinder with a conoid roof likened by Maguire to 'two half-oast-houses', sits nobly behind the Romanesque remains. It is the most powerful expression of his Wittkowerian belief in building the house of God in accordance with fundamental geometry, and followed the success of the pair's St Paul, Bow Common (see page 534). The concrete block walls resemble medieval ragstone in colour, but their smoothness highlights their shape, and contain two ringbeams which carry the weight of the roof to the walls, although internal columns were inserted in 1972.

In the centre is the nuns' church; to either side are low flat-roofed areas, one the nuns' entrance from the cloister, the other a side chapel for guests.

LISTED grade II*, 18 February 1999
ADDRESS West Malling, Kent
ACCESS guest chapel for services and special events only; call Sister Mary David on 01732 843309

Maguire and Murray 1964–66

LONG WALL
WEYBRIDGE

As work began on Leslie Gooday's Pools on the Park, Richmond (see page 720), so he began to build a new house for himself outside Weybridge. There are strong similarities between the two buildings, in the way the house is built up of differentiated volumes, some with flat roofs and others with a distinctive copper-clad mansard. Though quite a large house, the broken roof line ensures that it slots demurely into the side of a wooded hillside. The different roof levels are expressed internally in a series of double-height and lower spaces.

Gooday came to prominence as a Festival of Britain staff architect under Hugh Casson, from where he developed his primary interest in industrial and exhibition design. Casson's influence can be seen in the neatness of the design and its attention to details and finishes. This is the second house that Gooday built for himself, and is a good example of the evolution of the 'contemporary' style rooted in the legacy of Frank Lloyd Wright, with a sensitive use of contrasted materials and picturesque planning.

LISTED grade II, 15 July 1998
ADDRESS Golf Club Road, Weybridge, Surrey
ACCESS none

Leslie Gooday 1964–68

RC CHAPEL OF THE MOST HOLY NAME
FOLKESTONE

The Sir John Moore Barracks were rebuilt by the Westwoods from 1961 as a training school for 750 school leavers. It is rare for the army to build a Roman Catholic chapel, except where there are a lot of young trainees.

Zbigniew Jan Petruszewski came to Britain in 1945 and abbreviated his name after qualifying as an architect. His deeply-felt Catholicism led him to take personal responsibility for the chapel. It is roughly triangular in shape, with one curved wall giving form to the sanctuary at the narrow end. It is partly submerged in the ground and its concrete foundations are exposed internally to form low walls, which have a curious, fluid texture from being formed in shuttering lined in polythene. Above soars the roof, reminiscent of Frank Lloyd Wright's Unitarian church at Shorewood Hills, Wisconsin, but inspired, Piet says, by the scout camps of his boyhood. The timber comes from his native Poland. Stations of the Cross in fibreglass are set in rows along one wall, 'like a comic strip' says Piet; over which yellow glass in the sanctuary and concealed clerestory casts a warm glow. The building combines severe economy with boyish charm, and for Piet it represents nostalgia for the Poland of his youth mixed with a deep gratitude for what Britain has given him since his exile here.

LISTED grade II, 25 January 2000
ADDRESS Sir John Moore Barracks, East Road, Shorncliffe, Folkestone, Kent
NEAREST STATION Folkestone Centrals
ACCESS exterior only

Zbigniew Jan Piet of Bryan and Norman Westwood, Piet and Partners 1966–68

BENJAMIN'S MOUNT
WINDLESHAM

Although Goldfinger is best remembered for his massive Balfron and Trellick Towers in London (see pages 568 and 574), he also designed private houses, and Benjamin's Mount is the best preserved after his own. It was built for Jack Perry, one of the first English businessmen to trade with communist China. It is uncertain if this connection was an influence on the choice of timber as a building material and the emphatically expressed post-and-beam construction. It is superficially very different from Goldfinger's big blocks, but there is the same rigorous attention to structure and surfaces, and a monumentality that belies the house's tiny scale.

Benjamin's Mount is perched on a steep slope and is divided into two canted sections by a conservatory. One wing houses an open-plan living room, study and kitchen, the other has a suite of bedrooms situated off a long corridor. The full-height windows are set back behind the overhanging roof, so that the thick timber columns frame the wonderful views and give a unity between indoors and outdoors. All the rooms are lined in timber panels, while the living-room fireplace is set in a marble wall, of a similar colour to that at Balfron Tower.

A request for listing was made when the house was sold; however, the new owner rebuilt the conservatory on a much enlarged scale before the designation was made.

LISTED grade II*, 11 January 1999
ADDRESS Westwood Road, Windlesham, Surrey
NEAREST STATION Sunningdale
ACCESS none

Ernö Goldfinger 1967–69

THORNDIKE THEATRE
LEATHERHEAD

A flourishing repertory theatre was established in Leatherhead by Hazel Vincent-Wallace, with the support of Dame Sybil Thorndike and her husband Lewis Casson. Ham was invited to build a new theatre within the shell of the old Crescent cinema, with a new fly-tower and workshop. The frontage was sold for redevelopment as shops, and the theatre has only a narrow entrance under a boldly-lettered canopy.

Ham created two remarkable spaces, one sculptural, the other supremely practical. The generous foyers on three levels were designed to be open all day as a bar and café, their broad staircases and balconies making them a place to 'see and be seen' under dramatic top-lighting.

The auditorium established Ham's reputation as a theatre specialist. It holds 526 seats in a single steep tier, none of them more than 14 metres from the curved apron front to the stage. The 'continental' arrangement without a central aisle was novel, but has since become a common practice. There was also space for wheelchairs, served by a lift, well before disabled access became a requirement. The stage is a traditional one, with a flytower and defined curtain line, yet there is no moulded proscenium to make a 'frame' between actors and audience.

Listing has saved the theatre – closed in 1997 – from demolition, and it is now a church, the Pioneers People's Trust.

LISTED grade II, 8 July 1999
ADDRESS High Street, Leatherhead, Surrey
ACCESS contact Mike Hibberd on 01372 365128

Roderick Ham 1967–69

BRANKSOME CONFERENCE CENTRE
HASLEMERE

Edward Cullinan altered and James Stirling extended a house of 1901 by E J May as a training centre for Olivetti, one of the greatest post-war design patrons. It is Stirling's work which is exceptional, for it occupies a pivotal place between his earlier brutalist and neo-Victorian aesthetic, and his later post-modernism. Colin Rowe claims Thomas Hope's nearby Deepdene as an inspiration, with its similarly angled extension and glazed link. Stirling had begun collecting Hope artifacts, and his later work has affinities with early nineteenth-century explorations of new materials, historic styles and the interplay between spaces and light.

Nevertheless, the glazed link is reminiscent of those in his earlier Florey Building, Oxford. It gives on to a four-part lecture theatre with sliding screens, and classrooms. They are formed of glass-reinforced polyester (GRP), introduced around 1964 and used by Stirling in his notorious Runcorn housing, but which lent itself to the soft curves of this building just as it did to Olivetti's 1970s adding machines and typewriters, and to the firm's contemporary buildings in Italy by Mangiarotti and Gabetti. Stirling was moving towards a greater internationalism in his work.

The building would have been more startling had Stirling been allowed to use green and purple GRP, instead of buff. His vibrant greens and yellows are, however, still a dominant feature of the interior.

LISTED grade II*, 21 January 1997
ADDRESS formerly Olivetti International Education Centre, Hindhead Road, Haslemere, Surrey
ACCESS none

James Stirling 1970–72

CHRIST'S HOSPITAL ARTS CENTRE AND MUSIC SCHOOL
NEAR HORSHAM

The late 1960s saw the emergence of the ideal theatre as either a flexible black box or an adaptation of an older 'found' space. In part such architecturally minimal solutions were a reaction against the big-budget National and Barbican Theatres then under construction.

Christ's Hospital marks the revival of the historic courtyard theatre in England. It anticipates the Cottesloe Theatre inserted into the National Theatre complex (see pages 724–726) in 1973–77, and the Swan Theatre, Stratford upon Avon (1986). But Christ's Hospital combines architectural panache with its historic references, with a tough timber structure in brilliant red to the galleries that ring a central flat space. The stage can be set centrally or at one end of this using the plentiful schoolboy labour.

Howell's building surrounds a music block built c. 1910, on the axis of Aston Webb's baroque buildings of 1893–1902. Traditionally the school band marches the pupils into dinner twice a week, and Howell created a covered space where they could form up, set underneath a small recital hall on stilts. Spiral stairs on either side are among the firm's finest timber staircases. Behind they added more practice rooms, forming a symmetrical composition to which the theatre is an adjunct. The foyer commemorates Howell, who was killed in a car accident in 1974.

Listing was prompted by proposals to demolish the recital hall.

LISTED grade II*, 4 December 2000
ASSISTANT ARCHITECTS R J Murphy, N Catton, Di Haigh and R Barton
NEAREST STATION Christ's Hospital
ACCESS regular public performances: call 01403 247434 for details

Bill Howell of Howell, Killick, Partridge and Amis 1972–74

THORNCROFT MANOR
LEATHERHEAD

Thorncroft Manor is a compact villa of 1772 built by Sir Robert Taylor. It was converted to offices in the 1970s for a firm of engineers, who commissioned Manser to build an extension. Faced with the problem of adding to a distinguished full-square house in a 'Capability' Brown landscape, Manser and his team devised a set-back, three-storey addition clad entirely in mirror glass.

The mirror-glass building was the last statement in the development of the minimalist style, making only the most subliminal use of classical proportions. The first was the Bell Telephone Centre at Holmdel, New Jersey, of 1962 by Eero Saarinen. In Britain, mirror glass was pioneered by Norman Foster at his head office for IBM at Cosham, Hampshire, and it was he who first used reflective glass in a historic setting, with his Willis Corroon Building (see pages 322–324). Manser's solution is particularly neatly detailed, and the top floor – originally a restaurant – is angled to reflect the sky. Nevertheless, it took two years for the scheme to be approved by local planners. The tower to the rear was intended as a lift shaft but has never been used.

Manser made his reputation with a series of elegant steel-framed houses in the 1960s, built mainly in Surrey. This is his first major office building, tactful and yet confidently modern.

LISTED additions to house of 1772 included in listing at grade II*, 18 April 2002
ASSISTANT ARCHITECTS Vladimir Bogdanovich and Mark Ashmead
NEAREST STATION Leatherhead
ACCESS exterior on occasional open days; check local press for details

Michael Manser and Partners 1974–76

LONDON: NORTH OF THE THAMES

CANTEEN, RHÔNE-POULENC-RORER

The pharmaceutical industry contributed to the war effort: May and Baker, part of Rhône-Poulenc, produced the first commercial antibiotic, M+B 693, which cured Winston Churchill's pneumonia in 1941.

The canteen demonstrates both the personal hardships and building shortages experienced in wartime. Works canteens provided cheap nourishing meals off the ration and a social life, with amateur dramatics and music leavened by professional concerts organised by the Committee for the Encouragement of Music and the Arts, forerunners of the Arts Council. The stage was in the brick section at the south of the little building, which is otherwise fully glazed. Mills recalled that a V2 rocket shattered the glass just as it had been installed.

Reinforced concrete has an inherent strength when formed as a cone or cylinder, and was a cheap way of making large spans at a time of steel shortages. The technique was pioneered at Jena, Germany, in 1923 and this is among its first uses in England. The thin wavy roof, of five segmental arches, is only 51 millimetres thick. Such roofs became widespread after the war. The canteen is unusual in the care given to every detail, with projecting eaves and thin metal windows, and its delicacy has survived subsequent extensions. Mills subsequently designed several factory buildings here, but this remains his most appealing work.

LISTED grade II, 24 November 1995
ENGINEERS Dr Hajnal-Konyi and C V Blumfield
ADDRESS Rainham Road South, Dagenham
NEAREST STATION Dagenham East
ACCESS none

Edward D Mills 1943–44, extended 1953

SPA GREEN ESTATE

Berthold Lubetkin and Tecton were commissioned in 1938 to design two housing schemes for Finsbury MB, part of a progressive policy that included their health centre (1936–38).

The wartime hiatus did Spa Green nothing but good. Bomb damage expanded the site, and it enabled Ove Arup to develop a new and more sophisticated structural system. By 1942 his experiments at Highpoint II (1936–38) into providing large windows and balconies on the principal façades had evolved into a system where all the structure was carried on reinforced cross walls and floors. This he termed the box frame, claimed to be economical of materials, and to offer flexibility in grouping different types of flats in one block. It freed Lubetkin to orchestrate the façades in syncopated patterns of coloured bricks, tiled balconies and glass, based on Caucasian carpet designs.

In the heady days of 1945–47 there were government loans for ample lifts, wood-block floors and a Garchey refuse system. The roofs of the two taller blocks have aerodynamic enclosures for drying clothes. The lower block, with smaller flats and a projecting estate office, proves the adaptability of the box frame in its serpentine curve.

These flats were the most visually arresting and structurally innovative of the immediate post-war years and showed Lubetkin and Skinner's continued commitment and vivacity of design, despite the demise of their firm, Tecton, in 1947.

LISTED grade II*, 22 December 1998
ADDRESS Rosebery Avenue, London EC1
ENGINEER Ove Arup and Partners
NEAREST UNDERGROUND Angel
ACCESS exteriors only

Berthold Lubetkin and Francis Skinner 1946–50

NEWBURY PARK BUS STATION

In 1937 Oliver Hill was commissioned to rebuild Newbury Park Station as a transport inter-change with shops and a staff canteen, as part of the electrification of the future Central Line. Frank Pick, London Transport's design patron, had met Hill at the Council of Art and Industry, and they collaborated on Hill's British Pavilion for the 1937 Paris Exhibition. Etched glass panels from the show were earmarked for the station. However, the war intervened, and in 1947 only the bus shelter and canteen were deemed essential and secured a building licence.

Just as his Midland Hotel, Morecambe, defined the integration of modern art and architecture in the 1930s, so the simplicity of Hill's bus shelter symbolises post-war aus-terity. It is a concrete barrel vault of painful thinness, cast on seven round-arched ribs and sheathed in copper. The primitive concrete construction, with no prestressing, indicates its pre-war origins. The building won a Festival of Britain Merit Award in 1951, with the most votes of any entry, and its distinctive Poole pottery blue plaque faces the road.

It is such a striking local landmark that it was quietly listed as early as 1981 – in a resurvey of older Redbridge buildings – as a 1930s design. Hill's curved forecourt walls have been swept away with road widening, but the shelter was thoroughly restored in 1994–95.

LISTED grade II, 14 March 1981
ADDRESS Eastern Avenue, Ilford
NEAREST UNDERGROUND Newbury Park
ACCESS any reasonable time

Oliver Hill 1947–49

BARN FIELD AND WOOD FIELD

Hampstead Borough Council commissioned these two blocks to replace houses destroyed by the first bomb to land on the borough, on 9 September 1940. It determined that the new housing should have a traditional character to reflect the eighteenth-century architecture for which Hampstead is noted, and in Donald McMorran found a sympathetic yet inventive designer. These, his first and most lavish flats, combine Soanic and Scandinavian devices to create a lean, spare but exceptionally well-proportioned classicism.

The grouping of windows with areas of blank walling is distinctive in McMorran's work. So too is the device of setting little tiled gabled roofs behind a very high parapet – here they step down the sloping site. The dwellings were well equipped for their date, with lifts as well as staircases – exceptional for a four-storey block. Their position can be seen in the slight projection on the outer face of the staircase halls. The open semi-basement has a store for each flat and a covered play area. Many of the flats retain their original fireplaces and cupboards.

The names Barn Field and Wood Field were taken from old field names on the site.

Listing was prompted when residents opposed a scheme by the local council to replace McMorran's finely detailed sash windows with uPVC units.

LISTED grade II, 22 December 2000
ADDRESS Parkhill Road, Hampstead
NEAREST UNDERGROUND Belsize Park
ACCESS exteriors only

Farquharson and McMorran 1947–49

DANEGROVE INFANTS SCHOOL

Because parts of the London Borough of Barnet used to be in Hertfordshire, a handful of its schools were the product of that county's celebrated primary-school building programme, Danegrove among them.

Danegrove demonstrates all Herts County Council's care to create humane child-sized spaces, using the Hills 8-foot 3-inch system of a prefabricated cold-rolled steel frame clad in concrete panels. Most of the schools were designed by an in-house team of architects and educationalists, but because of the demand a few were farmed out to private architects. The seven members of the Architects' Co-Partnership had studied together at the Architectural Association in the late 1930s, and shared the Hertfordshire group's strong social commitment. Leo de Syllas, the partner in charge, put much effort into making the system more architectural than was usual, giving the building a rare presence. This can be seen in the uptilted canopy over the entrance and in the staggered line of classrooms to the rear. These are particularly effective early examples of semi-open classroom planning, with French windows on to a play terrace, individual cloakroom areas and no wasteful corridor space.

A particularly striking mural by Fred Millett in the main hall was overpainted before the building was listed, but the school remains an enjoyable composition, an austere little pavilion in an open park.

LISTED grade II, 30 March 1993
ADDRESS Ridgeway Avenue, East Barnet
NEAREST STATION Oakleigh Park
ACCESS none

Architects' Co-Partnership 1950–51

GREENSIDE SCHOOL

Greenside and Brandlehow (see page 672) schools were built by Goldfinger using the LCC's budget for temporary buildings, following a commission in 1949. Both built for 240 children, they cost £131 and £124 per place respectively. Goldfinger achieved this remarkably low cost by devising his own concrete-framed system, a personal answer to the cold-rolled steel chosen for Hertfordshire's prefabricated schools, whose system the LCC adopted in 1951 as a means of building quickly within the limited budgets then coming into force.

Goldfinger's portal frames were erected in only four weeks, and were then infilled with brick and large windows – some of them canted and originally with blinds. The corridor planning is very simple; the sinks for paints are later additions. Intended for both juniors and infants, his design has a strength and architectural presence found in few schools at any date. A sympathetic extension was added in 1992.

The unassuming appearance of Greenside School belies the activity and creativity found within. Though identical in design, apart from Brandlehow's use of red bricks and Greenside's gentler yellow brick, the latter is listed grade II* because its foyer has an exceptional mural by Gordon Cullen, urban designer and artist to the *Architectural Review*, which features cameos of nature scenes, boats and the Comet aircraft then being developed.

LISTED grade II*, 30 March 1993
ADDRESS Westville Road, London W12
NEAREST UNDERGROUND Goldhawk Road/Ravenscourt Park
ACCESS exterior only

Ernö Goldfinger 1950–51

TRINITY METHODIST CHURCH

Trinity was built as a Congregational church, replacing one destroyed by a rocket save for its bell. Stark's father, himself an architect, was a prominent member of the congregation, but passed the job to his son, an LCC schools' architect. The young Stark brought in Handisyde, his student contemporary, and may have helped secure a building licence by gaining its admission within Lansbury's 'Live Architecture' exhibition site. The LCC dictated the choice of brick.

Trinity was one of the first post-war churches with an extensive range of meeting rooms. The 'church centre' became a popular model for subsequent churches of all denominations, particularly in new towns and estates with few community facilities. The church itself is largely top-lit, to eliminate traffic noise. Its roof is hung from above: this avoids internal columns while creating the sloping side walls recommended for the perfect acoustics. Large balconies were provided for overflow congregations on special occasions. The tall tower was prompted by the surviving bell, but the Scandinavian styling was Handisyde's inspiration. The building succeeds as an unusually powerful and satisfying whole, with most of the church's contemporary fittings and character remaining intact.

Trinity passed to the Methodists in 1974, when Edward D Mills made alterations to include lodgings for Vietnamese students. It still combines the dual functions of church and hostel.

LISTED grade II, 25 September 1998
ADDRESS East India Dock Road, London E14
NEAREST STATION (DLR) All Saints
ACCESS Saturday coffee mornings and Sunday services; call 020 7987 1794 for information

Cecil Handisyde and Douglas Rogers Stark 1950–51

SUSAN LAWRENCE SCHOOL

Susan Lawrence School was one of the first buildings in the Lansbury Neighbourhood, the 'live' showcase for reconstruction and town planning for the Festival of Britain. George Lansbury, the late Labour Party leader, had been a local councillor and MP, as had Susan Lawrence.

Yorke, Rosenberg and Mardall, an international team widely experienced in prefabricated construction, became specialist school designers with their Barclay School, Stevenage (see page 216), and there is a Hills 8-foot 3-inch steel frame under the stone and brick cladding. Infants are on the ground floor and juniors above, their assembly halls set prominently one above the other. YRM's innovation was to top light the lower corridor by placing that for the juniors above to one side, with glazed spurs linking it to paired classrooms. Vivid, geometric tiles by Peggy Angus enliven the dining hall and entrance hall, where passers by can also enjoy their quintessential period design. They also feature in the single-storey nursery school – commemorating Lansbury's widow, Elizabeth – added alongside in 1952, the first built by the LCC after the war.

Susan Lawrence School was the most admired of the low-key, Scandinavian-inspired Festival buildings at Lansbury. Its former entrance makes an urban square next to Frederick Gibberd's shopping centre (rejected for listing), and the whole is an unusually architectural response to the growing interest in child-centred school design.

LISTED grade II, 5 March 1998
ADDRESS Cordelia Street, London E14
NEAREST STATION (DLR) All Saints
ACCESS exteriors only

Yorke, Rosenberg and Mardall 1950–52

RC CHURCH OF SS MARY AND JOSEPH

Of all the buildings erected within the Festival of Britain's 'Live Architecture' exhibition at Lansbury, this was singled out for particular condemnation. Yet in 1951 only its foundations had been laid and criticism was based on drawings. Now we can admire the building as one of the most powerful church compositions of the immediate post-war years and its architect's finest achievement.

SS Mary and Joseph was built to replace a bombed Victorian church nearby. The funding War Damages Commission insisted that the new church should be the same size as the old, even though many of the congregation had moved away. The site was tight, and a square Greek cross plan was adopted, which has subsequently been adapted with remarkable ease to post-Vatican II liturgical requirements. Scott's baldacchino has been brought closer to the congregation without disturbing the building's character.

Outside, the stepped brickwork, ascending to a central tower which makes it a striking local landmark, is reminiscent of St Alban's, Golders Green (1930), by Scott's older brother, Giles. The parabolic arches, within and without, are certainly derived from Giles' scheme of 1946–47 for Coventry Cathedral. Inside, the stone dado, into which the Stations of the Cross by Peter Watts are set, anticipates that at St Leonard, St Leonards-on-Sea (see page 440).

LISTED grade II, 5 March 1998
ADDRESS Upper North Street, London E14
NEAREST STATION (DLR) All Saints
ACCESS regular services; call 020 7987 4523 for details

Adrian Gilbert Scott 1950–54

ST COLUMBA

Thanks to its central location and some remarkable ministers, St Columba, founded in 1883, had become the pre-eminent Scottish Presbyterian church in London before its destruction by an incendiary bomb in 1941. Maufe exhibited designs for its replacement as early as 1944. These were closely followed in the built scheme.

The bold design is strongly Scandinavian in the form of its tower and the simplicity of its stretches of blank Portland stone walling. Maufe also suggested seventeenth-century Scottish churches as an inspiration for what remains one of his most inventive exteriors. Internally the most impressive features are the heavily moulded capitals that grace the columns of its entrance hall and the stairs that lead to the first-floor church. A particular feature of the worship here is the Sunday lunch provided in the ground-floor hall, where services were held before the church was finally completed and dedicated in December 1955.

The church has the narrow passage aisles characteristic of Maufe's Anglican designs, but it is otherwise wider and lighter. The simple round-arched arcades lack any residual Gothic traits, and heraldic panels provide the principal decoration. However, some of his favourite collaborators were brought in to provide decorative touches, including a rose window by Moira Forsyth and a figure of St Columba over the entrance by Vernon Hill.

LISTED grade II, 29 March 1988
ADDRESS Pont Street, London SW1
NEAREST UNDERGROUND Knightsbridge
ACCESS open for Sunday services; call 020 7584 2321 for details

Edward Maufe 1950–55

TECHNICAL BLOCK A, HEATHROW

Heathrow was acquired in 1943–44 by the Air Ministry as a prospective civil airport for London. In 1950 Williams was invited to design a hangar, maintenance and office complex in collaboration with the British Overseas Airways Corporation. The result is an extraordinarily egalitarian building, with aircraft, workshops, offices and boardrooms for 4000 staff under a single roof.

Williams had conjectured complex groups of hangars in the war. Here, however, he produced a simple yet logical piece of geometry, with a hangar or 'pen' set in each of the four corners. They are divided by a dramatic central spine of engineering workshops and a cross axis of offices. Offices also form the principal façade.

Williams showed that his preferred concrete was cheaper than steel. Most spectacular are the vast cantilever arches at the entrance to each pen, each with a span of 102 metres and with the eared counterbalances found in Williams's Empire Pool of 1934. Suspended between these is a complex beam 2.7 metres deep, a technique adapted from bridge building, to support the folding doors and concrete braced zigzag roof. All these entrances survive, but three of the pens were given unsightly extensions in 1980 to take 747 aircraft, aircraft having got longer but not significantly taller. The 'south pen' now used for storage survives perfectly and even retains its original folding doors.

The combination of technical virtuosity and dramatic scale makes this an outstanding building.

LISTED grade II*, 2 April 1996
NEAREST UNDERGROUND Hatton Cross
ACCESS none (but looks good from the air)

Sir E Owen Williams and Partners 1950–55

THE PHOENIX SCHOOL

The Phoenix School was built as an open-air school for delicate and asthmatic children, replacing a school developed in 1921–22 by the LCC out of First World War army huts which was bombed in the Second World War. Earlier open-air schools had comprised light-weight timber shelters, without glazing or heating; here a more substantial hall and two-storey classrooms were proposed – although heating remained minimal. Children received three substantial meals a day, rested in the afternoons and had many lessons outdoors in the pleasant tree-lined courtyards.

Horace Farquharson and Donald McMorran are best known for their neo-classical public buildings and flats. Here they produced a simple yet elegant design of brick and glass, cladding a precast concrete frame system of construction without extraneous ornamentation. Covered walkways, now glazed in, link the central hall with its commanding bellcote to two-storey classrooms to the north and a lower housecraft room, now the dining hall, to the south. This area has been sympathetically extended to make a courtyard for primary-school children. Although the site is a narrow one, the mature trees and shrubs still give the school a tranquil atmosphere set away from bustling Bow Road.

Phoenix is now a Supported National Curriculum school, serving students between the ages of five and 17.

LISTED grade II*, 30 March 1993
ADDRESS Bow Road, London E3
NEAREST STATION Bow Road
ACCESS none

Farquharson and McMorran 1951–52

AUBREY WALK

That the late-Georgian terrace was ideally suited to the immediate post-war era of austere brick building is nowhere better demonstrated than in this group by the master of the genre. Erith conceived the paved forecourt and simple railings as part of the composition, a careful massing of blank walls either side of round-headed relieving arches and blind windows. The three houses (two have now been united) have few windows facing the street because they overlook a large shared rear garden, and here Erith adopted a contrastingly vivacious Regency style of end bows and a first-floor verandah. The houses were built in the grounds of the adjoining Aubrey House and unfortunately the contrast of styles cannot be seen from the street.

Internally, the small scale is resolved by tightly planned staircases with curved ends and by Erith's carefully restrained detailing.

The design was suggested by nearby houses (nos 2–26) of c. 1826, but is a far more inventive composition. It was early admired by champions of modernism. In 1964 Ian Nairn called it 'not a copy or a pastiche, but the real thing, designed by somebody who is living a century and a half out of phase. It shows up the fussy modernity of the houses opposite, something I wish that I did not have to admit'.

LISTED grade II, 29 March 1988
ADDRESS 15, 17 and 19 Aubrey Walk, London W8
NEAREST STATIONS Notting Hill Gate/Holland Park
ACCESS exterior only

Raymond Erith 1951–52

BEVIN COURT

Skinner, Bailey and Lubetkin were the successor practice to Tecton, celebrated architects of the Penguin Pool (1934), who went on to build housing in Finsbury and Bethnal Green after the war. Their first involvement with blitzed Holford Square was to erect a bust to Lenin, who had stayed there in 1902–03. But it was vandalised, despite police protection, and was quietly buried in April 1951. When the replacement block was named after the first foreign minister of the Cold War period, Francis Skinner quipped that only two letters needed changing. In his third scheme for Finsbury, Lubetkin had to build at a high density while retaining a public open space. His scheme of staggered blocks was frustrated by the savage cuts in government housing subsidies introduced in August 1947, and a single seven-storey block proved cheaper.

Bevin Court has an innovative Y plan to allow maximum sunshine and minimal overlooking. The alternation of floor plans, made possible by the box frame, found full expression here in a chequer pattern of brick and precast panels, now painted. Holford House, four-storeys of maisonettes, provides a link with the surrounding Georgian street pattern. The climax of Bevin Court is its central staircase, a series of suspended half-landings in the central drum, between which stairs fly seemingly unsupported. It is the ultimate example of Lubetkin's obsession with pattern and movement – for humans. The entrance mural is by Peter Yates, later of Ryder and Yates (see Killingworth, page 114).

LISTED grade II*, 22 December 1998
ENGINEER Ove Arup and Partners
ADDRESS Cruickshank Street, London WC1
NEAREST UNDERGROUND Angel/King's Cross (also mainline station)
ACCESS exterior and stairwell only

Skinner, Bailey and Lubetkin 1951–54

ALL SAINTS

A new church was planned in the late 1930s, but was postponed by the war. Afterwards, shortages dictated that it be built in two phases. The entrance front containing the small baptistry and Chapel of the Blessed Sacrament was consecrated in 1951 and the body of the church followed only in 1957.

The main space is square, dramatically spanned by two reinforced-concrete arches which support a central cupola and a corona of pendant lights. Cachemaille-Day wrote as early as 1946 of the need to bring celebrant and congregation closer in worship, and his 1950s churches experimented with liturgical ideas when clients allowed. All Saints is among his most advanced designs. The choir was originally placed in the centre of the congregation, as pioneered at D F Martin-Smith's influential John Keble Church, Mill Hill (1936) but was soon moved to stalls at the back of the hall.

The sanctuary itself is a wide shallow apse lined in silver leaf, and exemplifies Cachemaille-Day's interest in light and shade. The abstract coloured glass in the cupola adds warmth and a hallowed quality to the space, while the figurative glass in the Lady chapel is unusally effective, for it is sandblasted, giving a shimmer to the painted details. Cachemaille-Day excelled at elaborate concrete fonts, and this example represents the Seven Sacraments. The stone carving over the main entrance is by Bainbridge Copnall.

LISTED grade II, 15 April 1991
ADDRESS Uxbridge Road, Hanworth, Feltham
NEAREST STATION Feltham
ACCESS daily; use side entrance on Woodlawn Drive

N F Cachemaille-Day 1951, 1956–57

YMCA INDIAN STUDENT HOSTEL

Tubbs' hostel is a gallant symbol of a newly independent nation, built with money from the Indian government and international sponsors as a base for Indian students new to England.

There is a ground-floor restaurant, and an ample staircase leads down to the Mahatma Gandhi Memorial Hall in the basement. Tubbs was anxious to avoid parallel lines where possible – hence the acute angles of the Festival-style stair and the hall's raking rear windows. The large first-floor windows light reading and television rooms and on the roof is a non-denominational prayer room. The hostel was intended as an important cultural centre, and the open planning and modern style, from the architect of the Dome of Discovery, were a striking contrast to the surrounding ruins seen in photographs of 1952.

The building's jewel-like image has been diluted with the subsequent building of the entire block in a similar style, but its relationship with Fitzroy Square remains critical. It sits on the corner between Robert Adam's two terraces, which governed its height and massing but not its style. The rooftop non-denominational prayer room gives weight to the corner of the square.

Tubbs' extension, at right-angles, is virtually identical in style and provides further bedrooms across an entirely glazed staircase link.

LISTED grade II, 6 March 1996
ADDRESS 41 Fitzroy Square, London W1
NEAREST UNDERGROUND Warren Street
ACCESS exterior and restaurant only

Ralph Tubbs 1952, 1962–64

HALLFIELD SCHOOL

Denys Lasdun was commissioned by Paddington MB to build its large Hallfield Estate on behalf of Tecton in 1946, and after the firm's disbandment he and Lindsay Drake took over the scheme. A school was also intended at Spa Green, but only here was one realised as part of the initial building campaign.

The patterning of the housing's ten- and six-storey blocks is reminiscent of Spa Green, but the school is more clearly Lasdun's. He reacted against system building with a design that is keenly architectural, while providing genuine intimacy for the smallest child.

Juniors and infants share a common entrance, which leads to a pair of assembly halls reminiscent of that by Gropius and Fry at Impington, Cambridge (1938), set one above the other. There is a mural by Gordon Cullen, himself a member of Tecton in the 1930s. The junior school comprises a two-storeyed spine, its cranked plan a miniature of that Lasdun was later to build at the University of East Anglia. The obtuse corners give a rippling effect to the long mullion windows lighting the corridors. Lasdun likened this spine to a branch, and the infants' rooms it shelters to its leaves or petals. These are four pairs of classrooms clustered around a low corridor, whose round windows are set at the height of the smallest children. The Lilliputian scale makes no compromises for grown-ups.

An extension by Caruso St John has recently been approved.

LISTED grade II, 29 March 1988; grade II*, 30 March 1993
ADDRESS Inverness Terrace, London W2
NEAREST UNDERGROUND Bayswater
ACCESS exterior only

Drake and Lasdun 1953–55

TRADES UNION CONGRESS MEMORIAL BUILDING

Congress House combines the functions of war memorial, public hall, offices, council chamber and education centre on a confined site abutting Lutyens's YWCA hostel. A competition was held in 1948, when there was little prospect of building. When it was finally completed, with little modification, *Architectural Design*, the Brutalists' mouthpiece, dedicated a special issue to it (December 1957). Such was its importance to the years of austerity.

The main façade is an honest curtain wall of committee rooms, dominated by a giant bronze figure by Bernard Meadow. The composition then spills down Dyott Street, in a surfeit of contrasting curves and volumes that define the cantilevered horseshoe staircase, the projecting library, and garaging. Inside, the council and secretariat rooms are elaborately panelled, mainly with Commonwealth timber, while the basement conference hall is toplit through hexagonal roof coffers. This hexagonal patterning dominates the courtyard around which the building is massed, and which is the memorial. The end wall of the YWCA was faced in Genoa marble and Jacob Epstein's giant *pietà* of a worker, carved from ten tons of stone, was unveiled early in 1958. The symphony of muted green-grey surfaces remains moving, despite the insertion of an extra glass membrane roof.

Listing in 1988 coincided with a substantial upgrading of this consistently elegant building to modern fire standards.

LISTED grade II*, March 1988
ENGINEER Ove Arup and Partners
ADDRESS Great Russell Street, London WC1
NEAREST UNDERGROUND Tottenham Court Road
ACCESS part open for special events and Open House

David du Rieu Aberdeen 1953–57

BOUSFIELD SCHOOL

Bousfield is full of wit and humanity as well as architectural invention. Geoffry Powell, who lived locally, described the difficulty of finding proprietary modern fittings such as windows and rooflights in the early 1950s and how every detail had to be designed from first principles.

The school comprises a single-storey infants' department and two-storey juniors' on either side of paired assembly halls, around which are the offices. The architects designed a steel frame on a 3-foot 4-inch grid, left exposed and infilled with aluminium-framed curtain walling similar to that at Great Arthur House, Golden Lane. The result is one of the most architectural schools of its day. Early Chamberlin, Powell and Bon schemes use brilliant colours: here the yellow verticals and blue horizontal panels, with green where they meet, are a beginners' guide to colour theory. The water tank in the playground resembles a giant lollypop or Belisha beacon. The entrance from The Boltons has a water jump instead of fencing – for deterring school inspectors, quipped Powell.

A plaque records that Beatrix Potter once lived in a house on the site. Eye-level slits in the wall alongside give good views over an open-air theatre with steps sloping down below ground level, and diving under a classroom block via a short tunnel.

The ensemble is one of the most charming of the post-war schools built by private architects for the LCC.

LISTED grade II, 30 March 1993
ADDRESS South Bolton Gardens, London SW5
NEAREST UNDERGROUND South Kensington
ACCESS exterior only

Chamberlin, Powell and Bon 1954–56

10 REGENT'S PARK ROAD

These small flats replaced a single bombed house in a stuccoed terrace. Goldfinger was required to make the proportions of his building fit with those of its neighbours, but the houses to either side were not quite in line, so while the flats adjoin the house to the right, their balcony fronts align with that to the left. His red brick and exposed wire-brushed concrete frame are nevertheless immediately striking.

Goldfinger was called in by ten friends who had formed a Housing Society. The 1936 Housing Act had created the forerunner of the modern housing association, which could raise a 90 per cent mortgage through a local authority. This was common practice in Scandinavia but was rarely adopted here for fear of legal disputes.

There were originally two flats per floor, the rooftop studios hidden behind a terrace and parapet so that the block appears no taller than its neighbours. The flats are compact, with folding partitions and timber fittings. The entrance, over a communal basement laundry and garden room, has square-paned surrounds reminiscent of Goldfinger's own Willow Road house. It leads to a cantilevered staircase without risers, a device Goldfinger was to repeat in later one-off private houses.

The block shows Goldfinger for the first time exploiting the sculptural possibilities of a frame-and-infill composition, as inspired by his tutor Auguste Perret.

LISTED grade II, 22 December 1998
ADDRESS Primrose Hill, London NW1
NEAREST UNDERGROUND Camden Town
ACCESS exterior only

Ernö Goldfinger 1954–56

USK STREET

From Columbia Market to the first LCC flats, the story of nineteenth-century charitable housing can be told within Bethnal Green. Peter Benenson, deputy head of the borough's Housing Committee and later founder of Amnesty International, sought to continue this tradition of quality housing, and was anxious that local people should be rehoused within the borough and not moved out to the suburbs. The area was popular with sociologists, who uncovered exceptionally strong surviving bonds of kinship within extended families. Denys Lasdun's was one of four modern practices appointed to an architects' panel in 1951.

The area granted Lasdun was bisected by roads and surviving buildings. Sulkin House replaced a Victorian church, and its basement contains the boiler house for the entire scheme of three slabs and two towers. The two listed towers have a butterfly plan, with 12 two-storey maisonettes set either side of a central lift and staircase. Lasdun successfully persuaded councillors that maisonettes were not only popular with tenants but saved money on lifts. The towers pioneered his 'cluster' concept, separating noisy services from flats, as Goldfinger was to do at Balfron Tower, while the facing lines of balconies on either side was a rare encouragement of neighbourliness. Lasdun developed these ideas subsequently at Keeling House (see page 528).

LISTED grade II, 22 December 1998
ADDRESS Sulkin House, Usk Street; Trevelyan House, Morpeth Street, London E2
NEAREST UNDERGROUND Bethnal Green
ACCESS exteriors only

Fry, Drew, Drake and Lasdun 1955–58

RC OUR LADY OF MOUNT CARMEL AND ST SIMON STOCK

A Carmelite church was established in Kensington by Father Hermann, a German Jewish musician who had converted to Catholicism. In 1862 he was invited to England, and in 1865–66 a church was built by E W Pugin. A monastery was added behind by Edward Goldie in 1888. This survives, but in 1943 the church was gutted by incendiaries, and the remains were struck by a rocket in 1944.

Scott's church is built of beautifully-laid pale brick. Its luminance is reminiscence of his first parish church, the Annunciation, Bournemouth, of 1906, but is more subtle. The sanctuary is made to seem higher than it is by concealed windows hidden behind the chancel arch, which light the high, gilded reredos. Passage aisles are cut through the broad concrete trusses that form the arches across the wide nave. They stop short of the roof, a distinctive feature comparable with those at Goodhart-Rendel's RC Our Lady of the Rosary (see page 616), so that light can freely enter from the clerestories above. For there are no windows in the nave walls.

The original church was noted for the quality of its Cavaillé Col organ, and in December 1965 a new organ was installed at the (liturgical) west end by Ralph Downes, designer of the organ in the Royal Festival Hall.

LISTED grade II, 25 September 1998
ADDRESS 41 Kensington Church Street, London W8
NEAREST UNDERGROUND High Street Kensington
ACCESS open daily; call 020 7937 9866 for more information

Sir Giles Gilbert Scott 1957–59

KEELING HOUSE

Denys Lasdun followed Usk Street (see page 524) with London's first post-war slum clearance project. Here he fulfilled his ambition to build a tall 'cluster block', inspired by his visit to the US in 1954 and the writings of Kevin Lynch.

The 'cluster' was identified as a visual and sociological unit of size and grain equivalent to an East End street, whose disappearing values were being recognised by sociologists such as Rattray Taylor. Lasdun conducted his own survey, and Claredale Street was early recognised as an alternative to new-town planning.

Keeling House required the demolition of just six houses, and fits neatly amid Victorian streets. At 16 storeys, it was one of the first tall blocks, with maisonette units grouped in four pairs around a central lift and stair tower. There was thus exceptional sound insulation, yet neighbours could call to each other across the balconies, and on alternate floors the staircase lobbies could be used for storage. On the fifth floor, the maximum height for firemen's ladders, there are bedsitters. The elevations, built of reinforced concrete with precast end panels, have the clean proportions found in 1930s modernism.

In 1992 the block was hastily emptied because of spalling concrete, and long sat empty. In 1999, however, it was sold for £1.3 million to a private developer, and restored by Munkenbeck and Marshall.

LISTED grade II*, 23 November 1993
ADDRESS Claredale Street, London E2
ENGINEER Ove Arup and Partners
NEAREST STATION Cambridge Heath/**UNDERGROUND** Bethnal Green
ACCESS exterior only

Fry, Drew, Drake and Lasdun 1957–59

THE FIRS

Patrick Gwynne designed this house for Mr and Mrs Otto Edler with his customary play-fulness, both in the materials selected and in its curvaceous plan. The Edlers wanted all the principal rooms to face south over the garden, so Gwynne made this elevation wider than the north, with bowed brick walls to either side. The roof, with a bold mosaic-clad fascia, tilts up towards the garden front, where it is supported on steel columns that also carry a projecting balcony.

The same richness of shapes and materials continues inside. There is a boldness of scale in The Firs that is rare in Gwynne's surviving domestic work, particularly in the living room, which has a sliding screen to separate it from the study when a single space is not required; and big steel windows and cupboards that revolve to conceal the television. The fireplace wall is lined in marble. The circular stairwell is another distinctive Gwynne feature, that was repeated in his house nearby for Max and Anne Bruh (see page 542 for Beechworth Close). Gwynne's sense of shape and proportion was particularly well seen in the kitchen, where he installed a kidney-shaped island table.

The client was introduced to Gwynne by the builder Leslie Bilsby (see page 722). The Edlers' house has a more distinctively 1950s character than Gwynne's later work.

LISTED grade II, 28 November 1996
ADDRESS Spaniard's End, Hampstead Heath, London NW3
NEAREST UNDERGROUND Hampstead
ACCESS none

Patrick Gwynne 1958

KENSINGTON CENTRAL LIBRARY

Vincent Harris claimed that Kensington did not want a modern design for its library. Nevertheless, in February 1959 it was targeted by 'Anti-Ugly Action' – students from the Royal College of Art opposed to traditional or bland new buildings. Today Harris is recognised as the leading town hall specialist of the century, and Kensington Central Library as one of his last great works.

Perhaps the design's conservatism owed something to the project's long genesis. A new library was first proposed in 1900, and Harris was commissioned in 1956 after a design by Percy Thomas was thwarted by the Second World War.

This is unmistakably a Harris building. The arched end openings are a signature, first seen in his County Hall competition entry of 1907 and in built form at Bristol Council House (1939–57). Here they carry busts of Chaucer and Caxton and the parapet is surmounted by a figure of Genius by William McMillan, who also did the large stone lion and unicorn pylons which symbolise the borough's royal status.

Inside, the planning is spacious and satisfying. The end pavilions, one the entrance, the other the children's library, are clad in Doulting stone; between them the lending library is simply finished, but the lofty proportions and columniation give great dignity. The first-floor reference library has sumptuous walnut panelling and both spaces retain original mahogany bookcases.

LISTED grade II*, 24 April 1998
ADDRESS Hornton Street, London W8
NEAREST UNDERGROUND High Street Kensington
ACCESS open Monday, Tuesday, Thursday and Friday, 9.30–20.00; Wednesday, 9.30–13.00; Saturday, 9.30–17.00

E Vincent Harris 1958–60

ST PAUL

St Paul (nearly always referred to as St Paul's Bow Common) is the vanguard of the Liturgical Movement in the Anglican church. In 1952 its bombed predecessor was taken on by Father Gresham Kirkby, a follower of Conrad Noel and an enthusiast for new churches. He admired the freestanding altar at the nearby Royal Foundation of St Katharine by the silversmith Keith Murray, who introduced him to Robert Maguire. Their partnership and the New Churches Research Group were founded as St Paul was under construction.

St Paul is a stepped cube, set round a central altar under a central pyramidal roof. The altar is raised up two steps under a baldacchino of black steel. Around it the congregation sit on benches, and around them the processional route runs behind a segmental arched arcade later decorated with mosaics by Charles Lutyens. Beyond this project side chapels and the entrance porch – where, symbolically, sits the font, formed from a Doulton's vat. The inscription outside is by Ralph Beyer: 'Truly this is none other but the House of God. This is the gate of heaven'.

Maguire brought to church building the Wittkowerian influence in geometric forms and use of industrial fittings that had inspired the New Brutalists. It was immediately heralded as a 'machine for worshipping in', for its building exactly coincided with Peter Hammond's campaign for liturgical planning, which culminated in his *Liturgy and Architecture* of 1960.

LISTED grade II*, 29 March 1988
ADDRESS Bow Common, Burdett Road, London E3
NEAREST UNDERGROUND Mile End
ACCESS regular services; groups by appointment on 020 7987 4941

Maguire and Murray 1958–60

30A HENDON AVENUE

Geoffry Powell of Chamberlin, Powell and Bon claimed that with the exception of the Ross-dales, for whom he designed this house, he never had a client who liked the practice's work. Dr Rossdale had practised in Germany, before 'getting a forewarning that Jews would be liquidated' as Powell put it. In France he was only allowed to practice in Algeria, so he came to Britain and requalified.

The firm's only private house, it adopted the plan, popular around 1960, of setting all the living accommodation in a single storey over garages. A brick core rises through the centre, culminating in a central clerestory, and it is surrounded on the first floor by a timber-framed structure, clad in weatherboarding and reached by an external stair.

The brick core forms a space more than 3-metres square, serving on the first floor as a partially open fireplace and sitting area. The living and dining areas are arranged to one side, with a kitchen beyond, accessible both from the dining end and from a passageway which serves the three bedrooms and two bathrooms.

The expression of materials and plan is intelligent and logical. As Ian Nairn said, the architects 'saw the problem fresh, and the result is delightful'.

LISTED grade II, 28 November 1996
ADDRESS Finchley, London N3
NEAREST UNDERGROUND Finchley Central
ACCESS none

Chamberlin, Powell and Bon 1959

COMMONWEALTH INSTITUTE

The Commonwealth Institute is one of the most carefully thought-out experiments in post-war English architecture. It replaced T E Collcutt's Imperial Institute of 1887–93, and was conceived as a modern educational exhibition in which each country in the Commonwealth devised their own displays on an equal footing. James Gardner, exhibition designer of the Dome of Discovery at the Festival of Britain, was involved from the first, and the uninterrupted central space, served by a circular ramped platform, is strongly reminiscent of that earlier synthesis of architecture and display. The youth-centred approach was close to the heart of Stirrat Johnson-Marshall, as architect to the Ministry of Education before this appointment. The concept of a 'tent in the park' was his, though the detailed design was by his assistant Roger Cunliffe.

The dominating feature is the roof, clad in copper given by Rhodesia and Nyasaland (now Malawi). In looking for a means of achieving a clear span, Cunliffe and the engineers Alan Harris and James Sutherland were particularly inspired by Félix Candela's anticlastic or double-curved roofs. This is the outstanding English example of the hyperbolic-paraboloid roof, which enjoyed a brief fashion in the early 1960s – most famously at the Sydney Opera House. While the unassuming wall-cladding and modest ancillary blocks reflect the low budget available, the entrance approach sequence across a water garden devised by Sylvia Crowe remains exhilarating.

LISTED grade II*, 12 October 1988
ADDRESS Holland Park, London W11
NEAREST UNDERGROUND High Street
Kensington
ACCESS exterior only; future uncertain

Robert Matthew, Johnson-Marshall and Partners 1960–62

ROYAL COLLEGE OF PHYSICIANS

The building which brought Lasdun to prominence was an exceptional commission, a rare modern ceremonial building constructed to an ample budget. The Royal College of Physicians was founded in 1518 as the highest of three 'orders' of doctors, and evolved as a regulatory and educational organisation until its premises off Trafalgar Square had become too small.

There the college officers had put on their robes in the censors' room and marched through to the library next door. Lasdun used this ritual to inform the entire plan of his building, extending the ritual from the censors' room at the heart of the building through the large staircase hall to the first-floor great library. On the other side are dining halls, which can be altered by means of a screen which rises into the wall at the touch of a switch.

The building is further defined by its materials: white, mosaic-clad concrete for the structural elements, and grey brick for infill walls and ancillary accommodation. The entrance, facing Regent's Park, is a good example of this, with mosaic for the principal entrance and brick for the kidney-shaped lecture theatre. Lasdun's additions in 1994 are subdued and elegant, and create a new axis across the hall.

The building is reminiscent of Frank Lloyd Wright, one of Lasdun's favourite architects, and particularly of the formality of the Guggenheim Museum. The planning has also been likened to William Harvey's seventeenth-century plans of blood circulation, which are hung in the library.

LISTED grade I, 24 April 1998
ADDRESS Outer Circle, Regent's Park, London NW1
NEAREST UNDERGROUND Regent's Park/Great Portland Street
ACCESS open for special events

Denys Lasdun and Partners 1960–64, 1994–96

HOUSE IN BEECHWORTH CLOSE

Max and Anne Bruh wanted a house that would be easy to run, 'with a certain toughness to withstand the mild ravages which even the nicest teenagers are liable to perpetrate'. Gwynne was the ideal choice, for few post-war architects of private houses have such a mastery of hard finishes, and here the dominating materials are natural timber, terrazzo and mosaic. The Bruhs were introduced to Gwynne's work when they saw The Firs nearby (see page 530).

The Bruhs had acquired part of a large garden with fine mature Victorian planting, facing north towards Hampstead Heath. Gwynne placed the living room across the end of the house so that it could have both north and south aspects. The dominant feature, however, is a central stairwell, lined in timber, generous in scale and style and lit by a circular skylight. The plan resembles a group of four houses he had built near Kingston-upon-Thames a year before (now mutilated), but here the larger scale enabled him to set back the upper storey, the difference emphasised by contrasting grey-black bricks and white render. Inside, Gwynne's built-in cupboards and wall finishes survive unaltered and give the house an astounding homogeneity. Their intricate detailing and clever contrivance demonstrate his exquisite finesse, and this is perhaps his finest surviving house after his own.

LISTED grade II, 26 April 1999
ADDRESS Hampstead Heath, London NW3
NEAREST UNDERGROUND Hampstead
ACCESS none

Patrick Gwynne 1961

BARKING STATION BOOKING HALL

The electrification of Eastern Region's suburban lines formed part of British Railways' 1955 Modernisation Plan. A number of new stations and signal boxes were required, but at Barking the trackside buildings were not rebuilt. A new booking hall was constructed on the bridge over the tracks, largely to advertise the railways' new modern image.

John Ward's design very closely resembles 'on an English smaller scale' – as *The Builder* condescendingly put it – the frontage block of Rome station, by Eugenio Montuori with the engineer Leo Calini. This was the result of a competition in 1947 to complete Angiolo Mazzoni's 1930s terminus. With its thin, concrete beams forming a dramatic canopy and upsweeping roof, infilled with glass, Barking – like Rome – entices the traveller with an expressionistic image of light and speed while keeping the actual locomotives and tracks out of view. There is a lively sense of movement despite its small scale, a lashing of red paint and the infiltration of shops into the concourse.

LISTED grade II, 24 November 1995
ADDRESS Station Parade, Barking
ACCESS any reasonable time

British Railways Eastern Region 1961

CENTRE POINT

Centre Point grew out of an LCC scheme for a roundabout at Tottenham Court Road. In October 1959 an alternative was offered, when Seifert proposed a 29-storey office block and an eight-storey block of shops, a bank and flats, linked by a bridge over the proposed road. His client was Harry Hyams, who held the land.

The tower was subsequently made narrower, but four storeys were added, with the top floors intended as a restaurant and open gallery. Its elevations date from 1962, after work had begun on the rear block. It was among the first towers entirely clad in precast concrete, in inverted 'T'-shaped sections, to a gently curved plan and with a progressive narrowing from bottom to top. This combination produced a genuine *brise-soleil* over which sunlight gently ripples, the movement suggesting a real piece of op-architecture worthy of Bridget Riley or Mary Quant. The block of flats is similarly precast but more solid in design above glazed first-floor showrooms. When its corner bank was converted to a bar a mosaic panel was revealed by Jupp Dernbach-Mayern, who also designed the mosaics for the fountain.

Centre Point was initially admired as the symbol of 'swinging London'. It acquired notoriety when Hyams set an unrealistically high rent, and it remained empty until the late 1970s. It is now fully occupied.

LISTED grade II, 24 November 1995
ADDRESS New Oxford Street, London WC1
NEAREST UNDERGROUND Tottenham Court Road
ACCESS exteriors only

Richard Seifert and Partners 1961–66

HEINZ UK HEADQUARTERS AND LABORATORIES

This pair of buildings are the only English work by America's leading office designer, and were one of the first greenfield headquarters here.

When in 1953 Loewy Engineering had built laboratories near Poole, it had contemplated building housing also. By 1960 there was sufficient car ownership for Heinz's move from Harlesden to be welcomed by its commuting workforce.

Gordon Bunshaft of Skidmore, Owings and Merrill first met H J Heinz II while working for Louis Skidmore on the New York World's Fair in 1939, and the two became lasting friends. Best known for his New York office towers, Bunshaft also pioneered the greenfield headquarters – the luxurious office and social complex in an idealised landscape – with his General Life Insurance Company of Bloomfield, Connecticut (1952–57). This was the formula applied to the ten-acre green-belt site at Hayes Park, with one difference. Around 1960 Bunshaft turned from steel framing in favour of concrete, then belatedly fashionable in the United States and inspired by his experiences in Turkey and Belgium.

The two buildings are set in echelon, the laboratories set back in a subordinate if complementary fashion and linked by a basement corridor. A condition of the planning permission was that the buildings should appear only two storeys in height, so the ground floor was sunk into the sloping hillside. While the entrance is at ground level, a cut-away bank brings light to the rear canteen, and other ground-floor rooms are lit principally from an internal courtyard, which has a shallow reflective pool. Contemporary critics were astounded that in the surrounding offices all the ceiling lights were symmetrically placed to give a perfect reflection by night. This epitomises the attention to detail that Bunshaft gave his clients: there is not a duct or extractor out of place. The external shell is crisply finished, although the concrete has darkened over the years. Its elegantly waisted concrete stanchions, on an American 4-foot 8-inch grid, stand forward of the glazing, so

Skidmore, Owings and Merrill 1962–65

HEINZ UK HEADQUARTERS AND LABORATORIES

they frame every view from the perimeter offices – a test of their precision. The inner areas are an early example of open planning in Britain. In the laboratories food-testing booths are deliberately dark so that tasters can concentrate their senses.

Heinz's headquarters sought to create a crisp pure image. It originally sat amid giant elms; since their destruction it has appeared to float over the landscape. It was described as 'ruthlessly benevolent' in 1965, a measure, perhaps, of how our working lives have changed thanks to American influences like those pioneered here.

LISTED grade II*, 24 November 1995
ADDRESS Hayes Park, Hillingdon
NEAREST STATION Hayes and Harlington, then bus
UNDERGROUND to Uxbridge or Hillingdon. Just north of A4020
ACCESS exterior only from public footpath

Skidmore, Owings and Merrill 1962–65

1 AYLMER CLOSE

This house suits the tougher architectural mood that emerged in the 1960s, despite being largely built of timber. Edward Samuel was never a prolific architect, and most of his private houses are in Ireland. At Aylmer Close he created a vocabulary of prefabricated timber units which he developed as a building system, called the Oliver Unit House, but which was not widely adopted.

The house is long and rectangular, with a small projection to the front forming an entrance terrace over a brick base, and a study projecting to the rear. It is divided into two parts, with an adults' area comprising an open-plan living and dining area, a master bedroom and the study, and a children's wing with its own playroom and eating area. A discreet small addition has been made to this, in the same timber idiom.

Samuel's system created a chunky idiom of broad timber cladding. This aesthetic is continued into the interior, with the frame expressed in varnished timber, fitted timber cupboards and room dividers. Samuel says that he was inspired by the exceptional landscape, with a lake, developed for a Georgian house which survives alongside as flats. The house is reminiscent of contemporary work by HKPA and Edward Cullinan.

Listing saved the building from proposed demolition.

LISTED grade II, 19 August 1996
ADDRESS Stanmore, Harrow
NEAREST UNDERGROUND Stanmore
ACCESS exterior only

Edward Samuel 1963

SWISS COTTAGE LIBRARY

The library and adjoining baths were all that were built of a civic centre proposed for the borough of Hampstead, a scheme aborted by local government reorganisation. The library was thus a memorial to Conservative Hampstead's civic pride before its absorbtion within LB Camden. It is the finest public library of the decade, and the first of a series of civic buildings which preoccupied Sir Basil Spence, Bonnington and Collins in later years.

The cigar-shaped library is set on a slope. This is emphasised by the contrast between the plain semi-basement and the upper floors, where precast black-basalt aggregate panels contrast with light concrete projecting fins. The public areas are planned at first- and second-floor levels around a double-height exhibition space, reached via a deliberately low ground-floor entrance. At either end are the lending and reference libraries, both with spiral stairs serving galleries. Between them are a children's library and music library. Spence planned the library to appear as open as possible, though the movement of books was tightly supervised. Glazed screens permit the penetration of light through the building, their vertical panels developed from the narrow windows and fins of the exterior. This verticality is a contrast to the strong horizontals of Spence's baths next door, which were rejected for listing by the DCMS and which are being demolished.

LISTED grade II, 2 December 1997
ADDRESS Avenue Road, London NW3
NEAREST UNDERGROUND Swiss Cottage
ACCESS library open Monday, Thursday, 10.00–19.00; Tuesday, Wednesday, Friday, 10.00–18.00; Saturday, 10.00–17.00

Sir Basil Spence, Bonnington and Collins 1963–64

JACK STRAW'S CASTLE

Such was Erith's success in recreating a historic landmark that in 1974 his building was listed as retaining eighteenth-century fabric. Yet only the cellars survive from the former coaching inn, first recorded in 1713, which was damaged by a landmine in 1941. By 1961 Charringtons wanted a smart restaurant. Erith was just completing his tasteful remodelling of No. 10 Downing Street, but he had long nursed an ambition to build in timber, and his application coincided with the height of interest in prefabrication then being popularised by buildings such as Centre Point, a comparison that amused him. The LCC and RFAC approved the design, although prim residents agitated for more sober Georgian proprieties. Frivolity prevailed. The frame took just eight weeks to erect, then the roof was completed before the walls were weatherboarded.

Like Centre Point, too, Jack Straw's is a stylistic palimpsest. A seventeenth-century cornice lurks between Gothick glazing and crenellations, while the canted bays, charming courtyard verandah and towers suggest early nineteenth-century additions. Only the Gothick arch in the rear garden is pure pastiche. The ground floor was originally three bars, the long room divided by a gentlemen's lavatory until 1971. The firebacks have the initials E R, tempting though it is to read them as R E.

In 2002 there were proposals to convert the building into flats.

LISTED grade II, 14 May 1974
ADDRESS North End Way, London NW3
NEAREST UNDERGROUND Hampstead
ACCESS pub opening hours

Raymond Erith 1963–64

SCHREIBER HOUSE

It was James Gowan's commission from C S Schreiber, the furniture manufacturer, that finally prompted the collapse of his partnership with James Stirling. It provided the perfect opportunity to refine the aesthetic of hard brick and glass which the pair had evolved through their Ham Common and Leicester jobs into a personal, smaller-scaled idiom. In the austerity of Gowan's independent work an overt kinship with early modern sources, particularly with German architecture of the 1920s, combines with an appreciation of classical proportions learned from Rudolf Wittkower and Colin Rowe.

The vertical bands of aluminium glazing and grey Staffordshire brick are the abiding and sombre image of the house, making it appear taller than its three storeys and basement. It is designed on a rigorous 3-foot grid, which determined not only the wall thicknesses but the exposed concrete trough ceilings and the panelling. Most of the rooms run right through the house, so that they can enjoy both the sun and views of Hampstead Heath to the north. A feature is the built-in furniture, designed by Gowan, made by Schreiber's factory. Money was spent not on ornament but on high-quality materials.

In 1967 Gowan returned to design a sunken pool house. This complements the angularity of the house by being entirely round, with a domed roof of glass and turf.

LISTED grade II, 15 July 1998
ADDRESS West Heath Road, London NW3
NEAREST UNDERGROUND Hampstead
ACCESS exterior only

James Gowan 1963–64, 1967

HORNSEY LIBRARY

Like Basil Spence's library at Swiss Cottage (page 554), the opulent scale of Hornsey Library is a valediction by a small, progressive Conservative authority before in 1965 it became part of larger, Labour Haringey. But Hornsey's architects and artists were local, and it was praised in librarians' periodicals rather than the architectural press.

The long frontage clad in rippling precast-concrete panels does not prepare one for the complex interior. It is a building of two halves, separated by an entrance set under the projecting first-floor reference library. To the left is the adult lending library for books and records, a double-height space with a gallery on two sides reached via a cantilevered staircase. The smaller rooms are set around a glazed courtyard. Another cantilevered stair leads to the reference library, with brightly patterned shelving and fixed desks, and a meeting hall with its own foyer and coffee bar. Below, the children's library was separate, with its own entrance and a story-telling room, but has since moved into the former news-paper reading room.

Works of art tell Hornsey's history. On the west wall the fountain behind T E Huxley Jones's attenuated bathing figure has plaques in the shape of the borough and its medieval church tower. Frederick Mitchell engraved a map of the borough on the staircase window, with a vignette of the new library at its centre.

LISTED grade II, 23 March 2001
ADDRESS Hornsey Library, Haringey Park, Crouch End, London
NEAREST UNDERGROUND Finsbury Park, then bus to Crouch End
ACCESS open Monday, Wednesday, 9.00–19.00; Tuesday, Thursday, Saturday, 9.00– 17.00; closed Friday. Call 020 8489 1427 for further information

Ley and Jarvis, Hornsey Borough Architects 1963–65

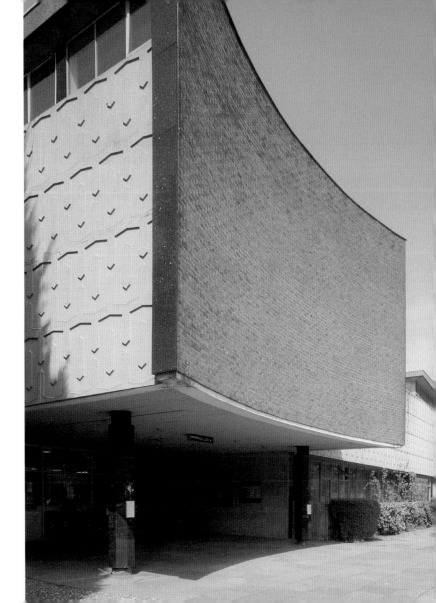

1 COLVILLE PLACE, FITZROVIA

Max Neufeld was an architect with the LCC and GLC for 25 years, working extensively in Covent Garden after an early specialisation in old-people's homes. He and his wife enjoyed living in central London, and when their flat was compulsorily purchased for demolition, they found a gap site with a 15-foot frontage left by a stray bomb. Neufeld got permission to build a gallery or photographer's studio, with a three-storey maisonette and roof garden on top.

The construction consists of timber joists on hangers spanning the party walls, with structural beams on the front and back to take the external walls. A spiral staircase sits in its own brick drum at the rear. What impresses is the simple, precise quality given to every detail - particularly of the internal timber fittings and built-in furniture, as well as the staircase, all designed by Neufeld himself. They make for an exceptionally calm, minimal interior – it was rejected for publication by the *Architectural Review* because it had so little furniture.

In both style and plan this house anticipates the present vogue for city living. Yet had it been built, the Smithsons' so-called 'House in Soho' – of which they first used the term New Brutalism in 1953 – would have been in the same street. A stronger contrast between two modern brick townhouses is hard to imagine.

LISTED grade II, 13 April 2000
NEAREST UNDERGROUND Goodge Street
ACCESS exterior only

Max Neufeld 1964

BLACKWALL TUNNEL VENTILATION TOWERS

When the young Terry Farrell worked briefly for the LCC in 1961–62 its Special Works Division was engrossed in detailing the South Bank Centre. He was therefore set to work unaided on the design of the ventilation towers urgently required for the second Blackwall Tunnel, then beginning construction.

The two structures, one either side of the river, are almost identical. Each houses shafts containing exhaust and blower fans discharging foul air. Farrell also designed a small supervisor's office at the northern end of the new tunnel, and worked on the tunnel lining. He admits that although the shafts' curvilinear funnel shape was hailed as aerodynamic and functional, it was actually inspired by the work of Oscar Niemeyer, whose first designs for Brasilia were beginning to be published. Marcel Breuer's contemporary UNESCO Building in Paris and Eero Saarinen's TWA terminal suggest too that that there was just then an international penchant for curvaceous forms. Farrell's funnels were made possible by the use of sprayed concrete or gunite, at that time beginning to be used for electricity cooling towers.

Long distinctive local landmarks, the southern tower was in 1998–99 enveloped by the Millennium Dome – unaltered, you can see its snout protruding on the west side.

LISTED grade II, 20 December 2000
LOCATION between Poplar and Greenwich (Millennium Dome)
NEAREST STATIONS north side Blackwall (DLR); south side North Greenwich (Underground)

LCC Architect's Department, job architect Terry Farrell 1964–67

8A FITZROY PARK

This house was built for engineer Peter Epstein, who had admired an earlier house built by Hal Higgins in Hampstead. Epstein's is a house of far greater scale and, indeed, is one of the relatively few 'luxury' modern-style houses of the 1960s.

Its complex plan comprises five 'pavilions' set around a central core of a large living room set over a swimming pool, which occupies the lowest part of the grounds. By exploiting the steeply sloping site Higgins was able to fit in a series of circulation levels, with movement between the pavilions made independent of the living room. The pavilions are constructed of brick, but are linked by 'bridges' of black steel and glass, also used to form the principal garden elevations of the living room.

Each pavilion houses a different function: one has the parents' suite of master bathroom and study; one the childrens' rooms, closely linked to the nanny's; one is for guests; and that to the rear serves the housekeeper and has the kitchen and projecting dining room. It is a rare, successful example of the 1960s enthusiasm for geometrical series of 'pods'.

The living room, by contrast, is high and light, and consequently it is strongly reminiscent of the California 'case study' houses from the late 1940s and 1950s.

LISTED grade II, 9 December 1999
ADDRESS Highgate, London N6
NEAREST UNDERGROUND Highgate
ACCESS none

Higgins and Ney 1965–67

BALFRON TOWER AND CARRADALE HOUSE

'I have wanted to build this for thirty years', claimed Goldfinger, when he lived in Balfron Tower briefly in 1967. The façades reflect Le Corbusier's 1938 plan for Algiers and Goldfinger's own projects of the 1930s and 1950s.

Urgent demands for housing in 1961 prompted the LCC to let private architects design its smaller schemes, and Goldfinger belatedly secured admittance to an approved list. Balfron Tower, a 26-storey block of 146 flats with a taller service tower, looks tough – and Carradale House at right-angles to it, its eleven storeys bisected by a free-standing lift tower, seems still stranger. But their concrete is perfectly finished, Balfron's entrance hall is lined in marble, and the flats are generously planned. The lifts serve every third floor, for speed, and doors off the connecting gallery lead up or down to larger flats as well as to those on the level. Larger balconies denote the larger flats. At Balfron Tower, the lowest floors, and the 15th and 16th floors, are combined as maisonettes. Goldfinger placed the oil-fired boiler house at the top of Balfron's service tower, well away from the ground floor gardens and playground. As construction began the LCC decided that it should also serve the next phase, Carradale House. Its exagerated form was thus accidental, but sculpturally satisfying. These themes were developed further at Trellick Tower (see page 574).

LISTED Balfron Tower grade II, 14 March 1996/Carradale House grade II, 4 December 2000
ADDRESS St Leonards' Road, Tower Hamlets, London E14
NEAREST STATIONS All Saints or Blackwall (DLR)
ACCESS exteriors only

Ernö Goldfinger Balfron Tower 1965–67/Carradale House 1967–68

THE BRUNSWICK CENTRE

In the late 1950s Leslie Martin and his associates made a series of studies of low-rise high-density housing, developing ideas begun for Habitat in 1954 and culminating in a scheme for St Pancras MB at West Kentish Town. When a 40-storey proposal for the redevelopment of the Foundling Estate by Covell and Matthews was rejected, Martin and Patrick Hodgkinson evolved this scheme. Hodgkinson developed the built scheme from 1961 onwards.

The Brunswick Centre is a 'megastructure', combining many functions within a single form. Two long ranges of small flats, each with its own balcony, are aligned either side of a shopping piazza, with car-parking below. Housing and shops are equally important to the scheme. Stepped terraces of flats face each other over the shop roofs; similar ranges look outwards. The result is an A-section to each block, the internal circulation space tapering upwards in a powerful composition of soaring columns laced with walkways. Opposite Brunswick Square, at the entrance to the shops, the flats are omitted and the supporting columns stand proud around the glazed entrance to a basement cinema; their scale is reminiscent of Antonio Sant'Elia's project for Milan Central Station (1914).

Hodgkinson was dismissed in 1970 and the shopping centre was finished cheaply, while the concrete was not painted as intended.

LISTED grade II, 24 September 2000
ADDRESS Brunswick Square and Marchmont Street, Camden
NEAREST UNDERGROUND Russell Square
ACCESS piazza with shops and cinema, plus exteriors, only

Patrick Hodgkinson 1967–72

RC ST MARGARET OF SCOTLAND

Austin Winkley had studied under Robert Maguire and was one of the first Roman Catholic members of the New Churches Research Group of architects interested in liturgical church planning. Father Sidney Thomason, who commissioned St Margaret's in 1965, wanted a building which would express the modern spirit that swept the Roman church with the conclusion of the Second Vatican Council and the elevation of Cardinal Heenan to Westminster. He did not live to see it completed.

The church was originally set amid elm trees. There is a weekday chapel and a hall, with the main worship space behind. This is diamond-shaped and is entered from the side under a low entrance, with higher roofs over the baptistry and the altar, placed in opposite corners. The use of concrete blocks follows that by Maguire and Murray at West Malling Abbey (see page 466). They and the opaque patent clerestory glazing impart a silvery coolness. This is enforced by the church's hidden position and two pieces of stained glass by Patrick Reyntiens in which greys and blues predominate. Stephen Sykes' hanging altar cross is of vivid gold mosaic.

Many Roman Catholic churches were built in the later 1960s, but few combine the innovation in planning with attention to detail and fixtures found at St Margaret's. It is Winkley's first and most appealing church.

LISTED grade II, 23 March 1999
ADDRESS St Margaret's Road, Twickenham
NEAREST STATION St Margaret's
ACCESS open most mornings; call 020 8987 4523 for details

Williams and Winkley 1968–69

TRELLICK TOWER

Trellick Tower signifies the LCC's western boundary as Goldfinger's earlier Balfron Tower (see page 568) does its eastern. Balfron is chunkier, Trellick taller and more elegant. It is the culmination of Goldfinger's lifelong study of mass housing, and although its opening coincided with the backlash against high flats it has since become one of London's trendiest addresses.

There are 217 flats and maisonettes set in a 31-storey tower and seven-storey wing. There is a ground-floor community centre, originally a nursery, shops and a doctor's surgery. There was also to have been a pub, but this projecting end unit became Goldfinger's office and is now an advice centre. Trellick, unlike Balfron, thus approaches the aims of Le Corbusier's *Unités d'Habitation* to fulfill a neighbourhood's needs in one building. The arrangement of a separate lift tower, giving access to every third floor of flats, with the twenty-third and twenty-fourth floors combined as maisonettes, is repeated from Balfron, but the surmounting boiler house is so exaggerated as to resemble Cyclops' eye. The building is immaculately detailed on a 2-foot 9-inch grid of double squares and built of scrupulously finished concrete with a cross-wall frame, and cedar panelling to the balconies. This trabeated idiom of perfect concrete is descended from that of Goldfinger's hero and master, Auguste Perret.

The tower has lost its parapets or 'cornices' but residents have recently restored the abstract glass panel in the foyer.

LISTED grade II*, 22 December 1998
ADDRESS Golborne Road, Kensington and Chelsea, London W10
NEAREST UNDERGROUND Westbourne Park
ACCESS exterior only

Ernö Goldfinger 1968–72

LONDON UNIVERSITY INSTITUTE OF EDUCATION

While the University of London was discouraged from major expansion in the post-war years, it was appreciated that its smaller departments, like Education, Law and the School of Oriental and African Studies (SOAS), needed better facilities. Lasdun was commissioned in 1960 to develop the concept of a spinal range along Bedford Way first proposed by Leslie Martin and Trevor Dannatt the year before. His task was to integrate new buildings with Bloomsbury's Georgian squares, then becoming appreciated. His scheme preserved more terraces than had Martin and Dannatt's, and created a new square between the Institute of Education and SOAS buildings.

The long elevations are among Lasdun's most formal compositions, demonstrating his mature language of horizontal strata and towers, beautifully finished concrete contrasted with bronze anodised aluminium panels and glazing. It has the sturdiness of Louis Kahn, but with details reminiscent of Wells Coates. The elevation facing SOAS is stepped, with seminar rooms and a library on the lower floors – an addition by the practice in 1990–93 is denoted by pyramidal roof lights. There is also one great spur wing, of five intended, with a striking silhouette of escape stairs. Most of the building is occupied by the Institute of Education, in which a broad stairwell leads to basement lecture theatres. The complex also includes the Clore Institute of Advanced Legal Studies and accommodation for University College.

Lasdun's SOAS building (1970–73), opposite, is itself under consideration for listing.

LISTED grade II*, 4 December 2000
ADDRESS Bedford Way, London
NEAREST UNDERGROUNDS Russell Square/Euston Square
ACCESS exterior, bookshop and foyers

Denys Lasdun and Partners 1970–76, 1990–93

ALEXANDRA ROAD ESTATE

Alexandra Road is the most formal and visually impressive of the distinctive low-rise, high-density schemes developed by young architects working for LB Camden in the 1960s and 1970s.

Camden took the site over from the private Eyre Estate, whose proposal for a tower block in 1959 was rejected because it interrupted protected views of St Paul's.

Neave Brown had already produced one scheme for Camden – four terraces of maisonettes set back to back at Fleet Road. Alexandra Road was similarly complex in its internal planning, yet its concept was simple: it was a Georgian terrace in modern dress. Devised in 1968, Brown resisted all attempts by the Housing Department to modify his concept and was supported by Sidney Cook, the tough Borough Architect.

The design was not begun until 1972 because of difficulties over road closures, and because local residents lobbied to keep the old houses. The brief also became more complex, with the addition of a park, a community centre, a home for the disabled, a special school and assessment centre, pubs and shops. Most of these extra facilities were squeezed on to the eastern half of the site so that Brown's scheme remained unsullied.

Two terraces face each other across a raised pedestrian street which has a gentle curve to enclose the view at either end. The third terrace, to the south, consists entirely of houses, their living rooms placed at the top for maximum light. The smaller terrace on Rowley Way has two tiers of maisonettes. The largest terrace is the most complex; designed as a noise barrier to the railway line alongside, it combines maisonettes with one-bedroom flats, each with a terrace set on the roof of the flat below.

One influence was Sir Leslie Martin and his associates, whose theoretical schemes from the late 1950s culminated in Patrick Hodgkinson's Brunswick Centre, designed from 1961 and begun as Alexandra Road was being finalised. Brown also drew on a low-rise

Camden Architects' Department 1972–78

tradition which originates with Mart Stam and Bruno Taut, Le Corbusier's Roq et Rob project of 1948 and Atelier 5's Siedlung Halen, Switzerland. Atelier 5's favourite stepped section became a feature of Camden's work. Brown had an underlying ideal of how city living could be, each home at the same time identifiable and part of a larger organism based on the street.

Above all, Alexandra Road is supremely crafted in fine white concrete, and it was to protect this quality in the face of insensitive repairs that the development was listed in 1993. However, despite Conservation Area status, Evans and Shalev's adjoining home for the disabled was demolished in 1999.

LISTED grade II*, 18 August 1993
ADDRESS Rowley and Ainsworth Ways, London NW8
NEAREST UNDERGROUND Swiss Cottage
ACCESS exteriors only

Camden Architects' Department 1972–78

LONDON: THE CITY AND WESTMINSTER

CHURCHILL GARDENS

In 1943 the London boroughs were ordered to produce housing plans for immediate implementation after hostilities ended. In Westminster Conservatives and Communists collaborated on an ambitious scheme for an exceptionally large site, and in 1945 held an international competition.

It was won by the young Philip Powell and Hidalgo Moya, with a *zeilenbau* plan of tall blocks set either side of a sinuously curved estate road, with lower ranges and terraced houses at right angles to them. Inspired by European rationalism, the first phase of four ten-storey blocks, named after poets, is also reminiscent of Lubetkin's 'working-class flats' project of 1935. It was the first estate with a district heating system, served by waste heat from Battersea Power Station, which was piped into a glazed accumulator tower. The contrast of square blocks and round lift-top details, together with the neat layout of paths and lawns, gives Churchill Gardens its character.

The next phases began with smaller flats at the western end of the site, at Gilbert and Sullivan houses, and worked inwards. The last and most easterly phase was replanned as lower, continuous terraces in 1960–62.

Since the LCC Architects' Department only began designing housing in 1950, only the boroughs enjoyed the exceptionally generous funding available for housing in the 1940s. Churchill Gardens won a Festival of Britain Merit Award.

LISTED grade II, 22 December 1998
ADDRESS Chaucer, Coleridge, Shelley, Keats, Gilbert and Sullivan Houses, with accumulator tower, Churchill Gardens, London SW1
NEAREST UNDERGROUND Pimlico
ACCESS exteriors only

Powell and Moya 1947–54

DUTCH CHURCH

Edward VI granted a charter to Dutch Protestants as early as 1550, and they occupied the former monastery of Augustinian Friars founded in 1253 until its total destruction in the raid of 15–16 October 1940.

The foundation stone of the new church was laid by the young Princess Irene, who had been born in exile here. It occupied only half the area of the original, for part of the site became an open space and rather more was developed as an office block. Bailey designed a chapel for 220 worshippers above a meeting hall, with a columbarium for bodies disinterred during excavations.

Arthur Bailey trained under E Vincent Harris and shares his master's facility for stone detailing and vaulting. The building's mixed use, as a community as well as religious centre, strengthens the feeling that this could be the architecture of a public building, although its crafted austerity is perfectly suited to the staunchly Calvinist worship.

There are many memorials. Glass was donated by the Church of Scotland (designed by W Wilson) and by the Worshipful Company of Carpenters (Hugh Easton). A window depicting the history of the church and Dutch worship in Britain is by Max Nauta, and another was dedicated to Queen Wilhelmina in 1962. The organ, with 2000 pipes and 26 stops, was imported from the Netherlands.

LISTED grade II, 25 September 1998
ADDRESS Austin Friars, London EC2
NEAREST UNDERGROUND Bank
ACCESS open for services

Arthur Bailey 1950–54

KNICKERBOX

It is unusual to find new offices and shops built before the end of building licensing (a form of rationing) in November 1954. This narrow block containing offices, a showroom and shop is still more unusual for also being a surviving memento of the 1951 Festival of Britain.

The first drawings for the scheme date from 1950. However, the developer Jack Salmon then began to make changes to his business, Oxford Street Properties Ltd. The delay led the design to be revised, and for plaques of precast Carrara stone to be incorporated into the façade. They are unique, and depict (from top to bottom), the Royal Festival Hall (see pages 668–670), the Festival of Britain logo devised by Abram Games, and the Dome of Discovery and Skylon. Their sculptor is unknown, but their quality is self-evident. They relate well to the banded metal windows of this corner composition.

Although the ground floor has been altered, there is great novelty to this little building, transitional in style between the 1930s and the 1950s. It is a rare example of a post-war building listed not only for its architecture but for its historic associations – here with the popular but short-lived exhibition dedicated to Britain's cultural and scientific achievements held on the South Bank between May and September 1951.

Listing was secured when the building was proposed for demolition.

LISTED grade II, 14 January 2002
ADDRESS 219 Oxford Street, Westminster, London
NEAREST UNDERGROUND Oxford Circus
ACCESS exterior only of interest

Ronald Ward and Partners 1951–52

TIME AND LIFE BUILDING

Time and Life International built their flagship European headquarters at a time when only government offices were being licensed, but it was made possible by American money.

The exterior reflects Rosenauer's expertise in designing compact flats. He made the corner site almost freestanding by placing a first-floor roof terrace between it and its neighbour, set behind a pierced abstract screen by Henry Moore. Moore's *Draped Reclining Figure* was placed on the terrace, which was landscaped by Peter Shepheard.

For the interior, Sir Hugh Casson and Misha Black approached many of the designers with whom they had worked on the Festival of Britain to create an unparalleled suite of offices and dining rooms. A grand staircase led to a double-height panelled reception room overlooking the roof terrace; this was truncated in 1983. Artists included Ben Nicholson, Geoffrey Clarke, R Y Goodden, Christopher and Robin Ironside, H T Cadbury-Brown, Leonard Manasseh and Oliver Cox, who recaptured the 'contemporary' spirit of the Festival in dignified colours and materials appropriate to an office building.

Few of the interiors remain. A small extension was permitted following a public inquiry, and another inquiry after Time Life's departure in 1992 determined that the fixed works of art, by Moore, Nicholson, Clarke and the Ironsides, should be returned to the building. What survives unaltered is Rosenauer and Moore's perfectly attuned external collaboration.

LISTED grade II, 29 March 1988
ADDRESS 153–7 New Bond Street, London W1
NEAREST UNDERGROUND Oxford Circus/Bond Street/Green Park
ACCESS exterior only

Michael Rosenauer 1951–53

1 DEAN TRENCH STREET

This house for Sir Michael Adeane replaces one built by Goodhart-Rendel in 1912 for the Adeane family, which was destroyed by bombing. The informality of the second design perhaps makes it superior to the first, which had a pilastered and pedimented front in brick.

The replacement building is a belated example of the Edwardian town house at its best. Its brick and strong white woodwork, with large projecting upper windows and dormers, is reminiscent – as is so much of Goodhart-Rendel's work – of Beresford Pite's domestic architecture in Marylebone, in its felicitous combination of arts and crafts and understated classical motifs. There are links, too, with the Chelsea houses of Norman Shaw and C R Ashbee. Although he is best remembered today for his reviving our appreciation of Victorian architecture as the author of English Architecture since the Regency (1953), there underlies all Goodhart-Rendel's work of the 1950s a profound sympathy with the underlying currents of architecture from the years before 1910 when he began in practice. Like Pite's, his is a very rational eclecticism.

Goodhart-Rendel built his own house and office at No. 60 Tufton Street in 1913, closing the vista of the newly created Dean Trench Street. This was also destroyed by bombs, but was not rebuilt.

LISTED grade II, 29 March 1988
ADDRESS London SW1
NEAREST UNDERGROUND Westminster
ACCESS exterior only

H S Goodhart-Rendel 1951–55

WESTMINSTER COLLEGE

The Westminster Technical Institute developed piecemeal. Its first building dates from 1893, the second from the 1930s and the steelwork of a third phase was abandoned in 1939. This enabled Harry Stuart Goodhart-Rendel to secure a building licence in 1951, although it dictated much of his design and an assembly hall had to wait until 1955. This now serves as the college library.

The college pioneered catering courses, which were founded by Monsieur Escoffier, chef at the Savoy, after whom the private dining room is named. This and the entrance hall have classical motifs, developed from those of the earlier building but more colourful in their use of black and red tiles and ebonised doors.

The exterior is more striking. The steel frame is clearly expressed, but Goodhart-Rendel embellished his brickwork with a pierced parapet and red diaper patterns – the latter harmonising with the building next door. The entrance is in green slate with an incised panel by J Ledger, while some of the windows have Gothic glazing details. The stair turret, begun in 1951, was extended to full height with the completion of the scheme.

The whole building typifies Goodhart-Rendel's exotic yet always harmonious mixture of sources and motifs. If in spirit it ultimately recalls the arts-and-crafts idiom of around 1900, it conveys a timeless sense of quality and pleasure.

LISTED grade II*, 24 April 1998
ADDRESS Vincent Square, London SW1
NEAREST UNDERGROUND Pimlico
ACCESS open for lunch; enquiries on 020 7828 1222

H S Goodhart-Rendel 1951–53, 1955–57

NOTRE DAME DE FRANCE

In 1865 a French church was opened to serve the community of hotel staff, chefs, musicians and milliners around Leicester Square, in an iron structure built in the remains of Burford's Panorama, a circular diorama of 1793. This church was hit by two bombs in November 1940.

Corfiato had studied in Paris before rising to become professor of architectural design at the Bartlett School. He retained the circular plan of the original, with an all-enveloping gallery supported on vast concrete piers, and reused some iron stanchions in the meeting room below. Above, a flat coffered roof opens to a central oculus lined with colonettes, which completes the sense of controlled modern classicism. It is a space of extraordinary solidity and refinement unparalleled in contemporary English church building.

The decoration of the church was entrusted to René Varin, the French Ambassador's cultural attaché. He commissioned the sculpture of Mater Misericordia over the entrance from Georges Saupique and the Aubusson tapestry behind the altar. The *art sacré* movement prominent in post-war France saw many leading artists and architects accepting church commissions in a remarkable integration of liturgical revival and avant-garde culture, and in 1960 the atheist poet Jean Cocteau offered to paint a mural for the Lady chapel. His self-portrait is to the left of the altar.

LISTED grade II, 25 September 1998
ADDRESS Leicester Place, Soho, London WC2
NEAREST UNDERGROUND Leicester Square
ACCESS open daily

Hector Corfiato 1953–55

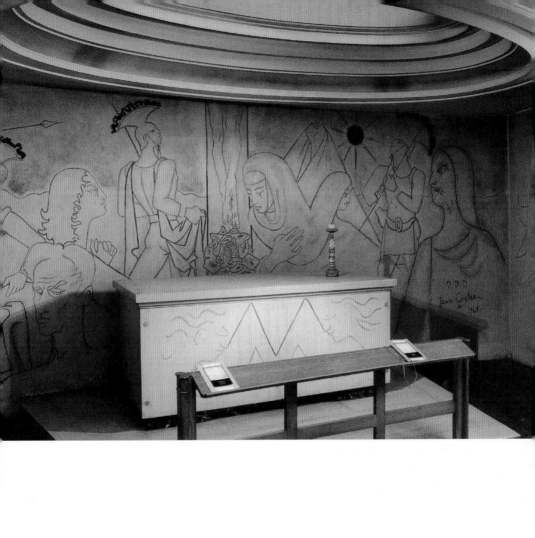

GOLDEN LANE ESTATE

In 1951 the City Corporation held a competition for housing on its northern fringes. Chamberlin, Powell and Bon submitted separate entries: when Geoffry Powell's won, the partnership was formed.

'There is no attempt at the informal in these courts', they explained in 1957 of the essential difference between Golden Lane and its contemporaries. To achieve the required density of 200 persons per acre two-bedroom maisonettes were placed in four- and six-storey ranges around a central tower of smaller flats, enlarged after the competition win and which at 16 storeys was briefly the tallest block in Britain. Today it stands out for its golden glass cladding, and especially for its oversailing 'aeroplane' fins masking rooftop water tanks and a garden with a pergola and pool. More small flats were built from 1958 when the site was extended westwards to Goswell Road. Crescent House, hugging the curve of the road, adopts a notably tougher aesthetic of pick-marked concrete and dark timber, and anticipates the style of Chamberlin, Powell and Bon's Barbican development then being designed next door.

No inch of space at Golden Lane is wasted. Deep basements left by bombed warehousing were exploited to make sunken gardens and tennis courts, while a circular tree-filled 'bastion' terminates the formal central axis preserved from the original scheme of more regular squares. There is a sports centre, community centre, tenant's hall, shops and a pub. It is indeed truly urban.

LISTED grade II (Crescent House II*), 4 December 1997
ADDRESS off Goswell Road, London EC1
NEAREST UNDERGROUND Barbican
ACCESS exteriors and sports centre only

Chamberlin, Powell and Bon 1953–63

45–46 ALBEMARLE STREET

These paired shops and offices are pivotal in Goldfinger's career, anticipating his more famous later works on a modest and elegant scale. It was among the first office schemes permitted following the abolition of building licences in 1954, and was built for the developer Imry, for whom Goldfinger was subsequently to design Alexander Fleming House, Elephant and Castle.

At Albemarle Street Goldfinger's combination of modernism and underlying classical proportions is at last wholly revealed, with a 'golden section' grid derived from his mentor, Auguste Perret. From him, too, comes the robustness of the frame. There is even a classical parapet – an expressive feature now lost from Balfron and Trellick towers – giving the building poise and setting it more easily among its neighbours. The cladding is of Portland stone and grey vitrolite panels.

There is additionally a constructivist ideology in the way Goldfinger expressed every element in the façade. To maximise its letting potential while meeting LCC regulations on height and set-backs, he set the whole block back, then cantilevered two bays forward. Clerestory glazing is, by contrast, set back to encourage more light into the building. This rhythm of different planes was to be repeated on an epic scale at Alexander Fleming House, which was rejected for listing in 1996 but which has subsequently been converted into flats.

Goldfinger designed the interior of No. 46, but only the shopfront survives.

LISTED grade II, 23 April 1991
ADDRESS 45–46 Albemarle Street, London W1
NEAREST UNDERGROUND Green Park
ACCESS exterior only

Ernö Goldfinger 1955–57

BRACKEN HOUSE

Bracken House, reviled as conservative when built, was in 1987 the first post-war building to be officially listed, saving it from demolition.

In later life Richardson, finding himself in an unsympathetic architectural climate, played the role of the 'last Georgian'. Yet his early London office buildings are clear expressions of their steel structure within a pure classical dress, inspired by pre-1914 Viennese models, and the same integrity is apparent here. Bracken House was built for the *Financial Times*, its pink brick and Hollington sandstone a symbolic reference requested by its chairman, Lord Brendan Bracken. The newspaper offices were in the north block, their entrance marked by an astrological clock whose central sun bears the features of Sir Winston Churchill, Bracken's former boss. The similar but skewed south block was rented out. The copper cornice is a distinctive late-Richardson feature that can also be seen in Clareville House (see page 632).

Richardson's central octagonal printing house was replaced in 1988–91 with offices by Michael Hopkins and Partners. It was a compromise, but a brilliant model of how a listed building can be reconciled with modern architecture. Hopkins's metal skeleton and tinted glass respect the proportions of Richardson's bookended composition within a 1990s aesthetic. Curiously, both elements have claimed Guarino Guarini's Palazzo Carignano in Turin as a source.

LISTED grade II*, 13 August 1987
ADDRESS Cannon Street, London EC4
NEAREST UNDERGROUND St Paul's
ACCESS exteriors only

Sir Albert Richardson 1955–59

100 PALL MALL

100 Pall Mall was Donald McMorran's only office building. He was a pupil of E Vincent Harris, and like him is best known for his public buildings, most of which are also listed.

100 Pall Mall features many of his favourite motifs. Here is his typical interplay of round arches, forming a distinguished entrance, contrasted with blank areas of Portland stone walling. The building had to fit in with London's most prestigious row of nineteenth-century clubs, and shares the same air of gentlemanly confidence without any extraneous detailing. Indeed, there is little save the predominance of stone walling to distinguish this building from one in a modern movement idiom. Perhaps the closest similarities are with the work of the novecento architects such as Giovanni Muzio active in Milan during the 1920s.

McMorran is not credited with designing the interior, but the groin-vaulted entrance hall is clearly by his hand.

LISTED grade II, 24 November 1995
ADDRESS London SW1
NEAREST UNDERGROUND Piccadilly Circus
ACCESS exterior only

McMorran and Armstrong-Smith 1956–58

ST VEDAST'S VICARAGE

This is an ingeniously planned building in a variety of styles, behind a simple frontage of yellow brick and artificial stone. St Vedast's had since 1885 accommodated its incumbent in a series of City houses, until the opportunity came to acquire the burnt-out Fountain Tavern next door. The purchase was made in 1952, although Dykes Bower's first designs date from 1950. Meanwhile, his restoration of Wren's St Vedast's began in 1953, and the church was reconsecrated in 1962.

An arched doorway between the church and vicarage leads to one of the most charming courtyards in London. Dykes Bower recreated a tiny two-storeyed wooden south cloister, with an open loggia below a sashed gallery, linking the vicarage with the rear hall of 1691. He extended the loggia along the rear of the rectory, in the end wall of which is a relief head by Jacob Epstein.

Dykes Bower believed that restorations need not be recreations so long as they were 'entirely appropriate.' This is the philosophy he applied to the vicarage. On the first floor an iron balustrade and French windows are in the style of c.1800, its witty domesticity reminiscent of Clough Williams-Ellis's work. The interior is a complex sequence of spaces on four levels. The first-floor living room has a mural of *Jacob's Dream* by Hans Feibusch, dated 1959.

LISTED grade II, 15 July 1998
ADDRESS Foster Lane, London EC2
NEAREST UNDERGROUND St Paul's
ACCESS wekdays, exterior and courtyard only

Stephen Dykes Bower c. 1957–59

SANDERSON HOUSE

A prestige headquarters and showrooms were built for Arthur Sanderson and Son, art-decorators and furnishers, in time for their centenary. Slater, Moberly and Uren, specialist designers of department stores, were also surveyors to the Berners Estate.

Sanderson House eschews unnecessary effects. A curtain-walled building no higher than its neighbours, without set backs or lavish decoration, it attracts attention by the subtly syncopated rhythm of its delicate mullions, more closely spaced in the centre of the long street frontage.

Natural light was the dominant theme of the extensive showrooms, on two floors, their deep floorplate lit by a courtyard to the side of the building. This semi-open roadway and gardens, contrasting curtain walling with foliage and water, is reminiscent of that at Gordon Bunshaft's Lever House (1952), and Sandersons wanted a share of this modern American image.

Like American office headquarters, this is an art building. The delicate staircase is backed by a glass mural in strong colours, designed by John Piper and made by Patrick Reyntiens – their largest secular work. There are also mosaics by Jupp Dernbach-Mayern (see page 546 for Centre Point), and his polished boulder in Philip Hicks's courtyard garden suggests Barbara Hepworth's natural forms.

Sandersons vacated the site in 1991, prompting the building's listing. It is now an hotel.

LISTED grade II*, 23 January 1991
ADDRESS 49–57 Berners Street, off Oxford Street, London W1
NEAREST UNDERGROUND Tottenham Court Road
ACCESS exterior and courtyard only

Slater, Moberly and Uren 1957–60

HALLS OF RESIDENCE, IMPERIAL COLLEGE

Imperial College was the flagship of scientific and technical education in the 1950s, with special government funding from 1952. This provided for the plain curtain-walled college by Norman and Dawbarn, but did not extend to the halls of residence.

It was left to the rector, Sir Patrick Linstead, to seek funding from industry for his vision of establishing a small residential community close to the college. In 1957 Vickers gave £150,000 for little Weeks Hall in Prince's Gardens, named after their former chairman. The building is quietly proportioned, with a glazed stair to the east. It makes a vertical accent behind the subsequent blocks, where instead the horizontals are heavily emphasised.

These blocks introduced the style of Le Corbusier to university architecture. Their plan is a compromise between long slabs, most economic to build, and the Oxbridge-born preference for arranging student accommodation in clusters around a staircase. Each block is divided vertically into units for about 150 students, with two narrow upper 'streets' or galleries set within them for common rooms and laundries. The larger southern block serves as a much-needed social centre for the whole college, with restaurants, butteries and bars that exploit the steep slope of the site to give these rooms high ceilings. On the east side Linstead Hall, completed last, combines accommodation with sports facilities. The long slabs appear particularly striking amid the stucco.

LISTED grade II, 30 March 1993
ADDRESS Prince's Gardens, London SW7
NEAREST UNDERGROUND South Kensington
ACCESS exteriors only

Richard Sheppard, Robson and Partners 1957–65

MARYLEBONE LOWER HOUSE

The former Rutherford Secondary School, for 780 boys, was built on a tight site adjoining a board school, subsequently demolished to provide the playground. The plan is similar to that of many LCC comprehensives, including Elliott School (see page 684), in placing all the teaching rooms in a single, curtain-walled block nearly 100 yards long, along with the kitchens, boiler house and caretaker's flat. From the central entrance a glazed link extends to an assembly hall and two gymnasia in a smaller building to the rear. This has a pyramidal roof; the main building's water tank is designed as an inverted pyramid.

The entire building is geometrical, through its use of structural concrete mullions, and this was emphasised by Manasseh in the precast sculpture at its entrance. Precasting allowed the school to be erected quickly; the mullions are thicker internally to support the glazing, and as well as giving strong rhythm to the façades shade the calssrooms from excessive glare. The library's coloured glass catches the late sun, and the entrance hall has a sculpture by Hubert Dalwood. Marble was one of Manasseh's favourite materials: elsewhere, quarry tiles, glazed bricks and solid timber were chosen as similarly 'boy-proof' surfaces.

The combination of structural innovation and carefully considered planning and finishes make this an exceptional school, which has been beautifully managed by an exceptional headmaster.

LISTED grade II*, 6 May 1998
ADDRESS North Westminster Community School, Penfold Street, London NW1
NEAREST UNDERGROUND Edgware Road (Bakerloo line)
ACCESS groups by application on 020 7262 8000

Leonard Manasseh 1958–60

26 ST JAMES'S PLACE

After his housing in Bethnal Green, Lasdun secured two prestigious West End commissions. One was the Royal College of Physicians (see page 540); this was the other, from the Malvin Investment Company, who had bought a derelict site overlooking Green Park and whose director wanted an 'all-glass' penthouse overlooking the park.

Lasdun designed eight luxury flats to a complex 3:2 plan, in which three storeys of smaller rooms to the north are set against two floors of high-ceiling living rooms on the south-west corner. These serve the four largest split-level flats. Lasdun had worked with Wells Coates on 10 Palace Gate (1939), which had first adopted the 3:2 plan pioneered by Mosei Ginsburg's Narkomfin flats in 1920s Moscow. He also knew Lubetkin's simpler 2:1 duplexes at Highpoint II.

The elevational treatment has the broad proportions of contrasting planes and strong horizontals found at Claredale Street, but transformed into granite, mosaic and bronze. To the park, the split levels are expressed by bands of granite and a vertical set back, and on the side elevations the levels are marked in dark brick. The flats are the more remarkable because they fit so happily into their setting, complementing John Vardy's grade I Spencer House (1752–54) next door, and confirm Lasdun's appreciation of urban 'grain' and context. It is Lasdun's first truly mature work.

LISTED grade II*, 22 December 1998
ENGINEER Ove Arup and Partners
ADDRESS 26 St James's Place, London SW1
NEAREST UNDERGROUND Green Park
ACCESS exterior only

Denys Lasdun and Partners 1959–60

RC OUR LADY OF THE ROSARY

Goodhart-Rendel left detailed designs in blue ballpoint pen for this church, built to replace a smaller church on the adjacent corner site. It was completed by his assistants Donald A Reid and H Lewis Curtis after his death.

The concealed site gave Goodhart-Rendel little opportunity for the brick patternings that are such a feature of Most Holy Trinity, Dockhead (see page 700), although blue headers lighten its blocky, north-facing profile. This elevation is based on his clear directions; the concealed side elevations were developed by Reid from rougher sketches. The interior, however, is more coherent, and is perhaps his most uplifting single space. As he intended, it is remarkable for its loftiness and simplicity. The effect of its stark transverse pointed arches across the nave, pierced at the crown by triple round arches, is monumental, and seems to have been inspired by use of the same motif at the Romanesque church of St Philibert Tournus, in Burgundy. With his preference for the round arch, southern Romanesque sources play an important part in Goodhart-Rendel's work.

Although light-brick facings were originally intended internally, the need to construct the arches and piers from reinforced concrete led to a plastered finish. This gives the church its coherence, and the tiled sanctuary under narrow lancets is both less altered and more imposing than that at Dockhead.

LISTED grade II, 25 September 1998
ADDRESS Old Marylebone Road, London NW1
NEAREST UNDERGROUND Edgware Road (Metropolitan, Circle and City lines)
ACCESS open daily; call 020 7723 5010 for information

H S Goodhart-Rendel 1959–63

NEW ZEALAND HOUSE

New Zealand House has for too long been decried for being 'in the wrong place', juxta-posed with Trafalgar Square and replacing Mewès and Davis's lamented Carlton Hotel. It is nevertheless London's finest 1960s office building, for the elegance of its tower as well as the sophistication of its diplomatic interiors.

Crown Estate immunity from most planning controls made the building possible, although RFAC and LCC pressure reduced the L-shaped tower originally proposed to the present slimline 18 storeys, albeit on a higher podium. The tower is an exceptionally light pattern of continuous horizontal bands of clear glazing set behind deep stone sills. Light shines through the corners on every floor. It houses both diplomatic and commercial offices, with a penthouse function suite, the Rainbow Room, that has some of the finest views in London.

The podium is more lavish and complex than is found in contemporary speculative offices. Passport offices and shops are on the ground and mezzanine floors, designed originally also to include a restaurant and expatriots' lounge. Above, the offices of the High Commission are set between glazed staircases and overlook luxuriantly planted rooftop courtyards. New Zealand marbles and hardwoods have been used extensively, both originally and in the refurbished roof-top Rainbow Room.

LISTED grade II, 24 November 1995
ENGINEER Kirkpatrick and Partners
ADDRESS 80 Haymarket, London SW1
NEAREST UNDERGROUND Piccadilly Circus
ACCESS exterior only

Robert Matthew, Johnson-Marshall and Partners 1959–63

WEST FOOTBRIDGE
LONDON ZOO

Franz Stengelhofen was appointed in 1947 to head the zoo's first Architect's Department, and to prepare a development plan. Then Lord Solly Zuckerman, Tecton's old patron, returned as Secretary to the Zoological Society. He was a facilitator and fundraiser, and commissioned a new plan from Casson, which concentrated on the areas adjoining the Regent's Canal. Their development was largely financed by the entrepreneur and architect, Jack Cotton, and was encouraged by the Duke of Edinburgh, president of the society.

The West Footbridge was one element of Stengelhofen's plan that was retained by Casson. It linked the two banks of the canal as part of the Cotton Terraces scheme.

The bridge has cantilevered side spans of the type pioneered for road bridges by those over the River Trent at Clifton, Nottingham, and over the Medway. They were adopted here because of the poor subsoil. The bridge is 17 metres long, with a suspended central span of 12.8 metres. The arched abutments are particularly elegant, and are unusual in having extra steps tucked between them so that pedestrians can climb from the canal edge directly on to the bridge. There are also two lightwells, enclosed by steel railings and teak handrails – a third has been replaced by benches on a raised plinth.

Visually, it relates very closely to the neighbouring Snowdon Aviary (see page 640).

(see page 640)

LISTED grade II, 29 May 1998
ENGINEER Stephen Revesz
ADDRESS Zoological Gardens, Regent's Park, London NW1
NEAREST UNDERGROUND Camden Town
ACCESS open daily; call 020 7449 6576 for information

Sir Hugh Casson, Neville Conder and Partners 1960–61

MILLBANK TOWER

The Vickers Tower, named after its first head lessees and principal occupants, is one of the few post-war buildings that makes the most of a Thameside location. Reflections from the river ripple across its grey-green curtain walling, as do changing cloud patterns. It shows the rapidity with which the British glass industry became sophisticated manufacturers of curtain walling by the early 1960s.

Much of the cleverness of the building lies in its diabolo shape. Douglas Marriott, the job architect, admitted that it grew out of an arrangement for the lifts that was superseded, but that as it allowed for a higher ratio of window space to floor space and the architects liked it, they stuck with it. It resembles Nervi's Pirelli tower in Milan, then just completed, while the projecting stainless-steel mullions are derived from Bunshaft's Union Carbide Tower, New York (1960). Although Ronald Ward and Partners are rarely credited for architectural sophistication, their sources here were up to the minute. A 'Y'-shaped eight-storey range alongside has a complementary concave curve.

Vickers made their board room on the thirtieth floor. It was designed by the Design Research Unit, with curved panelling. Despite the building's listing, this has been removed.

The LCC identified the Thames in 1956 as one area that could withstand tall buildings; only Millbank Tower demonstrated what could be achieved.

LISTED grade II, 24 November 1995
ADDRESS 21–24 Millbank, London SW1
NEAREST UNDERGROUND Pimlico
ACCESS exterior only

Ronald Ward and Partners 1960–63

ROYAL COLLEGE OF ART

The Royal College of Art developed out of ambitions to bring art into industry, and since 1851 occupied temporary workshops in South Kensington. Its prestige grew in the 1950s under the headship of Robert Darwin, who masterminded the new building. Robert Goodden, Professor of Silversmithing, prepared the brief; Hugh Casson, Professor of Interior Design, handled the committees. But the design was by H T Cadbury-Brown, then teaching in the sculpture department.

Cadbury-Brown sought to balance Albert Hall Mansions on the east of the Albert Hall with a corresponding block. The RCA is of dark brick because the mansions were then black with soot. The front workshop range has industrial floor loadings and a flexible plan. The tallest workshops, at the top, were for the prestigious glass workshops, which under Lawrence Lee had made the glass for Coventry Cathedral. The different heights of the workshops can be seen in the set-back central bay of the narrow side elevations. The pairing of the top-floor windows followed the 16-foot-6-inch grid of the building, although Cadbury-Brown also knew Louis Kahn's use of the motif in his Philadelphia laboratories.

To the west are offices and common rooms, including the elegant SCR with its distinctive timber detailing and high doors; to the east Cadbury-Brown added a gallery (now remodelled internally). Listing was prompted by proposals to replace this with a taller block.

LISTED grade II, 11 July 2001
ADDRESS Kensington Gore, London
NEAREST UNDERGROUND South Kensington
ACCESS exterior and galleries only (020 7590 4444 for details of exhibitions)

H T Cadbury-Brown, with Sir Hugh Casson and Robert Goodden 1960–63

1 GREYSTOKE PLACE

The architect's own office was a rare building type in the 1960s. The site was once occupied by the church of St Dunstan in the West, whose former graveyard provides the only long view of the building.

Yorke, Rosenberg and Mardall began to expand their firm when in 1955 they secured the commission for the new Gatwick Airport. F R S Yorke recruited a younger generation of partners – David Allford, Randall Evans and Brian Henderson – who steered the firm towards a specialism in office building, for which this served as a flagship. Their distinctive medium was white tiles – a means of achieving a pure white finish without the stains of concrete, and which also provided a module for modern or classical proportions. Rosenberg had used tiles in Prague in the 1930s, though a more probable source is Le Corbusier and, like him, YRM claimed never to cut a tile. With its six-and-a-half bays and constructivist set backs, Greystoke Place was one of the most sculptural of their tile designs.

There were originally five storeys of offices, the uppermost reserved for five of the six partners. Yorke asserted his supremacy with a penthouse flat on the floor above, which he filled with his extensive library on art, architecture, travel and pornography before his death in June 1962.

LISTED grade II, 24 November 1995
ADDRESS London EC4
NEAREST UNDERGROUND Chancery Lane
ACCESS exterior only

Yorke, Rosenberg and Mardall 1961

41 ALBEMARLE STREET

Moro and his assistant Michael Mellish designed this corner building of showrooms and offices for the furniture company, Hille, bringing to the site Moro's customary elegance and strong sense of geometry. The building reflects his personal character and style as assuredly as does his own house in Blackheath (see page 696).

Moro's brief was to build the maximum permitted accommodation on the site, including a small basement car park. The result is a curtain-walled building of seven storeys to the front, three to the rear, on a cantilevered concrete frame, with a glazed semi-circular staircase in between. The quality of the design lies in the refinement of its narrowly spaced black aluminium mullions, juxtaposed with silver-grey spandrel panels and a surprisingly rough-textured concrete frame where this is exposed at the rear. The original interior fittings, long gone, were by Robin Day.

LISTED grade II, 24 November 1995
ADDRESS 41 Albemarle Street, London W1
NEAREST UNDERGROUND Green Park
ACCESS exterior only

Peter Moro 1961–63

SMITHFIELD POULTRY MARKET

Smithfield was redeveloped in the 1860s as a market for carcases, having previously sold live animals too. New buildings for meat and poultry were designed by the City Architect, Horace Jones, followed by markets for fish and vegetables in the 1880s. In 1958 fire destroyed the poultry market.

Arup's designed a new clear-span market hall with a shell-concrete dome. It is flanked by covered driveways for deliveries, over which are first-floor offices with their own small shell cylinder roofs. Shell-concrete construction prospered in the post-war years of steel shortages. The Smithfield example is relatively late, but was when built the largest in Europe, with a span of 225 by 130 feet.

Externally the architects conceived a pattern of concrete and glass hexagons that is decorative while giving an opaque light to the unloading bays. Go inside, and the saucer dome invisible from the street is a real surprise, twinkling with lights. Below, the market hall is set out with stalls, all with blue fascias and contemporary-style signage – a coherent period piece with the tile and Formica surrounds to the balcony fronts and outer walls, as is the basement bar.

Concrete construction was popular in the 1960s for markets, which require a clear, unobstructed span, but Smithfield also has a rare architectural quality in its contemporary-style details. However, the building is underused and its future uncertain.

LISTED grade II, 24 July 2000
ADDRESS East and West Poultry Avenues, Smithfield, City of London
ENGINEER Ove Arup and Partners
NEAREST UNDERGROUND Barbican/Farringdon
ACCESS open weekdays until around 14.00

T P Bennett and Son 1961–63

CLAREVILLE HOUSE

Stone's Chop House was established in Panton Street in 1770, and until 1961 occupied two stuccoed terraced houses, with pub frontages to the street. In 1937 H E Popham wrote that 'Stone's seems never to change, and, consistent with its traditions, preserves its eminent respectability. On no account should it be missed by the lover of all that is good and old. Long may Stone's remain as it is.'

But changed it was, though if any architect was to invest a new building with an appropriate character it was Richardson, who in 1925 had written *The English Inn Past and Present* and in 1934 *The Old Inns of England*, among the first books to glorify the English pub. His partner and son-in-law, Eric Houfe, conducted the site meetings and correspondence on his behalf.

Richardson designed a five-storey office block, including his characteristic set-back attic, with a new Chop House in the middle of the Panton Street façade. Ground-floor columns and a Regency-style first floor hint at the style of the previous building. There were restaurants on both levels, with a lounge overlooking the street on the first floor.

Sadly, Stone's did not prosper in its new setting, and by 1986 it had become Maxim's Diner. However, the elevations remain little altered, with all the wit and idiosyncrasies of its designer.

LISTED grade II, 18 May 1995
ADDRESS 25–27 Oxendon Street/47 Whitcomb Street, London SW1
NEAREST UNDERGROUND Leicester Square
ACCESS exteriors only

Sir Albert Richardson and Eric Houfe 1962–64

THE ECONOMIST GROUP

> *The Economist* newspaper was a wonderful client. They had the nerve to commission and to
> build their own building, without any previous experience of how to do such a thing; allowing
> their architects to shape their work space from its presence in St James's Street to its filing
> systems and taps in the lavatories.

So wrote the Smithsons in 1989 of their masterpiece. Their clients were *The Economist*'s chairman, Geoffrey Crowther, who wanted to consolidate scattered offices with a penthouse for himself, and Peter Dallas-Smith, the joint manager who secured the tight, three-sided site and selected an architect from those engaged in the Churchill College competition. The Smithsons were commissioned in 1960. The complex land deal meant they had not only to accommodate *The Economist* offices, but a bank and shops, and serviced flats for Boodle's club next door. Each was given a separate tower rising from a low podium, which allowed the Smithsons to maintain a four-storey roofline to St James's Street, and to express their ideas of urban space with a plaza. The scheme has similarities with their proposals for Churchill College, where they also proposed a group of related towers. Here narrow towers with heavily serviced cores suited the clients' need for small flats and offices. The chamfered corners answered concerns for light levels in adjacent buildings, and unify the group – as does the bay on the side of Boodle's club, originally a lightwell.

The Economist building was one of the first offices to develop servicing as an integral part of the design, an antecedent of Willis Corroon. 'To make our mechanisms speak with our spaces is our central problem', the Smithsons wrote in 1970 of their search for a deliberately tranquil, even 'ordinary' architecture. There is also no separation between frame and cladding, unlike Mies's curtain walling. Windows and columns form a single

Alison and Peter Smithson 1962–64

shell, while the Roach-bed stone spandrels and mullions read clearly as cladding. The air conditioning is built in behind the windows.

In 1988 Skidmore, Owings and Merrill proposed to add two storeys to the 14-storey office tower. The group was listed, and the tower not raised, but substantial alterations were made to the plaza and office foyer, while the Smithsons' office interiors were entirely remodelled.

LISTED grade II*, 13 June 1988
ADDRESS St James's Street and Bury Street, London SW1
NEAREST UNDERGROUND Green Park
ACCESS exterior only

Alison and Peter Smithson 1962–64

CORRINGHAM

Corringham is the best of a group of London flats by an interesting practice, which included several architects who went on to greater renown as theorists and teachers. It has a special significance as the only building substantially designed by the critic Kenneth Frampton, who moved to the USA in 1966.

Corringham is striking for the adventurous planning of its 48 flats or maisonettes, and for the boldness of its external envelope. It adopted the scissor section to give each flat a dual aspect, by accessing them from a central corridor placed only on alternate floors. Ancillary rooms and landings step over or under this low corridor. Frampton says that the scissor section was invented by the LCC, where Margaret Dent (Mrs Douglas Stephen) had worked in the 1950s.

Externally the block is a slick curtain-walled composition, to a regular grid. The rear elevation, overlooking a grassy square, is relieved by balconies, and a projection on the upper five floors denotes larger, two-bedroomed units. But, as Goldfinger was to do, Frampton grouped the entrance, lifts, heating and waste-disposal shutes into a distinct unit that gives the block a powerful vertical emphasis. He acknowledges a stylistic debt to the tough aesthetic of Lyons Israel Ellis, but Corringham stands out as a private block of flats of rare quality.

LISTED grade II, 21 January 1998
ADDRESS 13–16 Craven Hill Gardens, London W2
NEAREST UNDERGROUND Paddington
ACCESS exterior only

Douglas Stephen and Partners 1962–64

SNOWDON AVIARY
LONDON ZOO

A walk-through aviary was a key component of Sir Hugh Casson's revised plan of 1958 for parts of London Zoo, and was inspired by San Diego Zoo. It was he who introduced Snowdon and Price, while Price brought in Newby.

The aviary consists of two aluminium tetrahedra, between which are pairs of wider-gauged tubes in another plane, anchored to the ground by heavy rocker bearings. This framework supports a web of steel cables in constant tension, covered by anodised aluminium netting. The falling ground, concreted to form a cliff face, gives the aviary a spectacular site and an illusion of greater structural complexity than it really has.

It belongs in the vigorous tradition of exhibition architecture, of which Price had experience through Joan Littlewood's 'Fun Palace' projects of 1961. The link with Casson to the Festival of Britain is telling. As then, Casson orchestrated a small body of designers to produce buildings intended to be lively, experimental and diverse in character. The Festival connection was enforced by Newby's pupillage under Felix Samuely – engineer of the Skylon, Britain's first sizeable tension structure, albeit a temporary one. Another possible source was Buckminster Fuller's transparent geodesic domes.

A tensile structure was not only novel, refreshing and exciting, but also offered the chance for a see-through effect in which the distinction between the inside and outside was blurred.

LISTED grade II*, 12 June 1998
ENGINEER Frank Newby
ADDRESS Zoological Gardens, Regent's Park, London NW1
NEAREST UNDERGROUND Camden Town
ACCESS open daily; call 020 7449 6576 for information

Lord Snowdon and Cedric Price 1962–64

ELEPHANT AND RHINO PAVILION
LONDON ZOO

> Elephants are such architectural animals that there is a temptation to look at a building
> housing them as a kind of analogy of themselves. This building, for example, could be
> described in terms of its massive curves, its wrinkled hide and its curious silhouette.

J M Richards (in 1965) was not the first to savour similarities between animals and buildings at London Zoo. The Penguin Pool made a theatrical display of its inhabitants, and Lubetkin and Tecton made an abortive design for an elephant house in 1939. Casson and Conder were indebted to Tecton's Elephant House at Whipsnade, which is developed from the 'turning circle' through which each elephant naturally moves. The difference is in the clustering of the pens here, the projecting skylights over each one providing a theatrical lighting while fixed benches and brick walkways gently corral the human audience. Outside the effect of their copper towers is reminiscent of a group of animals at a watering place. Casson himself called it 'a saucy thing'.

The external finishes have to withstand the rough tenants, and the corrugated texture of exposed aggregate resembles their hides. The finish had, however, already been perfected at Sidgwick Avenue (see page 266). Most compelling of all is the contrast between the Elephant and Rhino Pavilion and the contemporary Aviary – one deliberately heavy, the other almost weightless.

LISTED grade II*, 12 June 1998
ENGINEER Jenkins and Potter
ADDRESS Zoological Gardens, Regent's Park, London NW1
NEAREST UNDERGROUND Camden Town
ACCESS open daily; call 020 7449 6576 for information

Sir Hugh Casson, Neville Conder and Partners 1962–65

190 SLOANE STREET (FORMER SEKER'S BUILDING)

Lord Esher was an adviser to the Cadogan Estate, and Seker Silks' new showrooms were conceived as part of a proposed larger redevelopment of Sloane Street. They replaced Victorian shops, and the overhanging upper office floors were a compromise as part of a street-widening scheme.

The building is supported on just four main columns, with all the services placed against the party wall to the north. The west and south elevations are thus remarkably open and light. Note the set-back mezzanine floor, so that the entrance has a double height. This is the first of three extremely sophisticated curtain-walled elevations by Harry Teggin, who in his subsequent offices in Manchester and Portsmouth was to refine a black frame and dark-bronze glass aesthetics that defined sophistication in the early 1970s. Here the curtain walling of the upper office floors is of black aluminium, with double glazing.

Opening the new showroom, Sir Basil Spence pleaded for a 'warm humanity, richness and quality' in the London scene, and admired Seker's for the extrovert character of its mechanistic glass-and-concrete frame. Comparison with the Rosehill Theatre, Whitehaven (see page 68), shows the range of patronage of this enterprising firm.

The original internal fit-out was by Dennis Lennon, with door handles and other fittings by the sculptor Robert Adams, but these details are long gone.

LISTED grade II, 24 November 1995
ADDRESS London SW7
NEAREST UNDERGROUND Knightsbridge
ACCESS exteriors and shop only

Brett and Pollen 1963–65

CURZON MAYFAIR

The Curzon Mayfair replaced a 1930s art-house cinema of the same name by the same architects. A much-loved building, the high commercial value of its site saw its replacement by an office, flat and retail complex which included a larger auditorium at first-floor level.

The adoption of non-flammable film in the 1950s made it easier to build cinemas within larger complexes, and many West End cinemas were accordingly redeveloped. But only the Curzon scheme is distinguished. Hammond's cinema is expressed as an unglazed block across the front of the building that forms a strong contrast to the black-framed glazing above and below. The entrance foyer, to the side, retains original furnishings, including a fibre-glass screen that can be rolled across the box office when the building is closed.

The auditorium reacted against the stark simplicity of its predecessor. Its sculptured glass-fibre murals by William Mitchell disperse sound while giving a glowing cave-like effect, and the illuminated coffered ceiling is by Victor Vasarely. Patterns of light are also played on to the 12-metre screen – an example of the use of projection as an appropriate part of the architectural decoration. The cinema is unique for its architectural quality and state of preservation, particularly since Ernö Goldfinger's contemporary Odeon, Elephant and Castle, was demolished in 1988 while under consideration for listing.

LISTED grade II, 16 July 1997
ADDRESS Curzon Street, London W1
NEAREST UNDERGROUND Green Park
ACCESS daily performances

H G Hammond of Sir John Burnet, Tait and Partners 1963–66

WOOD STREET POLICE STATION

This is the last work built to the designs of Donald McMorran in his lifetime, and the culmination of 25 years spent designing fine traditional buildings for London's police forces. Even the modernist-minded *Architects' Journal* admitted that 'McMorran was a sincere and devoted architect who cared passionately about what he was doing. So, crazy though it is, this police station is in another class from the commercial trash nearby.' McMorran assessed the Golden Lane competition, and keenly supported the modernist winners Chamberlin, Powell and Bon. More recently Christof Bon celebrated the police station as 'post-modern before its time', and its heavy rustication and pedimented 13-storey tower do anticipate 1980s fashion.

This is a building of two halves. The four-storey front block accommodates the normal functions of a police station with larger offices for detectives and a largely ceremonial upper floor for the City's force of special constables. Behind it the tower has six floors of offices for traffic staff, with above it residential bed-sits for single constables and hobbies' rooms on the ninth floor. Tower and station are linked by a basement containing recreational and conference facilities, including the appropriately named McMorran Hall.

The closest analogies to what is probably McMorran's most imaginative work seem to be with the proto-modernism of pre-Fascist Italy, and more particularly with the 1920s Swedish architect Ivar Tengbom.

LISTED grade II*, 24 April 1998
ADDRESS Wood Street, London EC2
NEAREST UNDERGROUND St Paul's
ACCESS exterior only

McMorran and Whitby 1963–66

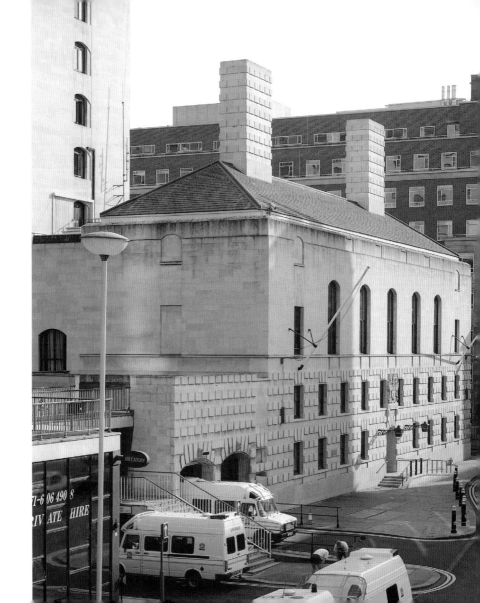

THE BARBICAN
BARBICAN CENTRE, GUILDHALL SCHOOL OF MUSIC AND DRAMA, AND CITY OF LONDON SCHOOL FOR GIRLS

The warehousing area north of St Paul's Cathedral was devastated in the Blitz. In 1953–54 the City produced plans for a new office district and ring road. But office rents were stagnant and the resident population just 48 when Duncan Sandys, Minister of Housing, suggested that the redevelopment include some housing and social facilities.

Chamberlin, Powell and Bon (CPB) were already designing flats at the adjacent Golden Lane site (see page 598). Working with an opposition group of the City's Common Council, they proposed high-density flats for middle- and high-income groups and the relocation of two of the City's schools. One was the Guildhall School of Music and Drama, and they suggested that its facilities could be shared with a small, local arts centre. CPB also suggested a gallery for the Lord Mayor's coach, the restitution of Temple Bar and the moving of J B Bunning's threatened Coal Exchange. But, as built, only St Giles Cripplegate and fragments of the medieval London Wall punctuate the new environment. The plan took shape in 1956 and assumed virtually its present form in 1959. A crescent of housing, inspired by Jewin Crescent previously on the site, was adapted as offices before completion. The towers took their triangular shape in 1959, and at 43 and 44 storeys were the tallest in Europe. Arup's recommended the curved balcony form as a way of expressing the massive edge beams required to support the external framework and of reducing wind resistance.

Work began in 1963 with Milton Court, the one detached element of the scheme. Its austere, rougher finish reflected its service functions, which included a fire station and coroners' court. Regrettably, it was excluded by Ministers from the listing.

In 1964 the City decided that a larger concert hall and theatre would be more financially viable, and secured the Royal Shakespeare Company as a tenant. Work on the Barbican Centre began in 1971. The insertion of a 2000-seat concert hall and 1500-seat

Chamberlin, Powell and Bon 1963–82

THE BARBICAN

theatre into a scheme already being constructed explains the congested plan. The Pit and the conference facilities are still later additions. But the views through the library are very dramatic, and the theatre is particularly successful. There is no seat more than 65 feet from the centre of the stage; no gangways to force parts of the audience to the peripheries as access is through individual doors at the end of each row. The two rows of balconies are cantilevered forward rather than stretched back. The 100-foot-high flytower and scene store is concealed by a conservatory wrapped around it.

The Barbican is one of the most ambitious new communities in Europe, executed without cutbacks over nearly 30 years. It combines CPB's fascination for social and land-use planning with detailed design and sophisticated structure. Listing was prompted by unsympathetic repairs proposed by the Corporation.

LISTED grade II, 5 September 2001
ENGINEER Ove Arup and Partners
LOCATION City of London
NEAREST UNDERGROUNDS Barbican/
Moorgate
ACCESS exteriors and Barbican Arts Centre
(Arts Centre 020 7638 4141; Barbican Theatre
020 7638 8891)

Chamberlin, Powell and Bon 1963–82

THE DELL RESTAURANT

Listing of The Dell in 1995 provided belated recognition of Patrick Gwynne as among the most sensitive of post-war designers, five years after his Serpentine Restaurant in Hyde Park had been demolished. Its listing coincided with the National Trust's acceptance into its care of Gwynne's own house, The Homewood.

In 1963 Geoffrey Rippon proposed new catering facilities for the Royal Parks, to be built by private caterers. Gwynne won an invited competition for Forte's two sites in Hyde Park. His first scheme resembled a two-storey wedding cake, but when car parking was refused the first-floor grill room was omitted, and the graceful, umbrella-like solution was the outcome. Its circular form took advantage of the outlook, with the catering facilities placed in the centre. The cantilevered raised terrace projecting over the lake balances the composition while leading the eye away from kitchens and lavatories hidden in the shrubbery.

The finishes of the building are particularly good. Best is the floor of Brescia Violetta marble, which runs unbroken from the inside café to the outside terraces. Precast terrazzo was used extensively for built-in tables, seats and counters, and these survive externally. The interior has been remodelled, with the loss of Gwynne's tables and swivel chairs and also a vitreous enamel panel by Stefan Knapp – removed in 1979.

LISTED grade II*, 11 January 1995
ADDRESS Hyde Park, London W2
NEAREST UNDERGROUND Hyde Park Corner
ACCESS open Monday, 11.00–19.00; Tuesday to Sunday, 10.00–18.00

Patrick Gwynne 1964

LILLINGTON GARDENS

In 1961 the City of Westminster held another housing competition, for a site close to Churchill Gardens (see page 584). The winner was John Darbourne, aged 26.

The modest height and dark red brick were determined by the presence of G E Street's church of St James the Less (1860–61). Otherwise, the housing forms a near-continuous wall around the site, creating secure play areas in the middle.

After a decade of rectangular housing blocks, Lillington startled by its complexity. Flats and maisonettes are different sizes and have complex plans. Some ground-floor units are back to back, with private gardens, while the upper flats have patios, and are reached from walkways planted with shrubs. Darbourne wanted the tenants to associate themselves with a particular element rather than feel lost in a big development.

Phases I and II, with an old-people's home and three pubs, are indistinguishable, but Phase III, begun in 1969 and including Pimlico Library, is differentiated by its tile-hung mansards. It has more large family units, more private gardens and little public space. Pensioners' flats are set on the rooftops.

Lillington inspired red-brick estates across England in the 1970s. Yet its sources are firmly of c. 1960, in Ham Common and the low-rise high-density projects by Leslie Martin's studio. Darbourne sought to make public housing less institutional, and in this he succeeded triumphantly.

LISTED phases I and II grade II*, 22 December 1998; phase III grade II, 20 December 2000
ADDRESS between Tachbrook Street and Vauxhall Bridge Road, London SW1
NEAREST UNDERGROUND Pimlico
ACCESS exteriors only

Darbourne and Darke 1964–72

PADDINGTON MAINTENANCE DEPOT

Two buildings were erected to garage and manage British Railway's fleet of parcel vans, in compensation for land taken for the M40 Westway. The buildings were amply funded but had to be built quickly, and the site between the Westway and Grand Union Canal was extraordinarily confined. Bicknell and Hamilton had worked for British Railways' Eastern and Midlands regions, and Paddington is the last and finest of their railway buildings inspired by the modernism of the 1920s.

The low east block is often overlooked, tucked next to the canal under the Harrow Road roundabout. It is a large oval garage with a dramatic precast roof, whose cranked beams incorporate a high clerestory. The west block pokes a distinctive snout over the Westway, like a tugboat with lift towers for funnels. Its lower service floors, designed for heavy loadings, are set down a steep ramp. The upper glazed floors had workshops, offices and mess-rooms, linked by a curving stairwell (detailed by Bicknell) sheathed in the same ceramic mosaic tiling as the exterior. There is a tactile muscularity in the building's curved corners, and a romanticism in its triangular plan – reminiscent of Hugo Häring's Garkau cowshed of 1925 – that extends to its triangular plan.

Listing saved the building from proposed demolition. After various unsuccessful proposals for office and restaurant use, in 2001 the depot was adapted for use as the headquarters of the Monsoon fashion company.

LISTED grade II*, 14 April 1994
ADDRESS 179 Harrow Road, London W2
NEAREST UNDERGROUNDS Warwick Avenue/
Royal Oak
ACCESS exteriors only

Bicknell and Hamilton 1966–68

125 PARK ROAD, REGENT'S PARK

In 1966 Terry Farrell and Nicholas Grimshaw joined the Mercury Housing Society, a co-ownership enterprise funded by the Housing Corporation and the Cheltenham and Gloucester Building Society. The Society had a site with planning permission, and Farrell and Grimshaw produced a scheme for 40 one- and two-bedroom flats that provided the maximum space within the Housing Corporation's financial yardsticks.

Though jointly designed, Farrell's influence is most clearly seen in his succinct plan, while the façade's continual strip windows and corrugated-aluminium cladding were to become distinctive in Grimshaw's subsequent work. Each floor comprised four flats round a large central service core that all the bathrooms back on to. Partitions can be altered, and some flats have been knocked together. Freestanding columns, continuous perimeter heating and regularly spaced electrical sockets encourage maximum flexibility. The architectural effect of this minimalism is of a finely proportioned, architecturally sensitive sense of space, with fantastic views across Regent's Park and west London. Both Farrell and Grimshaw occupied penthouse flats in the block's early years.

This was the first residential building in Britain to be designed as a central core entirely surrounded by flats, and pioneered Housing Corporation and building society co-funding. But it was for its simple, light-weight and technically inventive skin that the building first gained attention, singling it out as the vanguard of the high-tech movement.

LISTED grade II, 28 December 2000
ENGINEER Anthony Hunt
NEAREST STATION AND UNDERGROUND Marylebone
ACCESS exterior only

Farrell/Grimshaw Partnership 1968–70

LONDON: SOUTH OF THE THAMES

CLAPHAM SOUTH DEEP TUBE SHELTER

Eight deep tube shelters were built as secure headquarters for special organisations, such as the government's telephone service and staff, although seven were used briefly by the general public in the rocket raids of 1944. They were located and designed so that London Underground could have subsequently adopted them as express routes for the Northern and Central Lines had they been released. Shelters were built at Clapham South, Clapham Common, Clapham North and Stockwell; Camden Town and Belsize Park; Chancery Lane and Goodge Street.

Each shelter comprised twin concrete-lined tunnels, 5 metres in diameter and 427 metres in length, reached by a shaft at each end or stairs from the underground station above. The inelegant shaft heads had steel-reinforced pillboxes to minimise the risk of flooding from shattered water mains. The main tunnels were subdivided into two levels, with a canteen and lavatory tunnels, and were set out with triple-decker bunks.

After the Second World War the bunkers were refurbished. Camden Town, Clapham South, Goodge Street and Stockwell were used as transit camps for soldiers. Clapham South was used by school children on visits to London, and by the *Windrush* immigrants, until in 1951 LCC fire officers banned further use. Although other tunnels retain original metal bunks, only Clapham South also retains its wartime signage. Like many, it is now used for commercial storage.

LISTED grade II, 22 October 1998
ENGINEERS G W Ellis and H C Webb, with London Transport
ADDRESS Balham Hill, London SW12
NEAREST STATION Clapham South
ACCESS none

Mott, Hay and Anderson 1940–42

PASSFIELDS

Maxwell Fry was a pioneer of modern housing design in the 1930s, notably with Kensal House in North Kensington, but he built little housing in England after the war. This is a rare fusion of picturesque design with engineering innovation.

Lewisham MB had acquired and cleared the little site before the war, so building could begin early. It was, however, constrained by the busy Bromley Road, then still carrying trams and due for widening. Fry set the nearest blocks at right angles, and placed a bigger block behind as a buffer to the rear playground.

The variety of flats suggests an attempt at mixed development, particularly with the inclusion of some of the first maisonettes in public housing. The big block has two tiers of maisonettes, expressed by the use of box-frame construction, as pioneered by Arup at Spa Green (see page 486) but adapted here to incorporate projecting balconies. Again the system shows how it can be made to form a curve. Less funding was available than at Spa Green due to government cuts in 1947, and having the upper floors as maisonettes meant that only one lift was needed.

The laundrette behind the largest block was one of the first to be designed for automatic washing machines. The estate won a Festival of Britain Merit Award.

LISTED grade II, 22 December 1998
ENGINEER Ove Arup and Partners
ADDRESS Bromley Road, Catford, London SE6
NEAREST STATION Bellingham
ACCESS exteriors only

Fry, Drew and Partners 1949–50

ROYAL FESTIVAL HALL

The Royal Festival Hall was the only permanent building erected on the 1951 Festival of Britain's South Bank site. Though it superficially resembles the smaller concert halls at Gothenberg (1933) and Malmo (1940), it is a building of worldwide significance, an extraordinarily rich, sophisticated achievement for its date and the haste with which it was built.

It was a replacement for the bombed Queen's Hall in Langham Place, so was similarly required to hold a massive 3000 seats. The plan was Leslie Martin's. So tight was the site, and so noisy, that he enveloped the hall with foyers below and to either side. It was dubbed the 'egg in the box', and its drum clad in contrasting Derbyshire fossil stone, inside and out. The box was developed as a series of calm, open foyers linked by stairwells, with a restaurant overlooking the river. The novel idea of a public building that would be open for snacks and informal events all day was envisaged from the first, and the gallery area was originally conceived as a ballroom. Access was not from the river but from entrances to either side on different levels. The lower one was restored in the early 1990s and is the best way to experience the sequence of foyer spaces unfold.

The interiors defied the shortages of building materials. Their detailing is tactile: from the cyma-curved auditorium boxes reminiscent of Lubetkin's balconies at Highpoint I, to thick handrails with a continuous groove for your thumb, to the carpet motif. They were designed by Peter Moro and eight of his enthusiastic ex-students. In the absence of design catalogues, they had to devise every fixture themselves, from the door handles to the music stands, and this gave the building its richness. LCC architects were sidelined in their race against time and budget. The 'cold' auditorium acoustics were perhaps a reaction to the echoing Albert Hall, and were upgraded with resonators in the 1960s.

The exterior was rebuilt in a savvier, blander modernism in 1963–65, when walk-

LCC Architect's Department 1949–51

ways were installed across the complex ground levels between Waterloo Bridge and the river. The change has confused Martin's planning, but the building's significance as the prime monument of the Welfare State era remains unsullied. In the 1990s Allies and Morrison have restored much of the open character of Moro's foyers but in 2002 threaten to remove the central bar.

The initial brief included a smaller secondary hall, which was eventually built in 1963–67 in a subservient adjoining complex along with the Hayward Gallery. The change in aesthetics is striking, and is ripe for re-evaluation on its own terms.

LISTED grade I, 29 March 1988
ADDRESS Belvedere Road, London SE1
NEAREST STATION/UNDERGROUND Waterloo
ACCESS open daily

LCC Architect's Department 1949–51

BRANDLEHOW SCHOOL

Of Ernö Goldfinger's two low-budget schools for the LCC (see also Greenside School, page 494), built to his precast concrete-framed system, this is the more demure. Its qualities are not immediately apparent for, being a practical planner, he placed the kitchens and fuel stores where they were most accessible, and placed the assembly hall and a wing of classrooms overlooking the playground behind. We are left to admire the dominating water tower and boiler flue, concealed in a brick-and-concrete tower of clearly Festival of Britain character, and to squint behind for a glimpse of Goldfinger's constructivist concrete window patterns, set between the boldly expressed portal frame. Instead of a mural, the entrance hall has a varnished timber ceiling

Brandlehow is less altered by accretions than Greenside School. An aluminium sun screen has replaced Goldfinger's jaunty striped canvas blinds, but the school retains its charming simplicity, and a childish sense of pleasure that shines through all those austere, hard surfaces.

LISTED grade II, 30 March 1993
ADDRESS Brandlehow Road, Putney, London SW15
NEAREST STATION East Putney
UNDERGROUND Putney
ACCESS exterior only

Ernö Goldfinger 1950–51

STOCKWELL BUS GARAGE

As London's last trams were despatched to the Woolwich 'tramatorium' in 1952, so garages were urgently needed for buses. Where depots already existed steel was made available, but on new sites resort had to be made to concrete. Most of the work was entrusted to the commercial specialists George Adie and Frederick Button.

Peckham, now demolished, repeated the shell cylinder construction popularised at Bournemouth's Yellow Bus Garage (see page 328). Stockwell has ten concrete beams linked by thin barrel vaults and a ring beam. Its span of 59 metres makes it a third wider than Bournemouth, and it is longer by a similar factor. The difference is that the beams are arched portal frames, which rise from 4.8 to 16 metres at the centre, and between them the cylindrical curves soar still higher, their cathedral-like effect enhanced further by the incorporation of roof lights that cast an even, slightly ethereal glow. The roof is cantilevered from a giant beam at haunch level, and to ensure loadings, the frames' reinforcement bars were welded rather than lapped – perhaps the roof's greatest technical novelty.

Some 200 buses can be housed here, yet they are dwarfed by the giant roof, whose relatively thick frames and thin skins are impossible to appreciate from below. It is perhaps simpler than Pier Luigi Nervi's engineering, but similarily shows how concrete can be made sublime.

LONDON: SOUTH OF THE THAMES

LISTED grade II*, 29 March 1988
ENGINEER A E Beer
ADDRESS Lansdowne Way, Stockwell, London SW8
NEAREST UNDERGROUND Stockwell
ACCESS exterior only

Adie, Button and Partners 1951–54

ST JOHN'S VICARAGE AND CARETAKER'S HOUSE

These commissions provided Harry Stuart Goodhart-Rendel with a unique opportunity to build in an updated version of the secular Gothic style. They were inspired by the adjacent St John's (1871–74) by G E Street, which he had been commissioned to restore after it was gutted in 1941. Street was one of Goodhart-Rendel's idols, and both the restoration and the additional buildings show how fully attuned he was to gothic sensibilities. These characterful and strong houses avoid pastiche.

The vicarage was originally conceived as a convent, and a chapel in the gabled roof space is now a delightful library. It is lit by the rose window that is a prominent feature to the side of the asymmetrical gabled façade.

The caretaker's house forms a foil to the vicarage, resembling a lodge at its entrance, and with a hipped roof that serves to conceal its considerable size.

LISTED grade II, 15 July 1998
ADDRESS Vassall Road, London SW9
NEAREST UNDERGROUND Oval
ACCESS exterior only

H S Goodhart-Rendel 1952–54

ALTON ESTATE

The County of London Plan of 1943 established two principles that were fundamental to LCC housing policy. One was that people should be rehoused at lower densities, in the suburbs where possible, the other that new estates should provide a mix of different housing types and community facilities. Within the county boundary the only substantial sites for housing were at Roehampton, an area developed with large villas in the 1850s which had become derelict, and where some eighteenth-century houses and grounds survived. It was partly to protect these dream sites from unimaginative development that the LCC Architects' Department wrestled control of housing back from the Valuers' Department in 1950. The final scheme was described in 1961 as 'probably the finest low-cost housing development in the world'. Listing has recognised the importance of the most distinctive blocks, but the development and its landscaping should be appreciated as an entity.

Alton East, originally Portsmouth Road, was developed by a socially conscious team under Rosemary Stjernstedt, including some architects from the Hertfordshire schools programme. On the sites of the villas they placed point blocks of 11 storeys, inspired by Swedish models, and keeping the Victorian garden walls and trees they developed the lower slopes with houses and four-storey maisonettes, their red brick a contrast to the white brick and monochrome tile patterns of the points.

Alton West is sterner meat, developed by a younger generation who went on to practice as Howell, Killick, Partridge and Amis. There is the same variety of points, maisonettes and houses, with shops and a library, but the valley site is laid out more formally, and everything is uniformly clad in storey-high concrete panels, first refined here. On one hillside Mount Clare (1776) and its surrounding trees were retained and framed by old people's bungalows, their tall chimneys a cheerful anachronism in so modern a vista of point blocks and flat roofs.

LCC Architect's Department 1952–60

ALTON ESTATE

Still more striking is the hillside opposite. An LCC team, including Colin St John Wilson, had developed a design for a long slab, more cost-effective than narrow points and with scope for the two-bedroom maisonette units that were then a popular innovation. Elsewhere, less carefully detailed than here, they are unremarkable. But the Alton West team, inspired by a pilgrimage to Le Corbusier's *Unité d'Habitation*, slammed five blocks sideways into the recontoured hillside, after Harold Macmillan supported local objections to them being set in a line facing Richmond Park. At the price of more limited views for the residents, this is one of the great statements of modern architecture in London.

LISTED 22 December 1998: Blendworth, Cadnam, Dunhill, Eashing, Grayswood, Hilsea, Hindhead, Longmoor, Westmark and Witley Points, Alton East, grade II, 1952–55; Binley, Winchfield, Charcot, Denmead and Dunbridge Houses, Alton West, grade II*; old people's bungalows, Alton West, grade II, 1955–58
ADDRESS Wanborough Drive and Danebury Avenue, Roehampton, London SW15
NEAREST STATION Putney, or underground to Putney East, then bus; at junction of A3 and A306
ACCESS exteriors only

LCC Architect's Department 1952–60

ST LUKE'S CHURCH

St Luke's replaced a church of 1876–77 bombed in the war. It is a curious Byzantine design, belonging as much to the 1930s as the 1950s, yet its broad transepts and central domed crossing make it admirably suited to modern liturgy. The exterior is modest in scale and, although well massed, its simple brickwork presents rather a gaunt appearance. The interior, however, is surprisingly light and high, its central octagonal crossing and aisles defined by narrow columns on cushion capitals – a motif repeated in some of the fenestration and which gives an unexpected grace to the composition.

Most notable of all are the cross vistas produced by the combination of passage aisles with the angled transepts. These are a simplified and more successful version of Martin's earlier church, St Luke's, Milber, Newton Abbot, built for his brother, Keble Martin, in the 1930s and which has much larger transepts. For though Arthur Martin spent most of his working life as architect to the Duchy of Cornwall, he was from a strong high church background and this, his last work, is clearly a labour of love. Because such traditionally styled churches of the 1950s were never published, there may be several surprises awaiting rediscovery. But it is hard to imagine that there are as many as substantial and moving as St Luke's.

LISTED grade II, 13 April 2000
ADDRESS Diamond Street, Camberwell,
London SE5
NEAREST STATION Peckham Rye; or
underground to Elephant and Castle, then bus
ACCESS regular services only;
call 020 7703 5587 for details

Arthur Martin, with Milner and Craze (executants) 1953–54

ELLIOTT SCHOOL

Elliott School is recognised as the finest of the LCC's in-house comprehensive schools. George Trevett was the Group Architect, with Philip Rogers, N S Bahle and John Bancroft as his assisstants.

Elliott was built to serve the LCC's new housing at Roehampton, in line with the LCC's controversial decision in 1947 to build comprehensives. The main classrooms are in a single four-storey teaching block set into the slope, with a drama hall tucked under the pilotis at the lower end. The geography rooms are on the roof, with a compass design in the linoleum floor. On one side of this range are two single-storey gymnasia and a workshop block, and on the other an assembly hall for 1300 pupils. An open-air theatre is set into the lawn.

Elliott is a perfect example of the 'contemporary' style. At first sight a concise curtain-wall building, the variety of decorative detail is exceptional, with murals, busy tile and brick patterns, cyma balconies and wavy roofs. There are pilotis in the manner of Le Corbusier, while the wedge-shape of the hall, cantilevered entrance canopy and end balconies are reminiscent of Tecton's work.

Elliott's teachers are extremely proud of their building, and architectural education has become a part of their sixth-form design courses.

LISTED grade II, 30 March 1993
ADDRESS Pullman Gardens, Putney, London SW15
NEAREST STATION Putney, or underground to Putney East
ACCESS groups by appointment on 020 8788 3421

LCC Architect's Department 1953–56

PARKLEYS

The quality of public housing in the 1950s highlighted the dullness of most speculative developments. The exception was the work of Geoffrey Townsend, an architect turned developer, and Eric Lyons – close collaborators with remarkable tenacity when dealing with planning officers and whose attention to detail makes their simple design idiom special.

In 1954 Townsend formed Span Developments Ltd, a private company specialising in small units for first-time buyers in south London and Surrey. Parkleys was their first and most famous scheme, in which the key features of their successful package were established. There are 169 flats, plus a parade of shops and maisonettes, arranged in two-storey terraces and courtyards, and three-storey blocks. While the taller blocks have full-height glazed staircases and lattice detailing, the lower tile-hung ranges have the unassuming quality of Georgian terraces, and careful proportions that extend to the spaces between. The relatively high density (74 persons per acre) is masked by a clever layout and especially by the dense planting that became a feature of Span estates. Parkleys is on the site of a nursery, and mature trees were retained, as were the gardeners. Lyons' low mushroom courtyard lamp was also repeated subsequently.

Parkleys also pioneered endowment mortgages and the management company that is central to the Span concept, to which every leaseholder belongs and which elects a residents' committee to run the estate. This ensures that Parkleys has remained remarkably little altered.

LISTED grade II, 22 December 1998
ADDRESS Ham Common, Richmond-upon-Thames
NEAREST STATION Richmond or Kingston, then bus; off A307
ACCESS exteriors only

Eric Lyons 1954–56, 1958–59

ALL SAINTS

LONDON: SOUTH OF THE THAMES

All Saints was built with compensation from St George's, Canterbury, which was bombed in 1942 and not rebuilt. A reminder that Croydon was then part of the diocese of Canterbury, St George's is commemorated by fragments of surviving glass set into the southwest porch.

All Saints has a square nave, with a projecting baptistry at the west end and a long choir and sanctuary flanked by vestries and a Lady chapel. It closely resembles Curtis Green's nearby church of St George, Waddon (1932). The style is minimally Gothic, with lancet windows and unmoulded transverse arches, which define the main spaces and whose form is repeated in the narrow aisle arcades. More unusual is the Lady chapel, whose length is interrupted by six stone columns. The exterior is clad in hand-made bricks and has big tiled roofs.

In the excitement of the Liturgical Movement, which led to sudden and fundamental changes in church design, it is easy to ignore the long succession of well-crafted, traditionally planned churches that continued into the late 1950s. Certainly they were ignored by the architectural press. Curtis Green, his son and son-in-law were principally commercial architects, but their church work reflects their interest in good interior design. This building would have been elegant in the 1930s; for a 1950s building it is lavish.

LISTED grade II, 10 August 1998
ADDRESS Bridle Road, Spring Park, Croydon
NEAREST STATION West Wickham
ACCESS regular services

Curtis Green, Son and Lloyd 1955–56

LAMMAS GREEN

Donald McMorran chose a modern scheme when assessing the Golden Lane competition, yet his own work for the City Corporation remained firmly traditional.

Here he designed 27 houses and 30 flats around a small green on the southern slopes of Sydenham Hill. The high land and views of Kent give the scheme its character. It replaced three derelict houses long owned by the corporation, who insisted that their replacements should be no more than three storeys high and that the mature trees be kept. Who decided to arrange the family accommodation as two-storey houses is unclear. The result was an exceptionally low density, and McMorran claimed this was to ensure 'a community with its own life and identity'. He also included a small community hall in one corner, which seats about sixty people when not in use as a playgroup.

The flats protect the houses from the main road. They are among McMorran's most characterful designs, their blocky massing and proportions of the tall stacks and shallow gables – clad in timber – typical of his work. The use of Essex bricks affirms the contrast with the little colour-washed terraces, stepped in pairs like some of Tayler and Green's work, with occasional dormers to give an extra touch of the picturesque.

The result is some of the best-loved public housing in England.

LISTED grade II, 22 December 1998
ADDRESS Sydenham Hill, London SE26
NEAREST STATION Forest Hill
ACCESS exteriors only

Donald McMorran 1955–57

ST JAMES

Cachemaille-Day's church replaced a proprietary chapel of 1829 by Lewis Vulliamy, bombed in 1940. The exterior is a yellow-brick box, among the simplest of his post-war works and most unmannered. The interior is remarkable.

Nugent Francis Cachemaille-Day was chief assistant to Goodhart-Rendel before forming a partnership with Felix Lander and Herbert Welch. After setting up independently in 1935 he concentrated on designing churches until his retirement in about 1963. While Goodhart-Rendel sought to suggest mass in his brick and concrete volumes, Cachemaille-Day's churches are expressively 'thin' in their construction, depending for their effect on the treatment of light and shade within. This he expressed in remarkably vigorous drawings in coloured pencils on tracing paper.

In the late 1930s Cachemaille-Day began to experiment with exposed concrete construction for his internal vaulting, which is seen most effectively here. Each rib crosses the church diagonally, intersecting with three other ribs en route. This simple geometrical pattern of squares gives the optical effect of a true tierceron vault, made more convincing by the solid spandrels at their springing point from the wall. An extra set of columns denotes the chancel, in what was still a conventional plan. The brightly coloured glass is by J Wippell and Co.

LISTED grade II, 25 September 1998
ADDRESS Briarwood Road, London SW4
NEAREST UNDERGROUND Clapham Common
ACCESS Sunday services; call 020 7674 3973 for information

N F Cachemaille-Day 1957–58

THE FINNISH CHURCH

Cyril Sjöström was the son of a Finnish architect and an English opera singer. He adopted his mother's maiden name, Mardall, when in 1944 he formed a partnership with F R S Yorke and Eugene Rosenberg. His other work for YRM consisted chiefly of schools and housing schemes, but he had been involved since the 1930s in designing a new building for the Finnish Seamen's Mission, originally founded in 1882. In the 1950s the Surrey Docks were still the point of entry for Scandinavian timber, and Norwegian and Swedish churches are close to the present site, which was given by the LCC. The church aimed to serve a wider expatriot community from the first.

Mardall's original design dates from 1954 but was radically revised to become both more flexible and more compact, combining a church and meeting place within a single volume. A gallery café can be screened off or opened up as required, while a ground-floor reading room is separated from the church only by a freestanding stove and spiral staircase. The spaces are simple, yet beautiful, distinctively Finnish and uncluttered by 'contemporary' detailing. It is also the only church in England with a sauna, designed by Mardall's architect wife, June Park.

The church has a shop selling Finnish specialities, and the Christmas fair is an annual treat.

LISTED grade II, 25 September 1998
ADDRESS formerly Finnish Seamen's Mission, Albion Street, London SE16
NEAREST UNDERGROUND Rotherhithe
ACCESS open most afternoons

Yorke, Rosenberg and Mardall 1957–58

20 BLACKHEATH PARK

Peter Moro's own house is one of England's first 'upstairs bungalows'. Single-level houses were a vogue in the 1950s and 1960s, inspired by the Californian 'case study houses' which exalted in open-planned, servant-free spaces surrounded by shady gardens. Marcel Breuer was the first to use sloping land to create a semi-submerged plinth to house such necessities as a garage and utility room beneath living accommodation.

Moro developed this ideal notion for suburban living. He sliced his house along its long, central spine so that the living area and study overlooking the garden are a few steps lower than the dining area and kitchen. This enabled him to insert a clerestory to light the centre of the house. It was also Breuer who first articulated his cantilevered upper floor in different materials, but the internal timber finishes and overall calm simplicity here are more reminiscent of Alvar Aalto.

Moro worked for Tecton, and designed the interiors of the Royal Festival Hall (see pages 668–670). His own house is far cooler in its design, using a limited palette of favourite colours – black, white, grey, dark green and camelia red – with natural timber, dark steel and tiles. He died in 1999 and his collection of works of art (mostly by himself) was dispersed. However, the house has found sympathetic new owners.

LISTED grade II, 29 March 1988; upgraded 7 October 1999
ADDRESS London SE3
NEAREST STATION Blackheath
ACCESS exterior only

Peter Moro 1957–58

LANGHAM HOUSE CLOSE

In 1955 James Stirling was the first English architect to write on Le Corbusier's use of brick, contrasting the white-painted Villa Stein-de-Monzie at Garches (1927–28) with his boldly exposed brick and concrete at the Maisons Jaoul (1953–55). Here was the honest use of materials for which Stirling and Gowan's generation had been searching.

The 30 private flats at Langham House Close, for which Stirling and Gowan were commissioned in 1955 by the developer L E Manousso, adopted not only the materials of the Maisons Jaoul but many of Le Corbusier's details, notably his concrete water spouts. With a budget of only £1900 per flat an architecture of exposed concrete floor beams and brick walling was also cheap. It was not the first use of the aesthetic in Britain – the Smithsons' Sugden House (1954) was that – but its wholehearted celebration established the Maisons Jaoul as a model in British architecture as nowhere else.

Stirling and Gowan continued their inspiration into the interior, particularly in the fireplace, servery and kitchen fittings, but most residents preferred traditional furnishings. A vital sense of drama is captured only in the large foyers to the two smaller blocks, where the concrete first-floor landings form a bridge between glazed walls.

While Stirling moved on to more classical compositions, Gowan remained true to brick modernism in his later work.

LISTED grade II, 22 December 1998
ADDRESS Ham Common, Richmond-upon-Thames
GETTING THERE train to Richmond or Kingston, then bus
ACCESS limited; exteriors only

James Stirling and James Gowan 1957–58

RC MOST HOLY TRINITY, DOCKHEAD

This is one of the oldest post-reformation Catholic sites in London. The previous church and presbytery were bombed, and in 1951 Goodhart-Rendel planned an ambitious replacement, which was later simplified.

The exterior is particularly fascinating, as it is the culmination of his interest in patterned brickwork. The geometrical theme of hexagons and triangles, denoting the Trinity, continues through all aspects of the building. It is most readily apparent in the west front – a striking prospect from the road – where the twin hexagonal towers continue as a central arch, a device perhaps derived from the Garrison church at Ulm by Theodor Fischer (1908). The design is also a rationalisation of his uncompleted scheme for Prinknash Abbey, designed in 1938 following his conversion to Rome. The concentration of light from the south is developed from the work of G E Street; the round-arch windows are reminiscent of Beresford Pite, the closest of Goodhart-Rendel's affiliations.

The interior is high and surprisingly light, with relief panels of coloured sculpture behind the altar by Atri Brown, as are the Stations of the Cross. Its vault is of thin concrete, reinforced with Delta bronze for longevity. The church was completed after Goodhart-Rendel's death by H Lewis Curtis, his assistant since the 1920s, who also rebuilt the presbytery to Goodhart-Rendel's design.

LISTED grade II, 25 September 1998
ADDRESS Jamaica Road, London SE1
NEAREST UNDERGROUND Bermondsey
ACCESS regular services

H S Goodhart-Rendel 1957–60

HALLGATE

Hallgate was built as an entrance frontage to an earlier development of houses, The Hall, and has a sophistication not found in Eric Lyons' earlier work at Parkleys (see page 686) and The Priory, Blackheath. The Hall is reached via a covered passage through the block.

Span secured a number of gap sites on the Cato Estate at Blackheath, for which Lyons produced little developments of flats and houses, each managed by residents' committee. It is the best place in which to view the evolution of their collaboration through the 1950s and up to Span's financial collapse at New Ash Green in 1969; the subsequent work seldom satisfies. Lyons' schemes have relatively high densities, up to 70 persons per acre, controversial in leafy Blackheath but which is made to feel right by intense planting supervised by Ivor Cunningham.

Lyons' frustrations with planning inspectors are recorded at Hallgate. In a niche in the passageway wall is a sculpted figure by Keith Godwin, almost crushed under the concrete lintel he supports: its title is *The Architect in Society*. 'If it is not a good likeness, it is roughly the way I feel at times', Lyons explained in 1959. He argued with the LCC over the paint colour for Hallgate, and he had two other planning decisions pending at the time, one of them for South Row (see page 716).

LISTED grade II, 22 December 1998
ADDRESS Blackheath Park, London SE3
NEAREST STATION Blackheath
ACCESS exterior only

Span Developments Ltd 1958–59

ST CRISPIN

Thomas Ford rebuilt many of south London's bombed churches, including Coe and Robinson's St Crispin, gutted in 1940. Most of Ford's work is unassuming, and this is true externally of St Crispin's. However, the interior has a rare homogeneity. It has a Greek cross plan under a central dome, and a wide, shallow east end with choir stalls either side of the sanctuary. The church celebrates the Bermondsey leather industry in the coverings of the doors and pews, and particularly in the mural on the east wall by Hans Feibusch commemorating St Crispin and St Crispinian, patron saints of shoes and leather. A mural of sky and clouds fills the dome and was painted by Feibusch's protégé, Phyllis Dear. Stained-glass windows by M C Farrar Bell depicting leather working were salvaged from Christchurch, Jamaica Street, Rotherhithe, which was demolished in the 1960s.

Feibusch was a refugee of Jewish parentage who's work was exhibited in Hitler's exhibition of degenerate art in 1938. The success of a mural for Collier's Wood Methodist Church led to a career in church decoration, and that at St Crispin's is among his best. Feibusch and Ford collaborated regularly, as at St John, Waterloo Road, which they restored as the Festival of Britain church in 1951.

St Crispin's was listed when it was threatened with redundancy and demolition. Its future remains uncertain.

LISTED grade II, 4 December 2000
ADDRESS Southwark Park Road, Bermondsey, London
NEAREST UNDERGROUND Bermondsey
ACCESS exterior only at present

Thomas F Ford 1958–59

GEOFFREY CHAUCER SCHOOL

Chamberlin, Powell and Bon sought to 'avoid specialisation' in favour of 'fresh opportunities'. While we can see affinities between their work of the early 1950s (Golden Lane Estate and Bousfield School, see pages 598 and 520) and in their later work at the Barbican and Leeds University, there is a maverick quality to their middle period, particularly at New Hall, Cambridge (see pages 294–296), and here. Both buildings experiment with new concrete forms, and bring an architectural grand gesture to a simple brief. This tendency was first seen in Chamberlin's water tank at Golden Lane, and his may be the guiding hand here.

The school was originally built for 1260 girls, with a four-storey classroom block and four storeys of practical rooms set either side of three central gymnasia. Its most striking feature, however, is its pentagonal assembly hall, a stepped amphitheatre set over a broad walkway and topped by a hyperbolic paraboloid roof of five separate concrete shells with a central lantern. By supporting the shells at their low corners along the building's edge, the body of the 1300-square-metre hall could be free of columns. It is surrounded by five classrooms, originally designed as house rooms to encourage smaller social groups within the large school.

The school is now mixed, and the timber and tile interior, unusually well finished, is standing up excellently to rough treatment.

LISTED grade II, 30 March 1993
ENGINEER Flint and Neill
ADDRESS Theobald Street, London SE1
NEAREST UNDERGROUND/STATION Elephant and Castle
ACCESS none

Chamberlin, Powell and Bon 1958–60

ST PAUL

St Paul's replaced a church of 1854 damaged in the Second World War, and forms part of the Brandon Estate, the first major LCC scheme to combine new housing blocks with rehabilitated terraces.

The building takes its unusual form from two sources. One is the variety of materials: brick, concrete and copper are set over a high rubble stone plinth, symbolically reused from the old church. The other is the roof construction, a series of precast timber sections whose triangulation gives the church its dramatic, facetted appearance. The sections were delivered to the church ready-assembled and sheathed in copper, and were hoisted into place by large cranes.

The architects considered that the design stemmed naturally from this choice of structure. It may have partially determined the long, narrow plan, but so too did the desire to make the church a social centre for the estate. So the church is set over parish rooms, and opens into a hall at its west end.

The church's decoration is lavish and very complete. The sequence of acoustic panels at the west end and the altar cloths are the best surviving examples of the appliqué work of Gerald Holtom. The east-end sculpture is by Freda Skinner.

This quirky, highly decorative 1950s style rapidly became old fashioned with the Liturgical Movement, but is now being reappraised.

LISTED grade II, 11 July 2001
ADDDRESS Lorrimore Square, Kennington, London
NEAREST UNDERGROUND Kennington
ACCESS Sunday services; groups by appointment on 020 7701 4010

John Wimbleton and H G Coulter of Woodroffe, Buchanan and Coulter 1958–60

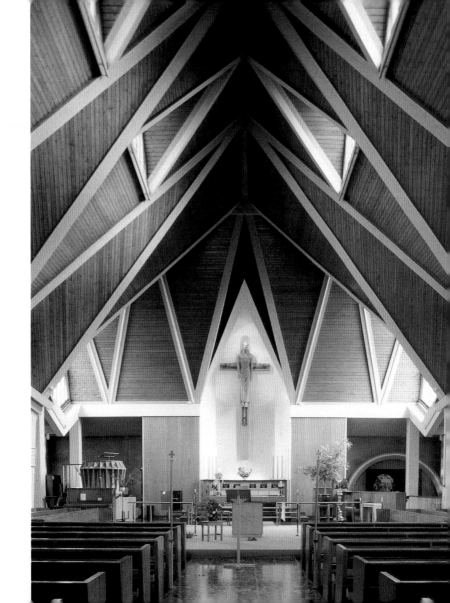

THE PAVILION

The Pavilion is a late example of the work of one of the most significant if eclectic architects of the mid century. Hill designed in both modern and traditional styles, a versatility often treated with suspicion by architectural historians today.

This late design is among his most whimsical. It shows him returning to the neo-Georgian style he had used for a series of London town houses in the early 1930s. In the 1950s he received few commissions, and his growing interest in history can be seen in his book with John Cornforth, *English Country Houses: Caroline* (Country Life, 1966). The Pavilion demonstrates the influences of this interest in early neo-Palladianism better than any other. Its resemblance to a garden temple also shows the growing interest in such buildings at this time.

The Pavilion has a three-bay front under a broad pediment, in which Hill placed the principal living room. This he flanked by small two-storey wings each housing a staircase as well as the principal bedrooms. The principal rooms retain distinctive Hill features, such as fireplaces and columned screens, with few alterations.

The house is an unusual example of a post-war building consciously inspired by the growing understanding of architectural history during this period.

LISTED grade II, 1 October 1999
ADDRESS Warren Road, Coombe, Kingston-upon-Thames
NEAREST STATION New Malden
ACCESS none

Oliver Hill 1959–60

MICHAEL FARADAY MEMORIAL

The Elephant and Castle was almost entirely redeveloped by the LCC from the late 1950s. When a new transformer station was required for the underground, its design was entrusted to the young Rodney Gordon, who subsequently joined Owen Luder and Partners.

Michael Faraday (1791–1867) was born at Elephant and Castle. He founded the science of electromagnetism, discovered electromotive power and first produced the formula for stainless steel. A transformer station was thus an appropriate commemoration, and stainless steel was chosen after a transparent glass design was rejected as too eye-catching for passing drivers.

Gordon realised that plain steel sheets would distort, so used dished panels whose refraction of light would contrast with a Miesian black steel frame. It is an early use of steel cladding in England, though Harrison and Abramowitz had used press-moulded panels on the Socony Mobil Building, New York, in 1956. The Faraday Memorial anticipates British 'high-tech' architecture of a decade later, but Gordon claims that his design was inspired by a Danish coffee table he owned, of black basalt supported on a steel frame.

Few people today realise that the little building in the middle of the Elephant and Castle roundabout is a transformer station, let alone a memorial. A floodlighting scheme was introduced in 1996 after a BBC *Blue Peter* competition.

LISTED grade II, 21 June 1996
ADDRESS Elephant and Castle, London SE1
NEAREST UNDERGROUND/STATION Elephant and Castle
ACCESS exterior only

LCC Architect's Department 1960–61

NATIONAL RECREATION CENTRE

In 1951 the LCC took over the derelict Crystal Palace Park. Sir Gerald Barry, Director of the Festival of Britain, suggested using the drained lakes in the middle of the site for sport. One lake became an athletics stadium; an indoor sports hall was designed for the other as early as 1953–54.

It was the first multi-purpose hall designed in Britain – though not the first to be built – at a time when such facilities did not exist in Europe, and was widely influential. Emphasis was given to swimming because there were few Olympic-sized pools in southern England.

The centre impresses by its planning and the homogeneous nature of the structural system and exterior design. It is divided in two by a central 'A'-frame, which supports the roof and banks of seating on its outer faces. The upper spectator walkways bisect a spine of concrete struts, with views over both halves of the building – swimming on one side, a sports hall on the other, and squash courts tucked below. Smaller spaces on lower levels have adapted to changing fashions.

The 'A'-frame dictated the building's form. Spurs continue as ribs across the roof and extend down the walls as glazing mullions, giving the building a sense of logic and drama – matched by the supremely architectural high diving board.

LISTED grade II*, 2 December 1997
ADDRESS Crystal Palace, London SE19
NEAREST STATION Crystal Palace
ACCESS open daily to users; 020 8778 0131 for enquiries

LCC Architect's Department 1960–64

3-35 SOUTH ROW

South Row is the sharpest and most confidently modern of Eric Lyons' work for Span. There are ten houses and 23 flats in two 'L'-shaped ranges round a private courtyard. There is a homogeneity in their proportions and in details such as the thick timber windows, while the dense courtyard planting that is a crucial Span ingredient has a unifying influence. But while the rear terrace of the houses are weatherboarded, and as unassuming as Lyons's earlier works, the flats at the front are massively executed in a dark-brown brick. Their concrete frame is also partially exposed, to form strong cornices and bands.

The difference is due to the prominence of the development. While concealed infill sites were Span's speciality at Blackheath, South Row faces square on to the Heath between large eighteenth-century houses. Lyons claimed an architectural and social affinity between Span and the speculative builders of Georgian terraces and squares, and thus justified his high densities and communal open spaces. It is therefore ironic that South Row should be his least terrace-like design. It is a square, which is revealed to outsiders through a broad two-bay entrance cut through the ground floor of the flats and simply glazed.

South Row was listed in 1996 when it was proposed to renew the windows in uPVC. A replacement scheme in timber has now been implemented.

LISTED grade II, 21 June 1996
ADDRESS Blackheath, London SE3
NEAREST STATION Blackheath
ACCESS exterior only

Span Developments Ltd 1962–63

LILIAN BAYLIS SCHOOL

Lilian Baylis was the first of a clutch of new secondary schools built by the LCC in the 1960s to replace small charitable institutions from the nineteenth century. Lilian Baylis replaced four such foundations, including the Beaufoy School on Newport Street whose name the new school originally took.

ACP had already built additions to a school in Islington, where they had rejected the form of a single, long slab popularised by London comprehensives such as Elliott School (see page 684) in favour of a series of low blocks set round courtyards. The partner in charge, Kenneth Capon, felt that such a plan was appropriate to a neighbourhood noted for its late-Georgian squares. At Lilian Baylis the pattern is repeated but the blocks are more closely interconnected and the detailing more sophisticated. Most of the school is of two storeys. There is a science wing with laboratories, three gymnasia, a double-height library, a drama room with a raked floor and music rooms set under the main hall. Two blocks built as house rooms, with their own kitchens, were adapted in 1999–2000 for special needs. Most striking of all is the first-floor assembly hall, a square space surrounded on three sides by staging, panelled and with a diagrid roof.

Listing was prompted by proposals to demolish the school as part of a comprehensive redevelopment of the Lambeth Walk area.

LISTED grade II, 20 December 2000
ADDRESS Lollard Street, Lambeth
NEAREST STATIONS/UNDERGROUNDS Vauxhall, Lambeth North and Waterloo
ACCESS exterior only

Architects' Co-Partnership 1962–64

POOLS ON THE PARK

Leslie Gooday, who lived in nearby Sheen for many years, specialised in exhibition design and private houses, and Richmond baths are correspondingly elegant in their detailing. The complex is also unusual in that in addition to the usual two indoor pools for adults and learners, plus slipper baths, there is also an outdoor pool. The slipper baths and high-level diving board have gone and the changing rooms reorganised, but otherwise the building functions with few alterations.

The breaking up of the entrance, changing and pool areas into distinctive masses serves to scale down the impact of what is already quite a small building on the historic landscape of the Old Deer Park. Most impressive is the copper roof with a deep-eaves fascia over the pool, and raised over the former diving area. Oxidised green, this again was designed to reduce the building's impact; it has recently been renewed, and so is again a 'copper' colour. Internally the large and small pools occupy a single space, broken only by a cantilevered mezzanine gallery which cuts across the hall at high level and which continues externally as a sunbathing terrace with steps to the open-air pool. This gallery originally served as a cafeteria.

Listing prevented a large extension to the building; instead additional sports facilities have been contained in the existing envelope.

LISTED grade II, 16 January 1996
ADDRESS Old Deer Park, Richmond
ENGINEER Stanley Weddle
NEAREST STATION/UNDERGROUND Richmond-on-Thames
ACCESS open Monday to Friday, 6.00–21.00; Saturday, Sunday, 8.00–18.00; call 020 8940 0561 for details

Leslie Gooday 1964–66

10 BLACKHEATH PARK

The builder Leslie Bilsby was an early friend and patron of Patrick Gwynne's. He commissioned three houses and was the contractor for several others; additionally he built much of the Span housing in Blackheath Park.

While radically different in style and materials, Gwynne's house maintains the symmetrical plan of the early nineteenth-century double-fronted villas to either side. The curtain walling of near-black slate and aluminium glazing was intended as a recessive contrast to these adjoining houses. The splayed plan unifies the composition and gives No. 10 angled views down the street. The staircases to the raised entrances at front and back add to the sophisticated space-age image.

The internal spaces are lined in Gwynne's favourite black plastic, save for the central core, which is rendered. The layout, a central staircase around which the principal rooms form a chain, was one Gwynne adopted regularly in the 1960s. But the Blackheath house has a particular logic, for Bilsby wanted a separate living room, dining room and study that could be opened into each other for the small drinks parties at which he excelled. Gwynne provided a pentagonal room of equal size in each corner of the house, connected by sliding doors to rectangular intermediate spaces. There were originally two basement garages, but one has been turned into a bedroom.

This is one of Gwynne's most sculptural and idiosyncratic houses.

LISTED grade II, 4 December 2000
NEAREST STATION Blackheath
ACCESS exterior only

Patrick Gwynne 1968–69

NATIONAL THEATRE

The first proposal to build a national theatre for England's pre-eminent art form was made in 1848, but it was only in 1942 that a site on the South Bank was offered by the LCC, who eventually co-funded the project. In 1962 Lasdun was chosen from 20 architects invited for interview, and after a proposed opera house and theatre scheme was aborted he designed the present building for its final site in 1967.

The National has to be seen in the context of post-war enthusiasm for repertory theatre and new forms of staging. Its company was founded in 1962 under Sir Laurence Olivier, reflecting an international movement in favour of an egalitarian company over the formula of individual production casts led by an outside star.

The three auditoria opened separately. The tiny Cottesloe is an adaptable galleried space devised by Iain Mackintosh, and rapidly developed an enthusiastic following. The building's architectural form, however, is derived from the other auditoria, their flytowers and foyers. While the Lyttelton has a conventional 'end-stage' proscenium, the larger Olivier Theatre (1160 seats) has a corner apron stage not unlike that at the Chichester Festival Theatre where Olivier had worked in 1962–64 (see page 454). Its light concrete and lavender fabrics produce a silvery shimmer, while the acoustic treatment of the ceiling gives a sense of the auditorium extending back into space. The backstage areas, although architecturally bare, are ample and inventive. The Olivier has a motorised flytower, drum revolve and, in the absence of wings, wagons on which sets can be held in waiting.

It is in the foyers that the importance of the building's structural geometry becomes apparent, for the axes of the two theatres are set at 45 degrees to each other. This geometry is picked up by a grid, set in line with the Olivier Theatre, that delineates the coffered ceiling and fixes such features as the lift towers, fly towers and principal walls. It means that while the Olivier is the most impressive auditorium, the lower-level Lyttelton foyers

Sir Denys Lasdun and Partners 1969–76

are spatially the more interesting. The grid also delineates the main stairs, with their half-hexagon landings cut through to provide unexpected views through the building. This interplay extends to the exterior where oversailing walkways provide an awning to the entrance and create lavish terraces above. They also permit the building to be entered at several levels.

The building was listed in 1994, when there were proposals to demolish an upper walkway. Instead Stanton Williams have extended the foyers underneath Lasdun's yawning porte-cochère and eased the circulation with minimum impact on his original concept.

LISTED grade II*, 23 June 1994
ADDRESS Upper Ground, South Bank, London SE1
NEAREST STATION/UNDERGROUND Waterloo
ACCESS foyers open daily except principal holidays

Sir Denys Lasdun and Partners 1969–76

INDEX

ENGLAND: A GUIDE TO POST-WAR LISTED BUILDINGS

All photographs are by Elain Harwood except:

Pete Smith, pages 27, 41, 109, 127, 145, 153, 157, 363

Mike Williams, pages 31; 35, 73, 81, 89, 221

Diane Kay, pages 61, 225, 235, 237, 239, 241, 299, 313, 555, 595

English Heritage (Nigel Corrie and John Critchley), pages 65, 67, 87, 91, 93, 107, 111, 133, 137, 149, 159, 167, 169, 185, 189, 243, 245, 249, 251, 253, 259, 261, 269, 275, 303, 339, 341, 343, 347, 349, 381, 383, 389, 399, 409, 415, 433, 451, 469, 511, 513, 533, 535, 537, 559, 561, 579, 603, 609, 621, 623, 649, 677, 701, 702, 727

Bill Smyth, pages 85, 191, 367, 369, 461

Julian Holder, page 125

English Heritage – National Monuments Record Centre, page 211

Alastair Ward, page 273

Alan Powers, pages 287, 355, 405, 447, 531, 677, 717

Bronwen Edwards, pages 315, 443

Every effort has been made to identify photographers correctly. The author would be grateful to be informed of any misattributions, which will be corrected in any future editions.